Thomas Hughes

Tom Brown at Oxford - A Sequel to School Days at Rugby

Part II

Thomas Hughes

**Tom Brown at Oxford - A Sequel to School Days at Rugby**
*Part II*

ISBN/EAN: 9783337141967

Printed in Europe, USA, Canada, Australia, Japan

Cover: Foto ©ninafisch / pixelio.de

More available books at **www.hansebooks.com**

# TOM BROWN AT OXFORD:

A SEQUEL TO

SCHOOL DAYS AT RUGBY.

BY
THE AUTHOR OF
"SCHOOL DAYS AT RUGBY," "SCOURING OF THE WHITE HORSE," ETC.

PART SECOND.

BOSTON:
TICKNOR AND FIELDS.
M DCCC LXII.

Entered according to Act of Congress, in the year 1861, by
TICKNOR AND FIELDS,
In the Clerk's Office of the District Court of the District of Massachusetts.

TO

# JAMES RUSSELL LOWELL,

OF

HARVARD COLLEGE, MASSACHUSETTS,

THE AMERICAN EDITION OF THIS BOOK

IS GRATEFULLY DEDICATED,

AS A SMALL ACKNOWLEDGMENT OF THE DELIGHT AND BENEFIT

WHICH THE AUTHOR HAS DERIVED FROM HIS WORKS.

LINCOLN'S INN, *June* 15, 1861.

MY DEAR LOWELL, — You will see by the foregoing that I have dedicated this book, at least the American edition of it, to you, at which I hope you will neither be surprised nor offended. It is one of the highest rewards an English author can hope for, to be read on your side of the Atlantic, and I have had so many proofs of hearty and kindly sympathy from over the water since I have taken to publishing, that I feel as though I had old friends scattered all about your States, and think of New England pretty much as I do of Yorkshire. To you, as the foremost of such friends, — though unhappily only known to me as yet on paper and by photograph, — I turn when I hear that the last sheets of proof are being made up for Messrs. Ticknor & Fields, and cannot resist the temptation of thus associating your name with a book of mine, as I have already over here had the honor of associating my name with a book of yours.

The book itself needs no comment. Superficially our youngsters no doubt differ from yours, and the lesson of life has to be learnt under very different surroundings at Harvard and Oxford, in New York or Boston and London. But at bottom it is the same battle, and the Devil, I doubt not, has just such subtle ways, with you as with us, of keeping them back from steady growth in purity, and manliness, and truthfulness. But, however unlike one another the young men of New England and Old England may be, they are a thousand times more like one another than they are like any other human creature the sun shines on. So if the book is, as I hope, one which will do some good to Oxford and Cambridge men if they will try to find out what it means to say, however feebly the meaning may be brought out, I have no fear but that it will do as much for your pupils at Harvard.

But enough about the book. It seems like fiddling while Rome is burning to be talking of such matters now to any American. My dear friend, you cannot know how deeply all that is soundest and noblest in England is sympathizing with you in your great struggle. You must not judge by newspapers or magazines, though so far as I see the best of them are speaking decidedly on the right side. Not so warmly or decidedly as I could wish ; for this our free-trade notions and some hasty and inconsiderate speaking and writing on your side will account. But be sure that the issues are appreciated here, and while we see the awfulness of the task you have in hand, we have faith in you, we believe that if it can be done you will do it, and we wish you, from the bottom of our hearts, God speed!

The great tasks of the world are only laid on the strongest shoulders. We, who have India to guide and train, who have for our task the educating of her wretched peoples into free men, who feel that the work cannot be shifted from ourselves and must be done as God would have it done, at the peril of England's own life, can and do feel for you. But as we hope to get through with our own work, as we would ask no meaner work for ourselves, so we rejoice that you, our brethren, have shaken yourselves up to your work, and have put your hands to it in such grim earnest as assures us that the old blood is still the same despite all difference of latitude or longitude.

And so, with firm faith that your country will quit herself as England's sister should in this fiery trial time, and with all good wishes to you and yours, believe me ever gratefully and most truly yours,

THOS. HUGHES.

# CONTENTS.

## VOLUME II:

### CHAPTER I.
The Schools, .................................................... 1

### CHAPTER II.
Commemoration, ................................................ 19

### CHAPTER III.
The Long Walk in Christ-Church Meadows, .................. 34

### CHAPTER IV.
Lecturing a Lioness, .......................................... 56

### CHAPTER V.
The End of the Freshman's Year, ............................. 73

### CHAPTER VI.
The Long Vacation Letter-Bag, ................................ 87

### CHAPTER VII.
Amusements at Barton Manor, ................................ 107

### CHAPTER VIII.
Behind the Scenes, ........................................... 117

### CHAPTER IX.
A Crisis, .................................................... 129

### CHAPTER X.
Brown Patronus, .............................................. 147

### CHAPTER XI.
Μηδὲν ἄγαν, .................................................. 173

### CHAPTER XII.
Second Year, ................................................. 193

## CONTENTS.

#### CHAPTER XIII.
The River Side, .................................................. 210

#### CHAPTER XIV.
The Night-Watch, ............................................... 224

#### CHAPTER XV.
Mary in Mayfair, ................................................ 239

#### CHAPTER XVI.
What came of the Night-Watch, ............................ 253

#### CHAPTER XVII.
Hue and Cry, .................................................... 269

#### CHAPTER XVIII.
The Lieutenant's Sentiments and Problems, ............ 283

#### CHAPTER XIX.
Third Year, ....................................................... 299

#### CHAPTER XX.
Afternoon Visitors, ............................................ 317

#### CHAPTER XXI.
The Intercepted Letter-Bag, ................................. 332

#### CHAPTER XXII.
Master's Term, .................................................. 354

#### CHAPTER XXIII.
From India to Englebourn, .................................. 366

#### CHAPTER XXIV.
The Wedding-Day, ............................................. 378

#### CHAPTER XXV.
A Meeting in the Street, ..................................... 391

#### CHAPTER XXVI.
The End, .......................................................... 405

#### CHAPTER XXVII.
The Postscript, .................................................. 419

# CHAPTER I.

### THE SCHOOLS.

There is no more characteristic spot in Oxford than the quadrangle of the schools. Doubtless in the times when the university held and exercised the privileges of infang-thief and outfang-thief, and other such old-world rights, there must have been a place somewhere within the liberties devoted to examinations even more exciting that the great-go. But since *alma mater* has ceased to take cognizance of "treasons, insurrections, felonies, and mayhem," it is here in that fateful and inexorable quadrangle, and the buildings which surround it, that she exercises her most potent spells over the spirits of her children. I suppose that a man being tried for his life must be more uncomfortable than an undergraduate being examined for his degree, and that to be hung,—perhaps even to be pilloried,—must be worse than to be plucked. But after all, the feelings in both cases must be essentially the same, only more intense in the former; and an institution which can examine a man (in literis humanioribus, in *humanities* so called) once a year for two or three days at a time, has nothing to complain of, though it has no longer the power of hanging him at once out of hand.

The schools' quadrangle is for the most part a lonely place. Men pass through the melancholy iron gates by which that quadrangle is entered on three sides,—from Broad Street, from the Ratcliffe, and from New College Lane,—when necessity leads them that way, with alert step and silently. No nursemaids or children play about it. Nobody lives in it. Only when the examinations are going on you may see a few hooded figures who walk as though conscious of the powers of academic life and death which they wield, and a good deal of shuddering undergraduate life flitting about the place, — luckless youths, in white ties and bands, who are undergoing the *peine forte et dure* with different degrees of composure ; and their friends who are there to look after them. You may go in and watch the torture yourself if you are so minded, for the *vivâ voce* schools are open to the public. But one such experiment will be enough for you, unless you are very hard-hearted. The sight of the long table, behind which sit Minos, Rhadamanthus, and Co., full-robed, stern of face, soft of speech, seizing their victim in turn, now letting him run a little way as a cat does a mouse, then drawing him back, with claw of wily question, probing him on this side and that, turning him inside out, — the row of victims opposite, pale or flushed, of anxious or careless mien, according to temperament, but one and all on the rack as they bend over the alloted paper, or read from the well-thumbed book, — the scarcely-less-to-be-pitied row behind, of future victims, "sitting for the schools," as it is called, ruthlessly brought hither by statutes, to watch the sufferings they must hereafter undergo, — should fill the friend of suffering humanity with thoughts too deep for tears. Through the long day till four o'clock, or later, the torture lasts. Then the last victim is dismissed; the men who are "sitting for the schools" fly all ways to their colleges, silently, in search of relief to their over-wrought feelings, — probably also of beer, the undergraduate's universal specific. The beadles close those ruthless doors for a mysterious half-hour on the examiners. Outside in the quadrangle collect by twos and threes the friends of the victims waiting for the re-opening of the door and the distribution of the " testamurs." The testamurs, lady readers will be pleased to understand, are certificates under the hands of the examiners, that your sons, brothers, husbands, perhaps, have successfully undergone the torture. But, if husbands, oh, go not yourselves, and send not your sons to wait for the testamur of the head of your house; for Oxford has seldom seen a sight over which she would more willingly draw the veil with averted face than that of the youth rushing wildly, dissolved in tears, from the schools' quadrangle, and shouting, "Mamma! papa's plucked; papa's plucked!"

On the occasion at which we have now arrived, the pass-schools are over already; the paper-work of the candidates for honors has been going on for the last week. Every morning our three St. Ambrose acquaintance have mustered with the rest for the anxious day's work, after such breakfasts as they have been able to eat under the circumstances. They take their work in very different ways. Grey rushes nervously back to his rooms whenever he is out of the schools for ten minutes, to look up dates and dodges. He worries himself sadly over every blunder which he discovers himself to have made, and sits up nearly all night cramming, always hoping for a better to-morrow. Blake keeps up his affected carelessness to the last, quizzing the examiners, laughing over the shots he has been making in the last paper. His shots, it must be said, turn out well for the most part; in the taste paper particularly, as they compare notes, he seems to have almost struck the bull's-eye in his answers to one or two questions which Hardy and Grey have passed over altogether. When he is wide of the mark he passes it off with some jesting remark " that a fool can ask in five minutes more questions than a wise man can answer in a week," or wish "that the examiners would play fair, and change sides of the table for an hour with the candidates, for a finish." But he, too, though he does it on the sly, is cramming with his coach at every available spare moment. Hardy had finished his reading a full thirty-six hours before the first day of paper-work, and had braced himself for the actual struggle by two good nights' rest and a long day on the river with Tom. He had worked hard from the first, and so had really mastered his books. And now feeling that he has fairly and honestly done his best, and that if he fails it will be either from bad luck or natural incapacity, and not from his own fault, he manages to keep a cooler head than any of his companions in trouble.

The week's paper-work passes off uneventfully; then comes the *vivâ voce* work for the candidates for honors. They go in in alphabetical order, four a day, for one more day's work, the hardest of all, and then there is nothing more to do but wait patiently for the class list. On these days there is a good attendance in the inclosed space to which the public are admitted. The front seats are often occupied by the private tutors of the candidates, who are there, like Newmarket trainers, to see the performances of their stables, marking how each colt bears pressing and comports himself when the pinch comes. They watch the examiners too, carefully, to see what line they take, whether science, or history, or scholarship is likely to tell most, that they may handle the rest of their starters accordingly. Behind them, for the most part, on the hindermost benches of the flight of raised steps, anxious younger brothers and friends sit, for a few minutes at a time, flitting in and out in much unrest, and making the objects of their solicitude more nervous than ever by their sympathy.

It is now the afternoon of the second day of the *vivâ*

*voce* examinations in honors. Blake is one of the men in. His tutor, Hardy, Grey, Tom, and other St. Ambrose men, have all been in the schools more or less during his examination, and now Hardy and Tom are waiting outside the doors for the issuing of the testamurs.

The group is small enough. It is so much of course that a class-man should get his testamur that there is no excitement about it; generally the man himself stops to receive it.

The only anxious faces in the group are Tom's and Hardy's. They have not exchanged a word for the last few minutes in their short walk before the door. Now the examiners come out and walk away towards their colleges, and the next minute the door again opens and the clerk of the schools appears with the slips of paper in his hand.

"Now you'll see if I'm not right," said Hardy, as they gathered to the door with the rest. "I tell you there isn't the least chance for him."

The clerk read out the names inscribed on the testamurs which he held, and handed them to the owners.

"Haven't you one for Mr. Blake of St. Ambrose?" said Tom, desperately, as the clerk was closing the door.

"No, sir; none but those I have just given out," answered the clerk, shaking his head. The door closed, and they turned away in silence for the first minute.

"I told you how it would be," said Hardy, as they passed out of the south gate into the Ratcliffe Quadrangle.

"But he seemed to be doing so well when I was in."

"You were not there at the time. I thought at first they would have sent him out of the schools at once."

"In his divinity, wasn't it?"

"Yes; he was asked to repeat one of the Articles, and didn't know three words of it. From that moment I saw it was all over. The examiner and he both lost their tempers, and it went from bad to worse, till the examiner remarked that he could have answered one of the questions he was asking when he was ten years old, and Blake replied, So could he. They gave him a paper in divinity afterwards, but you could see there was no chance for him."

"Poor fellow! what will he do, do you think? How will he take it?"

"I can't tell. But I'm afraid it will be a very serious matter for him. He was the ablest man in our year too. What a pity!"

They got into St. Ambrose just as the bell for afternoon chapel was going down, and went in. Blake was there, and one look showed him what had happened. In fact he had expected nothing else all day since his breakdown in the Articles. Tom couldn't help watching him during chapel, and afterwards, on that evening, acknowledged to a friend that whatever else you might think of Blake, there was no doubt about his gameness.

After chapel he loitered outside the door in the quadrangle, talking just as usual, and before Hall he loitered on the steps in well-feigned carelessness. Everybody else was thinking of his breakdown; some with real sorrow and sympathy; others as of any other nine-days' wonder, — pretty much as if the favorite for the Derby had broken down; others with ill-concealed triumph, for Blake had many enemies amongst the men. He himself was conscious enough of what they were thinking of, but maintained his easy gay manner through it all, though the effort it cost him was tremendous. The only allusion he made to what had happened which Tom heard was when he asked him to wine.

"Are you engaged to-night, Brown?" he said. Tom

answered in the negative. " Come to me, then," he went on. " You won't get another chance in St. Ambrose. I have a few bottles of old wine left; we may as well floor them; they won't bear moving to a Hall with their master."

And then he turned to some other men and asked them, every one in fact whom he came across, especially the dominant fast set with whom he had chiefly lived. These young gentlemen (of whom we had a glimpse at the outset, but whose company we have carefully avoided ever since, seeing that their sayings and doings were of a kind of which the less said the better) had been steadily going on in their way, getting more and more idle, reckless, and insolent. Their doings had been already so scandalous on several occasions as to call for solemn meetings of the college authorities; but, no vigorous measures having followed, such deliberations had only made matters worse, and given the men a notion that they could do what they pleased with impunity. This night the climax had come; it was as though the flood of misrule had at last broken banks and overflowed the whole college.

For two hours the wine party in Blake's large groundfloor rooms was kept up with a wild reckless mirth, in keeping with the host's temper. Blake was on his mettle. He had asked every man with whom he had a speaking acquaintance, as if he wished to face out his disaster at once to the whole world. Many of the men came feeling uncomfortable, and would sooner have stayed away and treated the pluck as a real misfortune. But after all Blake was the best judge of how he liked it to be treated, and, if he had a fancy for giving a great wine on the occasion, the civilest thing to do was to go to it. And so they went, and wondered as much as he could desire at the brilliant coolness of their host, speculating and doubting nevertheless in their own secret hearts whether it wasn't acting after all. Acting it was, no doubt, and not worth the doing; no acting is. But one must make allowances. No two men take a thing just alike, and very few can sit down quietly when they have lost a fall in life's wrestle, and say, "Well, here I am, beaten no doubt this time. By my own fault too. Now, take a good look at me, my good friends, as I know you all want to do, and say your say out, for I mean getting up again directly and having another turn at it."

Blake drank freely himself, and urged his guests to drink, which was a superfluous courtesy for the most part. Many of the men left his rooms considerably excited. They had dispersed for an hour or so to billiards, or a stroll in the town, and at ten o'clock reassembled at supper parties, of which there were several in college this evening, especially a monster one at Chanter's rooms — a "champagne supper," as he had carefully and ostentatiously announced on the cards of invitation. This flaunting the champagne in their faces had been resented by Drysdale and others, who drank his champagne in tumblers, and then abused it and clamored for beer in the middle of the supper. Chanter, whose prodigality in some ways was only exceeded by his general meanness, had lost his temper at this demand, and insisted that, if they wanted beer, they might send for it themselves, for he wouldn't pay for it. This protest was treated with uproarious contempt, and gallons of ale soon made their appearance in college jugs and tankards. The tables were cleared, and songs (most of them of more than doubtful character), cigars, and all sorts of compounded drinks, from claret cup to egg flip, succeeded. The company, recruited constantly as men came into college, was getting more and more excited every minute. The scouts cleared away and carried off all relics of the supper, and then left; still the revel went on, till, by midnight, the men were ripe for any mischief or folly which those among them who retained any brains at all could suggest. The signal for breaking up was given by the host's falling from his seat. Some of the men rose with a shout to put him to bed, which they accomplished with difficulty, after dropping him several times, and left him to snore off the effects of his debauch with one of his boots on. Others took to doing what mischief occurred to them in his rooms. One man, mounted on a chair with a cigar in his mouth which had gone out, was employed in pouring the contents of a champagne bottle with unsteady hand into the clock on the mantel-piece. Chanter was a particular man in this sort of furniture, and his clock was rather a speciality. It was a large bronze figure of Atlas, supporting the globe in the shape of a time-piece. Unluckily the maker, not anticipating the sort of test to which his work would be subjected, had ingeniously left the hole for winding up in the top of the clock, so that unusual facilities existed for drowning the world carrier, and he was already almost at his last tick. One or two men were morally aiding and abetting, and physically supporting the experimenter on clocks, who found it difficult to stand to his work by himself. Another knot of young gentlemen stuck to the tables, and so continued to shout out scraps of song, sometimes standing on their chairs, and sometimes tumbling off them. Another set were employed on the amiable work of pouring beer and sugar into three new pairs of polished leather dress boots, with colored tops to them, which they discovered in the dressing-room. Certainly, as they remarked, Chanter could have no possible use for so many dress boots at once, and it was a pity the beer should be wasted; but on the whole, perhaps, the materials were never meant for combination, and had better have been kept apart. Others had gone away to break into the kitchen, headed by one who had just come into college and vowed he would have some supper; and others, to screw up an unpopular tutor, or to break into the rooms of some inoffensive freshman. The remainder mustered on the grass in the quadrangle, and began playing leap-frog and larking one another. Amongst these last was our hero, who had been at Blake's wine and one of the quieter supper parties; and, though not so far gone as most of his companions, was by no means in a state in which he would have cared to meet the Dean. He lent his hearty aid accordingly to swell the noise and tumult, which was becoming something out of the way even for St. Ambrose's. As the leap-frog was flagging, Drysdale suddenly appeared carrying some silver plates which were used on solemn occasions in the common room, and allowed to be issued on special application for gentlemen commoners' parties. A rush was made towards him.

"Halloo, here's Drysdale with lots of swag," shouted one. "What are you going to do with it?" cried another. Drysdale paused a moment with the peculiarly sapient look of a tipsy man who has suddenly lost the thread of his ideas, and then suddenly broke out with —

"Hang it; I forget. But let's play at quoits with them."

The proposal was received with applause, and the game began, but Drysdale soon left it. He had evidently some notion in his head which would not suffer him to turn to any thing else till he had carried it out. He went off accordingly to Chanter's rooms, while the quoits went on in the front quadrangle.

About this time, however, the Dean and bursar, and the tutors who lived in college, began to be conscious that something unusual was going on. They were quite used to distant choruses, and great noises in the men's rooms, and to a fair amount of shouting and skylarking in the quadrangle, and were long-suffering men not given to interfering; but there must be an end to all endurance, and the state of things which had arrived could no longer be met by a turn in bed and a growl at the uproars and follies of undergraduates.

Presently some of the rioters on the grass caught sight of a figure gliding along the side of the quadrangle towards the Dean's staircase. A shout arose that the enemy was up, but little heed was paid to it by the greater number. Then another figure passed from the Dean's staircase to the porter's lodge. Those of the men who had any sense left saw that it was time to quit, and, after warning the rest, went off towards their rooms. Tom on his way to his staircase caught sight of a figure seated in a remote corner of the inner quadrangle, and made for it, impelled by natural curiosity. He found Drysdale seated on the ground with several silver tankards by his side, employed to the best of his powers in digging a hole with one of the college carving-knives.

"Hollo, Drysdale! what are you up to?" he shouted, laying his hand on his shoulder.

"Providing for poshterity," replied Drysdale, gravely, without looking up.

"What the deuce do you mean? Don't be such an ass. The Dean will be out in a minute. Get up and come along."

"I tell you, old fellow," said Drysdale, somewhat inarticulately, and driving his knife into the ground again, "the dons are going to spout the college plate. So I am burying these articles for poshterity—"

"Hang posterity," said Tom; "come along directly, or you'll be caught and rusticated."

"Go to bed, Brown — you're drunk, Brown," replied Drysdale, continuing his work, and striking the carving-knife into the ground so close to his own thigh that it made Tom shudder.

"Here they are then," he cried the next moment, seizing Drysdale by the arm, as a rush of men came through the passage into the back quadrangle, shouting and tumbling along, and making in small groups for the different staircases. The Dean and two of the tutors followed, and the porter bearing a lantern. There was no time to be lost; so Tom, after one more struggle to pull Drysdale up and hurry him off, gave it up, and leaving him to his fate, ran across to his own staircase.

For the next half-hour the Dean and his party patrolled the college, and succeeded at last in restoring order, though not without some undignified and disagreeable passages. The lights on the staircases, which generally burnt all night, were of course put out as they approached. On the first staircase which they stormed, the porter's lantern was knocked out of his hand by an unseen adversary, and the light put out on the bottom stairs. On the first landing the bursar trod on a small terrier belonging to a fast freshman, and the dog naturally thereupon bit the bursar's leg; while his master and other *enfants perdus*, taking advantage of the diversion, rushed down the dark stairs, past the party of order, and into the quadrangle, where they scattered amidst a shout of laughter. While the porter was gone for a light, the Dean and his party rashly ventured on a second ascent. Here an unexpected catastrophe awaited them. On the top landing lived one of the steadiest men in college, whose door had been tried shortly before. He had been roused out of his first sleep, and, vowing vengeance on the next comers, stood behind his oak, holding his brown George, or huge earthenware receptacle, half full of dirty water, in which his bed-maker had been washing up his tea-things. Hearing stealthy steps and whisperings on the stairs below, he suddenly threw open his oak, discharging the whole contents of his brown George on the approaching authorities, with a shout of, "Take that for your skulking."

The exasperated Dean and tutors rushing on, seized on their astonished and innocent assailant, and after receiving explanations, and the offer of clean towels, hurried off again after the real enemy. And now the porter appeared again with the light, and, continuing their rounds, they apprehended and disarmed Drysdale, collected the college plate, marked down others of the rioters, visited Chanter's rooms, held a parley with the one of their number who was screwed up in his rooms, and discovered that the bars had been wrenched out of the kitchen window. After which they retired to sleep on their indignation, and quietly settled down again on the ancient and venerable college.

The next morning at chapel many of the revellers met; in fact, there was a fuller attendance than usual, for every one felt that something serious must be pending. After such a night the dons must make a stand, or give up altogether. The most reckless only of the fast set were absent. St. Cloud was there, dressed even more precisely than usual, and looking as if he were in the habit of going to bed at ten, and had never heard of milk punch. Tom turned out not much the worse himself, but in his heart feeling not a little ashamed of the whole business; of the party, the men; but above all, of himself. He thrust the shame back, however, as well as he could, and put a cool face on it. Probably most of the men were in much the same state of mind. Even in St. Ambrose's, reckless and vicious as the college had become, by far the greater part of the undergraduates would gladly have seen a change in the direction of order and decency, and were sick of the wretched license of doing right in their own eyes, and wrong in every one's else.

As the men trooped out of chapel, they formed in corners of the quadrangle, except the reading set, who went off quietly to their rooms. There was a pause of a minute or two. Neither principal, dean, tutor, nor fellow, followed as on ordinary occasions. "They're hatching something in the outer chapel," said one.

"It'll be a coarse time for Chanter, I take it," said another.

"Was your name sent to the buttery for his supper?"

"No, I took d——d good care of that," said St. Cloud, who was addressed.

"Drysdale was caught; wasn't he?"

"So I hear, and nearly frightened the dean and the porter out of their wits by staggering after them with a carving-knife."

"He'll be sacked, of course."

"Much he'll care for that."

"Here they come, then; by Jove, how black they look!"

The authorities now came out of the antechapel door, and walked slowly across towards the principal's house in a body. At this moment, as ill-luck would have it, Jack trotted into the front quadrangle, dragging after him the light steel chain with which he was usually fastened up in Drysdale's scout's room at night. He came innocently towards one and another of the groups, and retired from each much astonished at the low growl with which his acquaintance was repudiated on all sides.

"Porter, whose dog is that?" said the Dean, catching sight of him.

"Mr. Drysdale's dog, sir, I think, sir," answered the porter.

"Probably the animal who bit me last night," said the bursar. His knowledge of dogs was small; if Jack had fastened on him he would probably have been in bed from the effects.

"Turn the dog out of college," said the Dean.

"Please, sir, he's a very savage dog, sir," said the porter, whose respect for Jack was unbounded.

"Turn him out immediately," replied the Dean.

The wretched porter, arming himself with a broom approached Jack, and after some coaxing managed to catch hold of the end of his chain, and began to lead him towards the gates, carefully holding out the broom towards Jack's nose with his other hand, to protect himself. Jack at first hauled away at his chain, and then began circling round the porter at the full extent of it, evidently meditating an attack. Notwithstanding the seriousness of the situation, the ludicrous alarm of the porter set the men laughing.

"Come along, or Jack will be pinning the wretched Copas," said Jervis, and he and Tom stepped up to the terrified little man, and, releasing him, led Jack, who knew them both well, out of college.

"Were you at that supper party," said Jervis, as they deposited Jack with an ostler, who was lounging outside the gates to be taken to Drysdale's stables.

"No," said Tom.

"I'm glad to hear it, there will be a pretty clean sweep after last night's doings."

"But I was in the quadrangle when they came out."

"Not caught, eh?" said Jervis.

"No, luckily I got to my own rooms at once."

"Were any of the crew caught?"

"Not that I know of."

"Well, we shall hear enough of it before lecture time.'

Jervis was right. There was a meeting in the common room directly after breakfast. Drysdale anticipating his fate, took his name off before they sent for him. Chanter and three or four others were rusticated for a year, and Blake was ordered to go down at once. He was a scholar, and what was to be done in his case would be settled at the meeting at the end of term.

For twenty-four hours it was supposed that St. Cloud had escaped altogether, but at the end of that time he was summoned before a meeting in the common room. The tutor, whose door had been so effectually screwed up that he had been obliged to get out of his window by a ladder to attend morning chapel, proved wholly unable to appreciate the joke, and set himself to work to discover the perpetrators of it. The door was fastened with long gimlets, which were screwed firmly in, and when driven well home their heads had been knocked off. The tutor collected the shafts of the gimlets from the carpenter, who came to effect an entry for him; and after careful examination, discovered the trade mark. So, putting them in his pocket, he walked off into the town, and soon came back with the information he required, which resulted in the rustication of St. Cloud, an event which was borne by the college with the greatest equanimity.

Shortly afterwards Tom attended in the schools' quadrangle again, to be present at the posting of the class list. This time there were plenty of anxious faces; the quadrangle was full of them. He felt almost as nervous himself as if he were waiting for the third gun. He thrust himself forward, and was amongst the first who caught sight of the document. One look was enough for him, and the next moment he was off at full speed to St. Ambrose, and, rushing headlong into Hardy's rooms, seized him by the hand, and shook it vehemently.

"It's all right, old fellow," he cried, as soon as he could catch his breath; "it's all right. Four firsts; you're one of them: well done!"

"And Grey, where's he? is he all right?"

"Bless me, I forgot to look," said Tom; "I only read the firsts, and then come off as hard as I could."

"Then he is not a first."

"No; I'm sure of that."

"I must go and see him; he deserved it far more than I."

"No, by Jove, old boy!" said Tom, seizing him again by the hand, "that he didn't; nor any man that ever went into the schools."

"Thank you, Brown," said Hardy, returning his warm grip. "You do one good. Now to see poor Grey, and to write to my dear old father before Hall. Fancy him opening the letter at breakfast the day after to-morrow! I only hope it won't hurt him."

"Never fear. I don't believe in people dying of joy, and any thing short of sudden death he won't mind at the price."

Hardy hurried off, and Tom went to his own rooms, and smoked a cigar to allay his excitement, and thought about his friend and all they had felt together and laughed and mourned over in the short months of their friendship. A pleasant dreamy half-hour he spent thus, till the hall bell roused him, and he made his toilette and went to his dinner.

It was with very mixed feelings that Hardy walked by the servitors' table and took his seat with the bachelors, an equal at last amongst equals. No man who is worth his salt can leave a place where he has gone through hard and searching discipline and been tried in the very depths of his heart without regret, however much he may have winced under the discipline. It is no light thing to fold up and lay by forever a portion of one's life, even when it can be laid by with honor and in thankfulness.

But it was with no mixed feelings, but with a sense of entire triumph and joy, that Tom watched his friend taking his new place, and the Dons one after another coming up and congratulating him, and treating him as the man who had done honor to them and his college.

## CHAPTER II.

#### COMMEMORATION.

The end of the academic year was now at hand, and Oxford was beginning to put on her gayest clothing. The college gardeners were in a state of unusual activity, and the lawns and flower-beds, which form such exquisite settings to many of the venerable grey-gabled buildings, were as neat and as bright as hands could make them. Cooks, butlers, and their assistants, were bestirring themselves in kitchen and butlery, under the direction of bursars jealous of the fame of their houses, in the preparation of the abundant and solid fare with which Oxford is wont to entertain all comers. Every thing the best of its kind, no stint but no nonsense, seems to be the wise rule which the University hands down and lives up to in these matters. However we may differ as to her degeneracy in other departments, all who have ever visited her will admit that in this of hospitality she is still a great national teacher, acknowledging and preaching by example the fact, that eating and drinking are important parts of man's life, which are to be allowed their due prominence, and not thrust into a corner, but are to be done soberly and thankfully, in the sight of God and man. The coaches were bringing in heavy loads of visitors; carriages of all kinds were coming in from the neighboring counties; and lodgings in the High Street were going up to fabulous prices.

In one of these High Street lodgings, on the evening

of the Saturday before Commemoration, Miss Winter and her cousin are sitting. They have been in Oxford during the greater part of the day, having posted up from Englebourne, but they have only just come in, for the younger lady is still in her bonnet, and Miss Winter's lies on the table. The windows are wide open, and Miss Winter is sitting at one of them, while her cousin is busied in examining the furniture and decorations of their temporary home, now commenting upon these, now pouring out praises of Oxford.

"Isn't it too charming? I never dreamt that any town could be so beautiful. Don't you feel wild about it, Katie?"

"It is the queen of towns, dear. But I know it well, you see, so that I can't be quite so enthusiastic as you."

"Oh, those dear gardens! what was the name of those ones with the targets up, where they were shooting? Don't you remember?"

"New College Gardens, on the old city walls, you mean?"

"No, no. They were very nice and sentimental. I should like to go and sit and read poetry there. But I mean the big ones, the gorgeous, princely ones; with wicked old Bishop Laud's gallery looking into them."

"Oh! St. John's, of course."

"Yes, St. John's. Why do you hate Laud so, Katie?"

"I don't hate him, dear. He was a Berkshire man, you know. But I think he did a great deal of harm to the Church."

"How do you think my new silk looked in the gardens? How lucky I brought it, wasn't it? I shouldn't have liked to have been in nothing but muslins. They don't suit here; you want something richer amongst the old buildings, and on the beautiful velvety turf of the gardens. How do you think I looked?"

"You looked like a queen, dear; or a lady in waiting, at least."

"Yes, a lady in waiting on Henrietta Maria. Didn't you hear one of the gentlemen say that she was lodged in St. John's when Charles marched to relieve Gloucester? Ah! can't you fancy her sweeping about the gardens, with her ladies following her, and Bishop Laud walking just a little behind her, and talking in a low voice about — let me see — something very important!"

"O Mary! where has your history gone? He was Archbishop, and was safely locked up in the Tower."

"Well, perhaps he was; then he couldn't be with her, of course. How stupid of you to remember, Katie. Why can't you make up your mind to enjoy yourself when you come out for a holiday?"

"I shouldn't enjoy myself any the more for forgetting dates," said Katie, laughing.

"Oh, you would though! only try. But, let me see, it can't be Laud. Then it shall be that cruel drinking old man, with the wooden leg made of gold, who was governor of Oxford when the king was away. He must be hobbling along after the queen in a buff coat and breast-plate, holding his hat with a long drooping white feather in his hand."

"But you wouldn't like it at all, Mary; it would be too serious for you. The poor queen would be too anxious to gossip, and you ladies in waiting would be obliged to walk after her without saying a word."

"Yes, that would be stupid. But then she would have to go away with the old governor to write dispatches; and some of the young officers with long hair and beautiful lace sleeves, and large boots, whom the king had left behind, wounded, might come and walk perhaps, or sit in the sun in the quiet gardens."

Mary looked over her shoulder with the merriest twinkle in her eye, to see how her steady cousin would take this last picture. "The college authorities would never allow that," she said, quietly, still looking out of the window; "if you wanted beaus, you must have them in black gowns."

"They would have been jealous of the soldiers, you think? Well, I don't mind; the black gowns are very pleasant, only a little stiff. But how do you think my bonnet looked?"

"Charmingly. But when are you going to have done looking in the glass? You don't care for the buildings, I believe, a bit. Come and look at St. Mary's; there is such a lovely light on the steeple!"

"I'll come directly, but I must get these flowers right. I'm sure there are too many in this trimming."

Mary was trying her new bonnet on over and over again before the mantel-glass, and pulling out and changing the places of the blush-rose buds with which it was trimmed. Just then a noise of wheels, accompanied by a merry tune on a cornopean, came in from the street.

"What's that, Katie?" she cried, stopping her work for a moment.

"A coach coming up from Magdalen bridge. I think it is a cricketing party coming home."

"Oh, let me see!" and she tripped across to the window, bonnet in hand, and stood beside her cousin. And then, sure enough, a coach covered with cricketers returning from a match, drove past the window. The young ladies looked out at first with great curiosity; but suddenly finding themselves the mark for a whole coach-load of male eyes, shrank back a little before the cricketers had passed on towards the "Mitre." As the coach passed out of sight, Mary gave a pretty toss of her head, and said, —

"Well, they don't want for assurance, at any rate. I think they needn't have stared so."

"It was our fault," said Katie; "we shouldn't have been at the window. Besides, you know you are to be a lady in waiting on Henrietta Maria up here, and of course you must get used to being stared at."

"Oh, yes! but that was to be by young gentlemen wounded in the wars, in lace ruffles, as one sees them in pictures. That's a very different thing from young gentlemen in flannel trousers and straw hats, driving up the High Street on coaches. I declare one of them had the impudence to bow, as if he knew you."

"So he does. That was my cousin."

"Your cousin! Ah, I remember! Then he must be my cousin too."

"No, not at all. He is no relation of yours."

"Well, I sha'n't break my heart. But is he a good partner?"

"I should say, yes. But I hardly know. We used to be a great deal together as children, but papa has been such an invalid lately."

"Ah! I wonder how uncle is getting on at the Vice-Chancellor's. Look, it is past eight by St. Mary's. When were we to go?"

"We were asked for nine."

"Then we must go and dress. Will it be very slow and stiff, Katie? I wish we were going to something not quite so grand."

"You'll find it very pleasant, I dare say."

"There won't be any dancing, though, I know; will there?"

"No; I should think certainly not."

"Dear me! I hope there will be some young men there, — I shall be so shy, I know, if there are nothing but wise people. How do you talk to a Regius Professor, Katie? It must be awful."

"He will probably be at least as uncomfortable as you, dear," said Miss Winter, laughing, and rising from the window; "let us go and dress."

"Shall I wear my best gown? — What shall I put in my hair?"

At this moment the door opened, and the maid-servant introduced Mr. Brown.

It was the St. Ambrose drag which had passed along shortly before, bearing the eleven home from a triumphant match. As they came over Magdalen bridge, Drysdale, who had returned to Oxford as a private gentleman after his late catastrophe, which he had managed to keep a secret from his guardian, and was occupying his usual place on the box, called out, —

"Now, boys, keep your eyes open, there must be plenty of lionesses about;" and thus warned, the whole load, including the cornopean player, were on the look-out for lady visitors, profanely called lionesses, all the way up the street. They had been gratified by the sight of several walking in the High Street or looking out of the windows, before they caught sight of Miss Winter and her cousin. The appearance of these young ladies created a sensation.

"I say, look! up there in the first floor."

"By George, they're something like."

"The sitter for choice."

"No, no, the standing-up one; she looks so saucy."

"Hollo, Brown! do you know them?"

"One of them is my cousin," said Tom, who had just been guilty of the salutation which, as we saw, excited the indignation of the younger lady.

"What luck!—You'll ask me to meet them—when shall it be? To-morrow at breakfast, I vote."

"I say, you'll introduce me before the ball on Monday? promise now," said another.

"I don't know that I shall see any thing of them," said Tom; "I shall just leave a pasteboard, but I'm not in the humor to be dancing about lionizing."

A storm of indignation arose at this speech; the notion that any of the fraternity who had any hold on lionesses, particularly if they were pretty, should not use it to the utmost for the benefit of the rest, and the glory and honor of the college, was revolting to the undergraduate mind. So the whole body escorted Tom to the door of the lodgings, impressing upon him the necessity of engaging both his lionesses for every hour of every day in St. Ambrose's, and left him not till they had heard him ask for the young ladies, and seen him fairly on his way up stairs. They need not have taken so much trouble, for in his secret soul he was no little pleased at the appearance of creditable ladies, more or less belonging to him, and would have found his way to see them quickly and surely enough without any urging. Moreover, he had been really fond of his cousin, years before, when they had been boy and girl together.

So they greeted one another very cordially, and looked one another over as they shook hands, to see what changes time had made. He makes his changes rapidly enough at that age, and mostly for the better, as the two cousins thought. It was nearly three years since they had met, and then he was a fifth-form boy and she a girl in the schoolroom. They were both conscious of a strange pleasure in meeting again, mixed with a feeling of shyness, and wonder, whether they should be able to step back into their old relations.

Mary looked on demurely, really watching them, but ostensibly engaged on the rosebud trimming. Presently Miss Winter turned to her and said, "I don't think you two ever met before; I must introduce you, I suppose;— my cousin Tom, my cousin Mary."

"Then we must be cousins too," said Tom, holding out his hand.

"No, Katie says not," she answered.

"I don't mean to believe her, then," said Tom; "but what are you going to do now, to-night? Why didn't you write and tell me you were coming?"

"We have been so shut up lately, owing to papa's bad health, that I really had almost forgotten you were at Oxford."

"By the by," said Tom, "where is uncle?"

"Oh! he is dining at the Vice Chancellor's, who is an old College friend of his. We have only been up here three or four hours, and it has done him so much good. I am so glad we spirited him up to coming."

"You haven't made any engagements yet, I hope?"

"Indeed we have; I can't tell how many. We came in time for luncheon in Balliol. Mary and I made it our dinner, and we have been seeing sights ever since, and have been asked to go to, I don't know how many luncheons, and breakfasts."

"What, with a lot of dons, I suppose?" said Tom, spitefully; "you won't enjoy Oxford then; they'll bore you to death."

"There now, Katie; that is just what I was afraid of," joined in Mary; "you remember we didn't hear a word about balls all the afternoon."

"You haven't got your tickets for the balls, then?" said Tom, brightening up.

"No; how shall we get them?"

"Oh! I can manage that, I've no doubt."

"Stop; how are we to go? Papa will never take us.'

"You needn't think about that; anybody will chaperon you. Nobody cares about that sort of thing at commemoration."

"Indeed I think you had better wait till I have talked to papa."

"Then all the tickets will be gone," said Tom. "You must go. Why shouldn't I chaperon you? I know several men whose sisters are going with them."

"No, that will scarcely do, I'm afraid. But really, Mary, we must go and dress."

"Where are you going then?" said Tom.

"To an evening party at the Vice-Chancellor's; we are asked for nine o'clock, and the half-hour has struck."

"Hang the dons; how unlucky that I didn't know before! Have you any flowers, by the way."

"Not one."

"Then I will try to get you some by the time you are ready. May I?"

"Oh! yes, pray do," said Mary. "That's capital, Katie, isn't it? Now I shall have something to put in my hair; I couldn't think what I was to wear."

Tom took a look at the hair in question, and then left them and hastened out to scour the town for flowers, as if his life depended on success. In the morning, he would probably have resented as insulting, or laughed at as wildly improbable, the suggestion that he would be so employed before night.

A double chair was thrown up opposite the door when he came back, and the ladies were coming down into the sitting room.

"Oh, look, Katie! What lovely flowers! How very kind of you."

Tom surrendered as much of his burden as that young lady's little round white hands could clasp, to her, and deposited the rest on the table.

"Now, Katie, which shall I wear — this beautiful white rose all by itself, or a wreath of these pansies? Here, I have a wire: I can make them up in a minute." She turned to the glass, and held the rich cream-white against her hair, and then turning on Tom, added, "What do you think?"

"I thought fern would suit your hair better than any thing else," said Tom; "and so I got these leaves," and he picked out two slender fern leaves.

"How very kind of you! Let me see, how do you mean? Ah! I see; it will be charming;" and so saying, she held the leaves each in one hand to the sides of her head, and then floated about the room for needle and thread, and with a few nimble stitches fastened together the simple green crown, which her cousin put on for her, making the points meet above her forehead. Mary was wild with delight at the effect, and full of thanks to Tom as he helped them hastily to tie up bouquets, and then, amidst much laughing, they squeezed into the wheel chair together, (as the fashions of that day allowed two young ladies to do), and went off to their party, leaving a last injunction on him to go up and put the rest of the flowers in water, and to call directly after breakfast the next day. He obeyed his orders, and pensively arranged the rest of the flowers in the china ornaments on the mantelpiece, and in a soup plate, which he got and placed in the middle of the table, and then spent some minutes examining a pair of gloves and other small articles of women's gear which lay scattered about the room. The gloves particularly attracted him, and he flattened them out and laid them on his own large brown hand, and smiled at the contrast, and took other unjustifiable liberties with them; after which he returned to college and endured much banter as to the time his call had lasted, and promised to engage his cousins, as he called them, to grace some festivities in St. Ambrose's at their first spare moment.

The next day, being Show Sunday, was spent by the young ladies in a ferment of spiritual and other dissipation. They attended morning service at eight at the cathedral; breakfasted at a Merton fellow's, from whence they adjourned to University sermon. Here, Mary, after two or three utterly ineffectual attempts to understand what the preacher was meaning, soon relapsed into an examination of the bonnets present, and the doctors and proctors on the floor, and the undergraduates in the gallery. On the whole, she was, perhaps, better employed than her cousin, who knew enough of religious party strife to follow the preacher, and was made very uncomfortable by his discourse, which consisted of an attack upon the recent publications of the most eminent and best men in the University. Poor Miss Winter came away with a vague impression of the wickedness of all persons who dare to travel out of beaten tracks, and that the most unsafe state of mind in the world is that which inquires and aspires, and cannot be satisfied with the regulation draught of spiritual doctors in high places. Being naturally of a reverent turn of mind, she tried to think that the discourse had done her good. At the same time she was somewhat troubled by the thought that somehow the best men in all times of which she had read seemed to her to be just those whom the preacher was in fact denouncing, although in words he had praised them as the great lights of the Church. The words which she had heard in one of the lessons kept running in her head, " Truly ye bear witness that ye do allow the deeds of your fathers, for they indeed killed them, but ye build their sepulchres." But she had little leisure to think on the subject, and, as her father praised the sermon as a noble protest against the fearful tendencies of the day to Popery and Pantheism, smothered the questionings of her own heart as well as she could, and went off to luncheon in a common room; after which her father retired to their lodgings, and she and her cousin were escorted to afternoon service at Magdalen, in achieving which last feat they had to encounter a crush only to be equalled by that at the pit entrance between the opera on a Jenny Lind night. But what will not a delicately nutured British lady go through when her mind is bent either on pleasure or duty?

Poor Tom's feelings throughout the day may be more easily conceived than described. He had called according to order, and waited at their lodgings after breakfast. Of course they did not arrive. He had caught a distant glimpse of them in St. Mary's, but had not been able to approach. He had called again in the afternoon unsuccessfully, so far as seeing them was concerned; but he had found his uncle at home, lying upon the sofa. At first he was much dismayed by this rencontre, but recovering his presence of mind he proceeded, I regret to say, to take the length of the old gentleman's foot, by entering into a minute and sympathizing inquiry into the state of his health. Tom had no faith whatever in his uncle's ill health, and believed, — as many persons of robust constitution are too apt to do when brought face to face with nervous patients, — that he might shake off the whole of his maladies at any time by a resolute effort, so that his sympathy was all sham, though, perhaps, one may pardon it, considering the end in view, which was that of persuading the old gentleman to entrust the young ladies to his nephew's care for that evening in the long walk; and generally to look upon his nephew, Thomas Brown, as his natural prop and supporter in the university, whose one object in life just now would be to take trouble off his hands, and who was of that rare and precocious steadiness of character that he might be as safely trusted as a Spanish duenna. To a very considerable extent the victim fell into the toils. He had many old friends at the colleges, and was very fond of good dinners, and long sittings afterwards. This very evening he was going to dine at St. John's, and had been much troubled at the idea of having to leave the unrivalled old port of that learned house to escort his daughter and niece to the long walk. Still he was too easy and good-natured not to wish that they might get there, and did not like the notion of their going with perfect strangers. Here was a compromise. His nephew was young, but still he was a near relation, and in fact it gave the poor old man a plausible excuse for not exerting himself as he felt he ought to do, which was all he ever required for shifting his responsibilities and duties upon other shoulders.

So Tom waited quietly till the young ladies came home, which they did just before hall-time. Mr. Winter was getting impatient. As soon as they arrived he started for St. John's, after advising them to remain at home for the rest of the evening, as they looked quite tired and knocked up; but if they were resolved to go to the long walk, his nephew would escort them.

"How can Uncle Robert say we look so tired?" said Mary, consulting the glass on the subject; "I feel quite fresh. Of course, Katie, you mean to go to the long walk?"

"I hope you will go," said Tom; "I think you owe me some amends. I came here according to order this morning, and you were not in, and I have been trying to catch you ever since."

"We couldn't help it," said Miss Winter; "indeed we have not had a minute to ourselves all day. I was very sorry to think that we should have brought you here for nothing this morning."

"But about the long walk, Katie?"

"Well, don't you think we have done enough for to-day? I should like to have tea and sit quietly at home, as papa suggested."

"Do you feel very tired, dear?" said Mary, seating herself by her cousin on the sofa, and taking her hand.

"No, dear; I only want a little quiet and a cup of tea."

"Then let us stay here quietly till it is time to start. When ought we to get to the long walk?"

"About half-past seven," said Tom; "you shouldn't be much later than that."

"There you see, Katie, we shall have two hours' perfect rest. You shall lie upon the sofa and I will read to you, and then we shall go on all fresh again."

Miss Winter smiled and said, "Very well." She saw that her cousin was bent on going, and she could deny her nothing.

"May I send you any thing from college?" said Tom; "you ought to have something more than tea, I'm sure."

"Oh! no, thank you. We dined in the middle of the day."

"Then I may call for you about seven o'clock," said Tom, who had come unwillingly to the conclusion that he had better leave them for the present.

"Yes, and mind you come in good time; we mean to see the whole sight, remember. We are country cousins."

"You must let me call you cousin then, just for the look of the thing."

"Certainly, just for the look of the thing, we will be cousins till further notice."

"Well, you and Tom seem to get on together, Mary," said Miss Winter, as they heard the front door close. "I'm learning a lesson from you, though I doubt whether I shall ever be able to put it in practice. What a blessing it must be not to be shy!"

"Are you shy, then?" said Mary, looking at her cousin with a playful loving smile.

"Yes, dreadfully. It is positive pain to me to walk into a room where there are people I do not know."

"But I feel that too. I'm sure now you were much less embarrassed than I last night at the Vice-Chancellor's. I quite envied you, you seemed so much at your ease."

"Did I? I would have given any thing to be back here quietly. But it is not the same thing with you. You have no real shyness, or you would never have got on so fast with my cousin."

"Oh! I don't feel at all shy with him," said Mary, laughing. "How lucky it is that he found us out so soon! I like him so much. There is a sort of way about him as if he couldn't help himself. I am sure one could turn him round one's finger. Don't you think so?"

"I'm not so sure of that. But he always was soft-hearted, poor boy! But he isn't a boy any longer. You must take care, Mary. Shall we ring for tea?"

## CHAPTER III.

#### THE LONG WALK IN CHRISTCHURCH MEADOWS.

Do well unto thyself and men will speak good of thee, is a maxim as old as King David's time, and just as true now as it was then. Hardy had found it so since the publication of the class list. Within a few days of that event, it was known that his was a very good first. His college tutor had made his own inquiries, and repeated on several occasions in a confidential way the statement that, "with the exception of a want of polish in his Latin and Greek verses, which we seldom get, except in the most finished public school men,— Etonians in particular, —there has been no better examination in the schools for several years." The worthy tutor went on to take glory to the college, and in a lower degree to himself. He called attention, in more than one common room, to the fact that Hardy had never had any private tuition, but had attained his intellectual development solely in the *curriculum* provided by St. Ambrose's College for the training of the youth intrusted to her. "He himself, indeed," he would add, "had always taken much interest in Hardy, and had, perhaps, done more for him than would be possible in every case, but only with direct reference to, and in supplement of, the college course."

The principal had taken marked and somewhat pompous notice of him, and had graciously intimated his wish, or, perhaps I should say, his will (for he would have been much astonished to be told that a wish of his could count for less than a royal mandate to any man who had been one of his servitors), that Hardy should stand for a fellowship, which had lately fallen vacant. A few weeks before, this excessive affability and condescension of the great man would have wounded Hardy; but, somehow, the sudden rush of sunshine and prosperity, though it had not thrown him off his balance, or changed his estimate of men and things, had pulled a sort of comfortable sheath over his sensitiveness, and given him a second skin, as it were, from which the principal's shafts bounded off innocuous, instead of piercing and rankling. At first, the idea of standing for a fellowship at St. Ambrose's was not pleasant to him. He felt inclined to open up entirely new ground for himself, and stand at some other college, where he had neither acquaintance nor association. But on second thoughts, he resolved to stick to his old college, moved thereto partly by the lamentations of Tom, when he heard of his friend's meditated emigration, but chiefly by the unwillingness to quit a hard post for an easier one, which besets natures like his to their own discomfort, but, may one hope, to the signal benefit of the world at large. Such men may see clearly enough all the advantages of a move of this kind — may quite appreciate the ease which it would bring them — may be impatient with themselves for not making it at once — but when it comes to the actual leaving the old post, even though it may be a march out with all the honors of war, drums beating and colors flying, as it would have been in Hardy's case, somehow or another, nine times out of ten, they throw up the chance at the last moment, if not earlier; pick up their old arms, — growling perhaps at the price they are paying to keep their own self-respect, — and shoulder back into the press to face their old work, muttering, "We are asses:

we don't know what's good for us; but we must see this job through somehow, come what may."

So Hardy stayed on at St. Ambose, waiting for the fellowship examination, and certainly, I am free to confess, not a little enjoying the changes in his position and affairs.

He had given up his low, dark, back rooms to the new servitor, his successor, to whom he had presented all the rickety furniture, except his two Windsor chairs and Oxford reading table. The intrinsic value of the gift was not great certainly, but was of importance to the poor raw boy, who was taking his place; and it was made with the delicacy of one who knew the situation. Hardy's good offices did not stop here. Having tried the bed himself for upwards of three long years, he knew all the hard places, and was resolved while he stayed up that they should never chafe another occupant as they had him. So he set himself to provide stuffing, and took the lad about with him, and cast a skirt of his newly acquired mantle of respectability over him, and put him in the way of making himself as comfortable as circumstances would allow; never disguising from him all the while that the bed was not to be a bed of roses. In which pursuit, though not yet a fellow, perhaps he was qualifying himself better for a fellowship than he could have done by any amount of cramming for polish in his versification. Not that the electors of St. Ambrose would be likely to hear of or appreciate this kind of training. Polished versification would no doubt have told more in that quarter. But we who are behind the scenes may disagree with them, and hold that he who is thus acting out, and learning to understand the meaning of the word "fellowship," is the man for our votes.

So Hardy had left his rooms and gone out of college, into

lodgings near at hand. The sword, epaulettes, and picture of his father's old ship — his tutelary divinities, as Tom called them — occupied their accustomed place in his new rooms, except that there was a looking-glass over the mantel-piece here, by the side of which the sword hung, instead of in the centre, as it had done while he had no such luxury. His Windsor chairs occupied each side of the pleasant window of his sitting-room, and already the taste for luxuries, with which he had so often accused himself to Tom, began to peep out in the shape of one or two fine engravings. Altogether Fortune was smiling on Hardy, and he was making the most of her, like a wise man, having brought her round by proving that he could get on without her, and was not going out of his way to gain her smiles. Several men came at once, even before he had taken his B.A. degree, to read with him, and others applied to know whether he would take a reading party in the long vacation. In short, all things went well with Hardy, and the Oxford world recognized the fact, and tradesmen and college servants became obsequious, and began to bow before him, and recognize him as one of their lords and masters.

It was to Hardy's lodgings that Tom repaired straightway, when he left his cousin by blood, and cousin by courtesy, at the end of the last chapter. For, running over in his mind all his acquaintance, he at once fixed upon Hardy as the man to accompany him in escorting the ladies to the Long Walk. Besides being his own most intimate friend, Hardy was the man whom he would prefer to all others to introduce to ladies now. "A month ago it might have been different," Tom thought; "he was such an old guy in his dress. But he has smartened up, and wears as good a coat as I do, and looks well enough for anybody, though he never will be much of a dresser.

Then he will be in a bachelor's gown too, which will look respectable."

"Here you are; that's all right; I'm so glad you're in," he said as he entered the room. "Now I want you to come to the Long Walk with me to-night."

"Very well; will you call for me?"

"Yes, and mind you come in your best get-up, old fellow: we shall have two of the prettiest girls who are up, with us."

"You wont want me, then; they will have plenty of escort."

"Not a bit of it. They are deserted by their natural guardian, my old uncle, who has gone out to dinner. Oh, it's all right; they are my cousins, more like sisters, and my uncle knows we are going. In fact, it was he who settled that I should take them."

"Yes, but you see I don't know them."

"That doesn't matter. I can't take them both myself—I must have somebody with me, and I'm so glad to get the chance of introducing you to some of my people. You'll know them all, I hope, before long."

"Of course I should like it very much, if you are sure it's all right."

Tom was as perfectly sure as usual, and so the matter was arranged. Hardy was very much pleased and gratified at this proof of his friend's confidence; and I am not going to say that he did not shave again, and pay most unwonted attention to his toilet before the hour fixed for Tom's return. The fame of Brown's lionesses had spread through St. Ambrose's already, and Hardy had heard of them as well as other men. There was something so unusual to him in being selected on such an occasion, when the smartest men in the college were wishing and plotting for that which came to him unasked, that he may be pardoned for feeling something a little like vanity, while he adjusted the coat which Tom had recently thought of with such complacency, and looked in the glass to see that his gown hung gracefully. The effect on the whole was so good, that Tom was above measure astonished when he came back, and could not help indulging in some gentle chaff as they walked towards the High Street arm in arm.

The young ladies were quite rested, and sitting dressed and ready for their walk when Tom and Hardy were announced, and entered the room. Miss Winter rose up, surprised and a little embarrassed at the introduction of a total stranger in her father's absence. But she put a good face on the matter, as became a well-bred young woman, though she secretly resolved to lecture Tom in private, as he introduced " My great friend, Mr. Hardy, of our college. My cousins." Mary dropped a pretty little demure courtesy, lifting her eyes for one moment for a glance at Tom, which said as plain as look could speak, " Well, I must say you are making the most of your new-found relationship." He was a little put out for a moment, but then recovered himself, and said, apologetically, —

" Mr. Hardy is a bachelor, Katie — I mean a Bachelor of Arts, and he knows all the people by sight up here. We couldn't have gone to the walk without some one to show us the lions."

" Indeed, I'm afraid you give me too much credit," said Hardy. " I know most of our dons by sight certainly, but scarcely any of the visitors."

The awkwardness of Tom's attempted explanation set every thing wrong again.

Then came one of those awkward pauses, which will occur so very provokingly at the most inopportune times. Miss Winter was seized with one of the uncontrollable fits of shyness, her bondage to which she had so lately been grieving over to Mary; and in self-defence, and without meaning in the least to do so, drew herself up, and looked as proud as you please. Hardy, whose sensitiveness, as we have seen, was as keen as a woman's, felt in a moment the awkwardness of the situation, and became as shy as Miss Winter herself. If the floor would have suddenly opened, and let him through into the dark shop, he would have been thankful; but, as it would not, there he stood, meditating a sudden retreat from the room, and a tremendous onslaught on Tom, as soon as he could catch him alone, for getting him into such a scrape. Tom was provoked with them all, for not at once feeling at ease with one another, and stood twirling his cap by the tassel, and looking fiercely at it, resolved not to break the silence. He had been at all the trouble of bringing about this charming situation, and now nobody seemed to like it, or to know what to say or do. They might get themselves out of it as they could, for any thing he cared; he was not going to bother himself any more.

Mary looked in the glass, to see that her bonnet was quite right, and then from one to another of her companions, in a little wonder at their unaccountable behavior, and a little pique that two young men should be standing there like unpleasant images, and not availing themselves of the privilege of trying, at least, to make themselves agreable to her. Luckily, however, for the party, the humorous side of the tableau struck her with great force, so that when Tom lifted his misanthropic eyes for a moment, and caught hers, they were so full of fun that he had nothing to do but to allow himself, not without a struggle, to break first into a smile and then into a laugh. This brought all eyes to bear on him, and the ice, being once broken, dissolved as quickly as it had gathered.

"I really can't see what there is to laugh at, Tom," said Miss Winter, smiling herself, nevertheless, and blushing a little, as she worked or pretended to work at buttoning one of her gloves.

"Can't you, Katie? Well then, isn't it very ridiculous, and enough to make one laugh, that we four should be standing here in a sort of Quaker's meeting, when we ought to be half-way to the Long Walk by this time?"

"Oh, do let us start," said Mary; "I know we shall be missing all the best of the sight."

"Come along, then," said Tom, leading the way downstairs, and Hardy and the ladies followed, and they descended into the High Street, walking all abreast, the two ladies together, with a gentleman on either flank. This formation answered well enough in High Street, the broad pavement of that celebrated thoroughfare being favorable to an advance in line. But when they had wheeled into Oriel Lane the narrow pavement at once threw the line into confusion, and after one or two fruitless attempts to take up the dressing they settled down into the more natural formation of close column of couples, the leading couple consisting of Mary and Tom, and the remaining couple of Miss Winter and Hardy. It was a lovely midsummer evening, and Oxford was looking her best under the genial, cloudless sky, so that, what with the usual congratulations on the weather, and explanatory remarks on the buildings as they passed along, Hardy managed to keep up a conversation with his companion without much difficulty. Miss Winter was pleased with his quiet, deferential manner, and soon lost her feeling of shyness, and, before Hardy had come to the end of such remarks as it occurred to him to make, she was taking her fair share in the talk. In describing their day's doings she spoke with enthusiasm of the beauty of Magdalen

4\*

Chapel, and betrayed a little knowledge of traceries and mouldings, which gave an opening to her companion to travel out of the weather and the names of colleges. Church architecture was just one of the subjects which was sure at that time to take more or less hold on every man at Oxford whose mind was open to the influences of the place. Hardy had read the usual text-books, and kept his eyes open as he walked about the town and neighborhood. To Miss Winter he seemed so learned on the subject, that she began to doubt his tendencies, and was glad to be re-assured by some remarks which fell from him as to the University sermon which she had heard. She was glad to find that her cousin's most intimate friend was not likely to lead him into the errors of Tractarianism.

Meantime, the leading couple were getting on satisfactorily in their way.

"Isn't it good of Uncle Robert? he says that he shall feel quite comfortable as long as you and Katie are with me. In fact, I feel quite responsible already, like an old dragon in a story-book watching a treasure."

"Yes, but what does Katie say to being made a treasure of? She has to think a good deal for herself; and I am afraid you are not quite certain of being our sole knight and guardian because Uncle Robert wants to get rid of us. Poor old uncle!"

"But you wouldn't object, then?"

"Oh, dear, no — at least, not unless you take to looking as cross as you did just now in our lodgings. Of course, I'm all for dragons who are mad about dancing, and never think of leaving a ball-room till the band packs up and the old man shuffles in to put out the lights."

"Then I shall be a model dragon," said Tom. Twenty-four hours earlier he had declared that nothing should induce him to go to the balls; but his views on the subject had been greatly modified, and he had been worrying all his acquaintance, not unsuccessfully, for the necessary tickets, ever since his talk with his cousins on the preceding evening.

The scene became more and more gay and lively as they passed out of Christchurch towards the Long Walk. The town turned out to take its share in the show; the citizens of all ranks, the poorer ones accompanied by children of all ages, trooped along cheek by jowl with members of the University of all degrees and their visitors, somewhat indeed to the disgust of certain of these latter, many of whom declared that the whole thing was spoilt by the miscellaneousness of the crowd, and that " those sort of people " ought not to be allowed to come to the Long Walk on Show Sunday. However, " those sort of people " abounded, nevertheless, and seemed to enjoy very much, in sober fashion, the solemn march up and down beneath the grand avenue of elms, in the midst of their betters.

The University was there in strength, from the vice-chancellor downwards. Somehow or another, though it might seem an unreasonable thing at first sight for grave and reverend persons to do, yet most of the gravest of them found some reason for taking a turn in the Long Walk. As for the undergraduates, they turned out almost to a man, and none of them more certainly than the young gentlemen, elaborately dressed, who had sneered at the whole ceremony as snobbish an hour or two before.

As for our hero, he sailed into the meadows thoroughly satisfied for the moment with himself and his convoy. He had every reason to be so, for though there were many gayer and more fashionably dressed ladies present than his cousin, and cousin by courtesy, there were none there whose faces, figures, and dresses carried more unmistakably the marks of that thorough, quiet, high breeding, that refinement which is no mere surface polish, and that fearless unconsciousness which looks out from pure hearts, which are still, thank God, to be found in so many homes of the English gentry.

The Long Walk was filling rapidly, and at every half-dozen paces Tom was greeted by some of his friends or acquaintance, and exchanged a word or two with them. But he allowed them one after another to pass by without effecting any introduction.

"You seem to have a great many acquaintances," said his companion, upon whom none of these salutations were lost.

"Yes, of course; one gets to know a great many men up here."

"It must be very pleasant. But does it not interfere a great deal with your reading?"

"No; because one meets them at lectures, and in Hall and Chapel. Besides," he added in a sudden fit of honesty, "it is my first year. One doesn't read much in one's first year. It is a much harder thing than people think to take to reading, except just before an examination."

"But your great friend who is walking with Katie — what did you say his name is?"

"Hardy."

"Well, he is a great scholar, didn't you say?"

"Yes, he has just taken a first class. He is the best man of his year."

"How proud you must be of him! I suppose now he is a great reader?"

"Yes, he is great at every thing. He is nearly the best oar in our boat. By the way, you will come to the procession of boats to-morrow night? We are the head boat on the river."

"Oh, I hope so. Is it a pretty sight? Let us ask Katie about it."

"It is the finest sight in the world," said Tom, who had never seen it; "twenty-four eight oars, with their flags flying, and all the crews in uniform. You see the barges over there, moored along the side of the river. You will sit on one of them as we pass."

"Yes, I think I do," said Mary, looking across the meadow in the direction in which he pointed; "you mean those great gilded things. But I don't see the river."

"Shall we walk round there? It wont take us ten minutes."

"But we must not leave the walk and all the people. It is so amusing here."

"Then you will wear our colors at the procession to-morrow?"

"Yes, if Katie doesn't mind. At least if they are pretty. What are your colors?"

"Blue and white. I will get you some ribbons to-morrow morning."

"Very well, and I will make them up into rosettes."

"Why, do you know them?" asked Tom, as she bowed to two gentlemen in masters' caps and gowns, whom they met in the crowd.

"Yes; at least we met them last night."

"But do you know who they are?"

"Oh, yes; they were introduced to us, and I talked a great deal to them. And Katie scolded me for it when we got home. No; I wont say scolded me, but looked very grave over it."

"They are two of the leaders of the Tractarians."

"Yes. That was the fun of it. Katie was so pleased and interested with them at first; much more than I was. But when she found out who they were, she fairly ran away, and I stayed and talked on. I don't think they said any thing very dangerous. Perhaps one of them wrote No. 90. Do you know?"

"I dare say. But I don't know much about it. However, they must have a bad time of it, I should think, up here with the old dons."

"But don't you think one likes people who are persecuted? I declare I would listen to them for an hour, though I didn't understand a word, just to show them that I wasn't afraid of them, and sympathized with them. How can people be so ill-natured? I'm sure they only write what they believe, and think will do good."

"That's just what most of us feel," said Tom; "we hate to see them put down because they don't agree with the swells up here. You'll see how they will be cheered in the theatre."

"Then they are not unpopular and persecuted after all?"

"Oh, yes, by the dons. And that's why we all like them. From fellow-feeling you see, because the dons bully them and us equally."

"But I thought they were dons too?"

"Well, so they are, but not regular dons, you know, like the proctors, and deans, and that sort."

His companion did not understand this delicate distinction, but was too much interested in watching the crowd to inquire further.

Presently they met two of the heads of houses walking with several strangers. Every one was noticing them as they passed, and of course Tom was questioned as to who they were. Not being prepared with an answer he appealed to Hardy, who was just behind them talking to Miss Winter. They were some of the celebrities on whom honorary degrees were to be conferred, Hardy said; a famous American author, a foreign ambassador, a well-known Indian soldier, and others. Then came some more M.A.'s, one of whom this time bowed to Miss Winter.

"Who was that, Katie?"

"One of the gentlemen we met last night. I did not catch his name, but he was very agreeable."

"Oh, I remember. You were talking to him for a long time after you ran away from me. I was very curious to know what you were saying, you seemed so interested."

"Well, you seem to have made the most of your time last night," said Tom; "I should have thought, Katie, you would hardly have approved of him either."

"But who is he?"

"Why, the most dangerous man in Oxford. What do they call him — a Germanizer and a rationalist; isn't it, Hardy?"

"Yes, I believe so," said Hardy.

"Oh, think of that! There, Katie; you had much better have stayed by me after all. A Germanizer, didn't you say? What a hard word. It must be much worse than Tractarian. Isn't it now?"

"Mary, dear, pray take care; everybody will hear you," said Miss Winter.

"I wish I thought that everybody would listen to me," replied Miss Mary. "But I really will be very quiet, Katie, — only I must know which is the worst, my Tractarians or your Germanizer?"

"Oh, the Germanizer of course," said Tom.

"But why?" said Hardy, who could do no less than break a lance for his companion. Moreover he happened to have strong convictions on these subjects.

"Why? Because one knows the worst of where the Tractarians are going. They may go to Rome and there's an end of it. But the Germanizers are going into the abysses, or no one knows where."

"There, Katie, you hear, I hope," interrupted Miss Mary, coming to her companion's rescue before Hardy could bring his artillery to bear, "but what a terrible place Oxford must be. I declare it seems quite full of people whom it is unsafe to talk with."

"I wish it were, if they were all like Miss Winter's friend," said Hardy. And then the crowd thickened, and they dropped behind again. Tom was getting to think more of his companion and less of himself every minute, when he was suddenly confronted in the walk by Benjamin, the Jew money-lender, smoking a cigar and dressed in a gaudy-figured satin waistcoat and water fall of the same material, and resplendent with jewellery. He had business to attend to in Oxford at this time of the year. Nothing escaped the eyes of Tom's companion.

". Who was that?" she said; "what a dreadful-looking man! Surely, he bowed as if he knew you?"

"I dare say. He is impudent enough for any thing," said Tom.

" But who is he?"

"Oh, a rascally fellow who sells bad cigars and worse wine."

Tom's equanimity was much shaken by the apparition of the Jew. The remembrance of the bill scene at the public house in the Corn-market, and the unsatisfactory prospect in that matter, with Blake plucked and Drysdale no longer a member of the University and utterly careless as to his liabilities, came across him, and made him silent and absent.

He answered at hazard to his companion's remarks for the next minute or two, until, after some particularly inappropriate reply, she turned her head and looked at him for a moment with steady, wide-open eyes, which brought him to himself, or rather drove him into himself, in no time.

"I really beg your pardon," he said; "I was very rude, I fear. It is so strange to me to be walking here with ladies. What were you saying?"

"Nothing of any consequence — I really forget. But is it a very strange thing for you to walk with ladies here?"

"Strange! I should think it was! I have never seen a lady that I knew up here, till you came."

"Indeed! but there must be plenty of ladies living in Oxford?"

"I don't believe there are. At least, we never see them."

"Then you ought to be on your best behavior when we do come. I shall expect you now to listen to every thing I say, and to answer my silliest questions."

"Oh, you ought not to be so hard on us."

"You mean that you are not used to answering silly questions? How wise you must all grow, living up here together."

"Perhaps. But the wisdom doesn't come down to the first-year men; and so —"

"Well, why do you stop?"

"Because I was going to say something you might not like."

"Then I insist on hearing it. Now, I shall not let you off. You were saying that wisdom does not come so low as first-year men; and so — what?"

"And so — and so, they are not wise."

"Yes, of course; but that was not what you were going to say; and so —"

"And so they were generally agreeable, for wise people are always dull; and so — ladies ought to avoid the dons."

"And not avoid first-year men?"

"Exactly so."

"Because they are foolish, and therefore fit company for ladies. Now, really —"

"No, no; because they are foolish, and therefore, they ought to be made wise; and ladies are wiser than dons."

"And, therefore, duller, for all wise people, you said, were dull."

"Not all wise people; only people who are wise by cramming, — as dons; but ladies are wise by inspiration."

"And first-year men, are they foolish by inspiration and agreeable by cramming, or agreeable by inspiration and foolish by cramming?"

"They are agreeable by inspiration in the society of ladies."

"Then they can never be agreeable, for you say they never see ladies."

"Not with the bodily eye, but with the eye of fancy."

"Then their agreeableness must be all fancy."

"But it is better to be agreeable in fancy than dull in reality."

"That depends upon whose fancy it is. To be agreeable in your own fancy is compatible with being as dull in reality as —"

"How you play with words; I see you wont leave me a shred either of fancy or agreeableness to stand on."

"Then I shall do you good service. I shall destroy your illusions; you cannot stand on illusions."

"But remember what my illusions were,— fancy and agreeableness."

"But your agreeableness stood on fancy, and your

fancy on nothing. You had better settle down at once on the solid baseness of dulness, like the dons."

"Then I am to found myself on fact, and try to be dull? What a conclusion! But perhaps dulness is no more a fact than fancy;— what is dulness?"

"Oh, I do not undertake to define; you are the best judge."

"How severe you are! Now, see how generous I am. Dulness in society is the absence of ladies."

"Alas, poor Oxford! Who is that in the velvet sleeves? Why do you touch your cap?"

"That is the proctor. He is our Cerberus; he has to keep all undergraduates in good order."

"What a task! He ought to have three heads."

"He has only one head, but it is a very long one. And he has a tail like any Basha, composed of pro-proctors, marshals, and bull-dogs, and I don't know what all. But to go back to what we were saying—"

"No don't let us go back. I'm tired of it; besides, you were just beginning about dulness. How can you expect me to listen now?"

"Oh, but do listen, just for two minutes. Will you be serious? I do want to know what you really think when you hear the case."

"Well, I will try, for two minutes, mind."

Upon gaining which permission Tom went off into an interesting discourse on the unnaturalness of men's lives at Oxford, which it is by no means necessary to inflict on my readers. As he was waxing eloquent and sentimental, he chanced to look from his companion's face for a moment in search of a simile, when his eyes alighted on that virtuous member of society, Dick, the factotum of the Choughs, who was taking his turn in the Long Walk with his betters. Dick's face was twisted into an uncomfortable grin; his eyes were fixed on Tom and his companion; and he made a sort of half motion towards touching his hat, but couldn't quite carry it through, and so passed by.

"Ah! aint he a going of it again," he muttered to himself; "jest like 'em all."

Tom didn't hear the words, but the look had been quite enough for him, and he broke off short in his speech, and turned his head away, and, after two or three flounderings which Mary seemed not to notice, stopped short, and let Miss Winter and Hardy join them.

"It's getting dark," he said, as they came up; "the walk is thinning; ought we not to be going? Remember, I am in charge."

"Yes, I think it is time."

At this moment the great Christ Church bell — Tom, by name — began to toll.

"Surely, that can't be Tom?" Miss Winter said, who had heard the one hundred and one strokes on former occasions.

"Indeed it is, though."

"But how very light it is."

"It is almost the longest day in the year, and there hasn't been a cloud all day."

They started to walk home all together, and Tom gradually recovered himself, but left the laboring oar to Hardy, who did his work very well, and persuaded the ladies to go on and see the Ratcliffe by moonlight, — the only time to see it, as he said, because of the shadows, — and just to look in at the old quadrangle of St. Ambrose.

It was almost ten o'clock when they stopped at the lodgings in High Street. While they were waiting for the door to be opened, Hardy said, —

"I really must apologize, Miss Winter, to you, for my

intrusion to-night. I hope your father will allow me to call on him."

"Oh, yes! pray do; he will be so glad to see any friend of my cousin."

"And if I can be of any use to him; or to you, or your sister —"

"My sister! Oh, you mean Mary? She is not my sister."

"I beg your pardon. But I hope you will let me know if there is any thing I can do for you."

"Indeed we will. Now, Mary, papa will be worrying about us." And so the young ladies said their adieus, and disappeared.

"Surely, you told me they were sisters," said Hardy, as the two walked away towards college.

"No, did I? I don't remember."

"But they are your cousins?"

"Yes; at least Katie is. Don't you like her?"

"Of course; one can't help liking her. But she says you have not met for two years or more."

"No more we have."

"Then I suppose you have seen more of her companion lately?"

"Well, if you must know, I never saw her before yesterday."

"You don't mean to say that you took me in there to-night when you had never seen one of the young ladies before, and the other not for two years! Well, upon my word, Brown —"

"Now don't blow me up, old fellow, to-night — please don't. There, I give in. Don't hit a fellow when he's down. I'm so low." Tom spoke in such a deprecating tone, that Hardy's wrath passed away.

"Why, what's the matter?" he said. "You seemed to

be full of talk. I was envying your fluency, I know, often."

"Talk; yes, so I was. But didn't you see Dick in the walk? You have never heard any thing more?"

"No; but no news is good news."

"Heigho! I'm awfully down. I want to talk to you. Let me come up."

"Come along then." And so they disappeared into Hardy's lodgings.

The two young ladies, meanwhile, soothed old Mr. Winter, who had eaten and drunk more than was good for him, and was naturally put out thereby. They soon managed to persuade him to retire, and then followed themselves — first to Mary's room, where that young lady burst out at once, "What a charming place it is! Oh! didn't you enjoy your evening, Katie?"

"Yes; but I felt a little awkward without any chaperone. You seemed to get on very well with my cousin. You scarcely spoke to us in the Long Walk till just before we came away. What were you talking about?"

Mary burst into a gay laugh. "All sorts of nonsense," she said. "I don't think I ever talked so much nonsense in my life. I hope he isn't shocked. I don't think he is. But I said any thing that came into my head. I couldn't help it. You don't think it wrong?"

"Wrong, dear? No, I'm sure you could say nothing wrong."

"I'm not so sure of that. But, Katie dear, I know there is something on his mind."

"Why do you think so?"

"Oh! because he stopped short twice, and became quite absent, and seemed not to hear any thing I said."

"How odd! I never knew him do so. Did you see any reason for it?"

"No; unless it was two men we passed in the crowd. One was a vulgar-looking wretch, who was smoking — a fat black thing, with such a thick nose, covered with jewellery — "

"Not his nose, dear?"

"No, but his dress; and the other was a homely, dried-up little man, like one of your Englebourn troubles. I'm sure there is some mystery about them, and I shall find it out. But how did you like his friend, Katie?"

"Very much indeed. I was rather uncomfortable at walking so long with a stranger. But he was very pleasant, and is so fond of Tom. I am sure he is a very good friend for him."

"He looks a good man; but how ugly!"

"Do you think so? We shall have a hard day to-morrow. Good-night, dear."

"Good-night, Katie. But I don't feel a bit sleepy." And so the cousins kissed one another, and Miss Winter went to her own room.

# CHAPTER IV.

### LECTURING A LIONESS.

THE evening of Show Sunday may serve as a fair sample of what this eventful Commemoration was to our hero. The constant intercourse with ladies, — with such ladies as Miss Winter and Mary, — young, good-looking, well-spoken, and creditable in all ways, was very delightful, and the more fascinating, from the sudden change which their presence wrought in the ordinary mode of life of the place. They would have been charming in any room, but were quite irresistible in his den, which no female presence, except that of his blowsy old bedmaker, had lightened since he had been in possession. All the associations of the freshman's rooms were raised at once. When he came in at night now, he could look sentimentally at his arm-chair (christened "The Captain," after Captain Hardy), on which Katie had sat to make breakfast; or at the brass peg on the door, on which Mary had hung her bonnet and shawl, after displacing his gown. His very teacups and saucers, which were already a miscellaneous set of several different patterns, had made a move almost into his affections; at least, the two — one brown, one blue — which the young ladies had used. A human interest belonged to them now, and they were no longer mere crockery. He thought of buying two very pretty China ones, the most expensive he could find in Oxford, and getting them to use these for the first time, but rejected the idea. The fine new ones, he felt, would never be the same to him. They had come in and used his own rubbish; that was the great charm. If he had been going to give *them* cups, no material would have been beautiful enough; but for his own use after them, the commoner the better. The material was nothing, the association every thing. It is marvellous the amount of healthy sentiment of which a naturally soft-hearted undergraduate is capable by the end of the summer term. But sentiment is not all one-sided. The delights which spring from sudden intimacy with the fairest and best part of the creation, are as far above those of the ordinary unmitigated, undergraduate life, as the British citizen of 1860 is above the rudimentary personage in prehistoric times from whom he has been gradually improved, up to his present state of enlightenment and perfection. But each state has also its own troubles as well as its pleasures; and, though the former are a price which no decent fellow would boggle at for a moment, it is useless to pretend that paying them is pleasant.

Now, at Commemoration, as elsewhere, where men do congregate, if your lady-visitors are not pretty or agreeable enough to make your friends and acquaintance eager to know them, and to cater for their enjoyment, and try in all ways to win their favor and cut you out, you have the satisfaction at any rate of keeping them to yourself, though you lose the pleasures which arise from being sought after, and made much of for their sakes, and feeling raised above the ruck of your neighbors. On the other hand, if they are all this, you might as well try to keep the sunshine and air to yourself. Universal human nature rises up against you; and, besides, they will not stand it themselves. And, indeed, why should they?

Women, to be very attractive to all sorts of different people, must have great readiness of sympathy. Many have it naturally, and many work hard in acquiring a good imitation of it. In the first case it is against the nature of such persons to be monopolized for more than a very short time; in the second, all their trouble would be thrown away if they allowed themselves to be monopolized. Once in their lives, indeed, they will be, and ought to be, and that monopoly lasts, or should last, forever; but instead of destroying in them that which was their great charm, it only deepens and widens it, and the sympathy which was before fitful, and, perhaps, wayward, flows on in a calm and healthy stream, blessing and cheering all who come within reach of its exhilarating and life-giving waters.

But man of all ages is a selfish animal, and unreasonable in his selfishness. It takes every one of us in turn many a shrewd fall in our wrestlings with the world to convince us that we are not to have every thing our own way. We are conscious in our inmost souls that man is the rightful lord of creation; and, starting from this eternal principle, and ignoring, each man-child of us in turn, the qualifying truth that it is to man in general, including woman, and not to Thomas Brown in particular, that the earth has been given, we set about asserting our kingships each in his own way, and proclaiming ourselves kings from our own little ant-hills of thrones. And then come the strugglings and the downfallings, and some of us learn our lesson and some learn it not. But what lesson? That we have been dreaming in the golden hours when the vision of a kingdom rose before us? That there is, in short, no kingdom at all, or that, if there be, we are no heirs of it?

No — I take it that, while we make nothing better than that out of our lesson, we shall have to go on spelling at it and stumbling over it, through all the days of our life, till we make our last stumble, and take our final header out of this riddle of a world, which we once dreamed we were to rule over, exclaiming "vanitas vanitatum!" to the end. But man's spirit will never be satisfied without a kingdom, and was never intended to be satisfied so; and a wiser than Solomon tells us day by day that our kingdom is about us here, and that we may rise up and pass in when we will at the shining gates which He holds open, for that it is His, and we are joint heirs of it with Him.

On the whole, however, making allowances for all drawbacks, those Commemoration days were the pleasantest days Tom had ever known at Oxford. He was with his uncle and cousins early and late, devising all sorts of pleasant entertainments and excursions for them, introducing all the pleasantest men of his acquaintance, and taxing all the resources of the college, which at such times were available for undergraduates as well as their betters, to minister to their comfort and enjoyment. And he was well repaid. There was something perfectly new to the ladies, and very piquant in the life and habits of the place. They found it very diverting to be receiving in Tom's rooms, presiding over his breakfasts and luncheons, altering the position of his furniture, and making the place look as pretty as circumstances would allow. Then there was pleasant occupation for every spare hour, and the fêtes and amusements were all unlike every thing but themselves. Of course the ladies at once became enthusiastic St. Ambrosians, and managed in spite of all distractions to find time for making up rosettes and bows of blue and white, in which to appear at the procession of the boats, which was the great event of the Monday. Fortunately,

Mr. Winter had been a good oar in his day, and had pulled in one of the first four-oars in which the University races had commenced some thirty-five years before; and Tom, who had set his mind on managing his uncle, worked him up almost into enthusiasm and forgetfulness of his maladies, so that he raised no objection to a five o'clock dinner, and an adjournment to the river almost immediately afterwards. Jervis, who was all-powerful on the river, at Tom's instigation got an arm-chair for him in the best part of the University barge, while the ladies, after walking along the bank with Tom and others of the crew, and being instructed in the colors of the different boats, and the meaning of the ceremony, took their places in the front row on the top of the barge, beneath the awning and the flags, and looked down with hundreds of other fair strangers on the scene, which certainly merited all that Tom had said of it on faith.

The barges above and below the University barge, which occupied the post of honor, were also covered with ladies, and Christchurch meadow swarmed with gay dresses and caps and gowns. On the opposite side the bank was lined with a crowd in holiday clothes, and the punts plied across without intermission loaded with people, till the groups stretched away down the towing-path in an almost continuous line to the starting-place. Then, one after another, the racing-boats, all painted and polished up for the occasion, with the college flags drooping at their sterns, put out and passed down to their stations, and the bands played, and the sun shone his best. And then after a short pause of expectation, the distant bank became all alive, and the groups all turned one way, and came up the towing-path again, and the foremost boat with the blue and white flag shot through the Gut and came up the reach, followed by another, and another, and another, till they were tired of counting, and the leading boat was already close to them before the last had come within sight. And the bands played up altogether, and the crowd on both sides cheered as the St. Ambrose boat spurted from the Cherwell, and took the place of honor at the winning-post, opposite the University barge, and close under where they were sitting.

"Oh, look, Katie dear; here they are. There's Tom, and Mr. Hardy, and Mr. Jervis;" and Mary waved her handkerchief and clapped her hands, and was in an ecstasy of enthusiasm, in which her cousin was no whit behind her. The gallant crew of St. Ambrose were by no means unconscious of, and fully appreciated, the compliment.

Then the boats passed up one by one; and, as each came opposite to the St. Ambrose boat, the crews tossed their oars and cheered, and the St. Ambrose crew tossed their oars and cheered in return; and the whole ceremony went off in triumph, notwithstanding the casualty which occurred to one of the torpids. The torpids being filled with the refuse of the rowing-men,— generally awkward or very young oarsmen,— find some difficulty in the act of tossing; no very safe operation for an unsteady crew. Accordingly, the torpid in question, having sustained her crew gallantly till the saluting point, and allowed them to get their oars fairly into the air, proceeded gravely to turn over on her side, and shoot them out into the stream.

A thrill rang along the top of the barges, and a little scream or two might have been heard even through the notes of Annie Laurie, which were filling the air at the moment; but the band played on, and the crew swam ashore, and two of the punt-men laid hold of the boat and collected the oars, and nobody seemed to think any thing of it.

Katie drew a long breath.

"Are they all out, dear?" she said; "can you see? I can only count eight."

"Oh, I was too frightened to look. Let me see; yes, there are nine; there's one by himself, the little man pulling the weeds off his trousers."

And so they regained their equanimity, and soon after left the barge, and were escorted to the hall of St. Ambrose by the crew, who gave an entertainment there to celebrate the occasion; which Mr. Winter was induced to attend and pleased to approve, and which lasted till it was time to dress for the ball, for which a proper chaperone had been providentially found. And so they passed the days and nights of Commemoration.

But it is not within the scope of this work to chronicle all their doings — how, notwithstanding balls at night, they were up to chapel in the morning, and attended flower-shows at Worcester and musical promenades in New College, and managed to get down the river for a picnic at Nuncham, besides seeing every thing that was worth seeing in all the colleges. How it was done, no man can tell; but done it was, and they seemed only the better for it all. They were waiting at the gates of the theatre amongst the first, tickets in hand, and witnessed the whole scene, wondering no little at the strange mixture of solemnity and license, the rush and crowding of the undergraduates into their gallery, and their free and easy way of taking the whole proceedings under their patronage, watching every movement in the amphitheatre and on the floor, and shouting approval or disapproval of the heads of their republic of learning, or of the most illustrious visitors, or cheering with equal vigor the ladies, Her Majesty's ministers, or the prize poems. It is a strange scene certainly, and has probably puzzled many persons besides young ladies. One can well fancy the astonishment of the learned foreigner, for instance, when he sees the head of the University, which he has reverenced at a distance from his youth up, rise in his robes in solemn convocation to exercise one of the highest of university functions, and hears his sonorous Latin periods interrupted by " three cheers for the ladies in pink bonnets!" or, when some man is introduced for an honorary degree, whose name may be known throughout the civilized world, and the vice-chancellor, turning to his compeers, inquires, " Placetne vobis, domini doctores, placetne vobis, magistri," and he hears the voices of doctors and masters drowned in contradictory shouts from the young Demos in the gallery, " Who is he?" " Non placet!" " Placet!" "Why does he carry an umbrella?" It is thoroughly English, and that is just all that need, or indeed can, be said for it all; but not one in a hundred of us would alter it if we could, beyond suppressing some of the personalities which of late years have gone somewhat too far.

After the theatre there was a sumptuous lunch in All Souls', and then a fête in St. John's Gardens. Now, at the aforesaid luncheon, Tom's feelings had been severely tried; in fact, the little troubles which, as has been before hinted, are incident to persons, especially young men in his fortunate predicament, came to a head. He was separated from his cousins a little way. Being a guest, and not an important one in the eyes of the All Souls' fellows, he had to find his level; which was very much below that allotted to his uncle and cousins. In short, he felt that they were taking him about, instead of he them — which change of position was in itself trying; and Mary's conduct fanned his slumbering discontent into a flame. There she was, sitting between a fellow of All Souls', who was a collector of pictures and an authority in fine-art matters, and the Indian officer who had been so recently promoted to the degree of D.C.L. in the theatre. There she sat, so absorbed in their conversation that she did not even hear a remark which he was pleased to address to her.

Whereupon he began to brood on his wrongs, and to take umbrage at the catholicity of her enjoyment and enthusiasm. So long as he had been the medium through which she was brought in contact with others, he had been well enough content that they should amuse and interest her; but it was a very different thing now.

So he watched her jealously, and raked up former conversations, and came to the conclusion that it was his duty to remonstrate with her. He had remarked, too, that she never could talk with him now without breaking away after a short time into badinage. Her badinage certainly was very charming and pleasant, and kept him on the stretch; but why should she not let him be serious and sentimental when he pleased? She did not break out in this manner with other people. So he really felt it to be his duty to speak to her on the subject—not in the least for his own sake, but for hers.

Accordingly, when the party broke up, and they started for the fête at St. John's, he resolved to carry out his intentions. At first he could not get an opportunity while they were walking about on the beautiful lawn of the great garden, seeing and being seen, and listening to music, and looking at choice flowers. But soon a chance offered. She stayed behind the rest without noticing it, to examine some specially beautiful plant, and he was by her side in a moment, and proposed to show her the smaller garden, which lies beyond, to which she innocently consented; and they were soon out of the crowd, and in comparative solitude.

She remarked that he was somewhat silent and grave, but thought nothing of it, and chatted on as usual, remarking upon the pleasant company she had been in at luncheon.

This opened the way for Tom's lecture.

"How easily you seem to get interested with new people!" he began.

"Do I?" she said. "Well, don't you think it very natural?"

"Wouldn't it be a blessing if people would always say just what they think and mean, though?"

"Yes, and a great many do," she replied, looking at him in some wonder, and not quite pleased with the turn things were taking.

"Any ladies, do you think? You know we haven't many opportunities of observing."

"Yes, I think quite as many ladies as men. More, indeed, as far as my small experience goes."

"You really maintain deliberately that you have met people — men and women — who can talk to you or any one else for a quarter of an hour quite honestly, and say nothing at all which they don't mean — nothing for the sake of flattery, or effect, for instance?"

"Oh dear me! yes, often."

"Who, for example?"

"Our Cousin Katie. Why are you so suspicious and misanthropical? There is your friend Mr. Hardy, again; what do you say to him?"

"Well, I think you may have hit on an exception. But I maintain the rule."

"You look as if I ought to object. But I sha'n't. It is no business of mine if you choose to believe any such disagreeable thing about your fellow-creatures."

"I don't believe any thing worse about them than I do about myself. I know that I can't do it."

"Well, I am very sorry for you."

"But I don't think I am any worse than my neighbors."

"I don't suppose you do. Who are your neighbors?"

"Shall I include you in the number?"

"Oh, by all means, if you like."

"But I may not mean that you are like the rest. The man who fell among thieves, you know, had one good neighbor."

"Now, Cousin Tom," she said, looking up with sparkling eyes, "I can't return the compliment. You meant to make me feel that I *was* like the rest — at least, like what you say they are. You know you did. And now you are just turning round, and trying to slip out of it by saying what *you* don't mean."

"Well, Cousin Mary, perhaps I was. At any rate, I was a great fool for my pains. I might have known by this time that you would catch me out fast enough."

"Perhaps you might. I didn't challenge you to set up your palace of truth. But, if we are to live in it, you are not to say all the disagreeable things and hear none of them."

"I hope not, if they must be disagreeable. But why should they be? I can't see why you and I, for instance, should not say exactly what we are thinking to one another without being disagreeable."

"Well, I don't think you made a happy beginning just now."

"But I am sure we should all like one another the better for speaking the truth."

"Yes; but I don't admit that I haven't been speaking the truth."

"You wont understand me. Have I said that you don't speak the truth?"

"Yes, you said just now that I don't say what I think and mean. Well, perhaps you didn't exactly say that, but that is what you meant."

"You are very angry, Cousin Mary. Let us wait till — "

"No, no. It was you who began, and I will not let you off now."

"Very well, then. I did mean something of the sort. It is better to tell you than to keep it to myself."

"Yes, and now tell me your reasons," said Mary, looking down and biting her lip. Tom was ready to bite his tongue off, but there was nothing now but to go through with it.

"You make everybody that comes near you think that you are deeply interested in them and their doings. Poor Grey believes that you are as mad as he is about rituals and rubrics. And the boating-men declare that you would sooner see a race than go to the best ball in the world. And you listened to the dean's stale old stories about the schools, and went into raptures in the Bodleian about pictures and art with that fellow of Allsouls'. Even our old butler and the cook — "

Here Mary, despite her vexation, after a severe struggle to control it, burst into a laugh, which made Tom pause.

"Now you can't say that I am not really fond of jellies," she said.

"And you can't say that I have said any thing so very disagreeable."

"Oh, but you have, though."

"At any rate, I have made you laugh."

"But you didn't mean to do it. Now, go on."

"I have nothing more to say. You see my meaning, or you never will."

"If you have nothing more to say you should not have said so much," said Mary. "You wouldn't have me rude to all the people I meet, and I can't help it if the cook thinks I am a glutton."

"But you could help letting Grey think that you should like to go and see his night schools."

"But I should like to see them of all things."

"And I suppose you would like to go through the manuscripts in the Bodleian with the dean. I heard you talking to him as if it was the dearest wish of your heart, and making a half engagement to go with him this afternoon, when you know that you are tired to death of him, and so full of other engagements that you don't know where to turn."

Mary began to bite her lips again. She felt half inclined to cry, and half inclined to get up and box his ears. However, she did neither, but looked up after a moment or two, and said,—

"Well, have you any more unkind things to say?"

"Unkind, Mary?"

"Yes, they *are* unkind. How can I enjoy any thing now when I shall know you are watching me, and thinking all sorts of harm of every thing I say and do. However, it doesn't much matter, for we go to-morrow morning."

"But you will give me credit at least for meaning you well?"

"I think you are very jealous and suspicious."

"You don't know how you pain me when you say that."

"But I must say what I think."

Mary set her little mouth, and looked down, and began tapping her boot with her parasol. There was an awkward silence while Tom considered within himself whether she was not right, and whether after all, his own jealousy had not been the cause of the lecture he had been delivering much more than any unselfish wish for Mary's improvement.

"It is your turn now," he said presently, leaning forward with his elbows on his knees, and looking hard at the gravel. "I may have been foolishly jealous, and I thank you for telling me so. But you can tell me a great deal more if you will, quite as good for me to hear."

"No, I have nothing to say. I dare say you are open and true, and have nothing to hide or disguise, not even about either of the men we met in the Long Walk on Sunday."

He winced at this random shaft as if he had been stung, and she saw that it had gone home, and repented the next moment. The silence became more and more embarrassing. By good luck, however, their party suddenly appeared strolling towards them from the large garden.

"There's Uncle Robert and Katie, and all of them. Let us join them."

She rose up and he with her, and as they walked towards the rest he said quickly in a low voice, "Will you forgive me if I have pained you? I was very selfish, and am very sorry."

"Oh, yes; we were both very foolish. But we wont do it again."

"Here you are at last. We have been looking for you everywhere," said Miss Winter, as they came up.

"I'm sure I don't know how we missed you. We came straight from the music tent to this seat, and have not moved. We knew you must come by sooner or later."

"But it is quite out of the way. It was quite by chance that we came round here."

"Isn't Uncle Robert tired, Katie?" said Tom; "he doesn't look well this afternoon."

Katie instantly turned to her father, and Mr. Winter declared himself to be much fatigued. So they wished their hospitable entertainers good-by, and Tom hurried off and got a wheel chair for his uncle, and walked by his side to their lodgings. The young ladies walked near the chair also, accompanied by one or two of their acquaintance; in fact, they could not move without an escort. But Tom never once turned his head for a glance at what was going on, and talked steadily on to his uncle, that he might not catch a stray word of what the rest were saying. Despite of all which self-denial, however, he was quite aware somehow when he made his bow at the door that Mary had been very silent all the way home.

Mr. Winter retired to his room to lie down, and his daughter and niece remained in the sitting-room. Mary sat down and untied her bonnet, but did not burst into her usual flood of comments on the events of the day. Miss Winter looked at her and said, —

"You look tired, dear, and over-excited."

"Oh, yes, so I am. I've had such a quarrel with Tom."

"A quarrel — you're not serious?"

"Indeed I am, though. I quite hated him for five minutes at least."

"But what did he do?"

"Why he taunted me with being too civil to everybody, and it made me so angry. He said I pretended to take an interest in ever so many things, just to please people, when I didn't really care about them. And it isn't true now, Katie; is it?"

"No, dear. He never could have said that. You must have misunderstood him."

"There, I knew you would say so. And if it were true, I'm sure it isn't wrong. When people talk to you, it is so easy to seem pleased and interested in what they are saying — and then they like you, and it is so pleasant to be liked. Now, Katie, do you ever snap people's noses off, or tell them you think them very foolish, and that you don't care, and that what they are saying is all of no consequence?"

"I, dear? I couldn't do it to save my life!"

"Oh, I was sure you couldn't. And he may say what he will, but I'm quite sure he would not have been pleased if we had not made ourselves pleasant to his friends."

"That's quite true. He has told me himself half a dozen times how delighted he was to see you so popular."

"And you, too, Katie?"

"Oh, yes. He is very well pleased with me. But it is you who have turned all the heads in the college, Mary. You are queen of St. Ambrose beyond a doubt just now."

"No, no, Katie; not more than you, at any rate."

"I say yes, yes, Mary. You will always be ten times as popular as I; some people have the gift of it; I wish I had. But why do you look so grave again?"

"Why, Katie, don't you see you are just saying over again, only in a different way, what your provoking cousin — I shall call him Mr. Brown, I think, in future — was telling me for my good in St. John's Gardens. You saw how long we were away from you: well, he was lecturing me all the time, only think; and now you are going to tell it me all over again. But go on, dear; I sha'n't mind any thing from you."

She put her arm round her cousin's waist, and looked up playfully into her face. Miss Winter saw at once that no great harm, perhaps some good, had been done in the passage of arms between her relatives.

"You made it all up," she said, smiling, "before we found you."

"Only just, though. He begged my pardon just at last, almost in a whisper, when you were quite close to us."

"And you granted it?"

"Yes, of course; but I don't know that I shall not recall it."

"I was sure you would be falling out before long, you got on so fast. But he isn't quite so easy to turn round your finger as you thought, Mary."

"Oh, I don't know that," said Mary, laughingly; "you saw how humble he looked at last, and what good order he was in."

"Well, dear, it's time to think whether we shall go out again."

"Let me see; there's the last ball. What do you say?"

"Why, I'm afraid poor papa is too tired to take us, and I don't know with whom we could go. We ought to begin packing, too, I think."

"Very well. Let us have tea quietly at home."

"I will write a note to Tom to tell him. He has done his best for us, poor fellow, and we ought to consider him a little."

"Oh, yes, and ask him and his friend Mr. Hardy to tea, as it is the last night."

"If you wish it, I should be very glad; they will amuse papa."

"Certainly, and then he will see that I bear him no malice. And now I will go and just do my hair."

"Very well; and we will pack after they leave. How strange home will seem after all this gayety."

"Yes; we seem to have been here a month."

"I do hope we shall find all quiet at Englebourn. I am always afraid of some trouble there."

# CHAPTER V.

#### THE END OF THE FRESHMAN'S YEAR.

On the morning after Commemoration, Oxford was in a bustle of departure. The play had been played, the long vacation had begun, and visitors and members seemed equally anxious to be off. At the gates of the colleges groups of men in travelling-dresses waited for the coaches, omnibuses, dog-carts, and all manner of vehicles, which were to carry them to the Great Western railway station, at Steventon, or elsewhere to all points of the compass. Porters passed in and out with portmanteaus, gun-cases, and baggage of all kinds, which they piled outside the gates, or carried off to the Mitre or the Angel, under the vigorous and not too courteous orders of the owners. College servants flitted round the groups to take last instructions, and, if so might be, to extract the balances of extortionate bills out of their departing masters. Dog-fanciers were there also, holding terriers; and scouts from the cricketing-grounds, with bats and pads under their arms; and hostlers, and men from the boats, all on the same errand of getting the last shilling out of their patrons — a fawning, obsequious crowd for the most part, with here and there a sturdy Briton who felt that he was only come after his due.

Through such a group, at the gate of St. Ambrose, Tom and Hardy passed soon after breakfast time, in cap and gown, which costume excited no small astonishment.

"Hullo, Brown, old fellow! aint you off this morning?"

"No, I shall be up for a day or two yet."

"Wish you joy. I wouldn't be staying up over to-day for something."

"But you'll be at Henley to-morrow?" said Diogenes, confidently, who stood at the gate in boating coat and flannels, a big stick and knapsack, waiting for a companion, with whom he was going to walk to Henley.

"And at Lord's on Friday," said another. "It will be a famous match; come and dine somewhere afterwards, and go to the Haymarket with us."

"You know the Leander are to be at Henley," put in Diogenes, "and Cambridge is very strong. There will be a splendid race for the cup, but Jervis thinks we are all right."

"Bother your eternal races; haven't you had enough of them?" said the Londoner. "You had much better come up to the little village at once, Brown, and stay there while the coin lasts."

"If I get away at all, it will be to Henley," said Tom.

"Of course, I knew that," said Diogenes, triumphantly; "our boat ought to be on for the ladies' plate. If only Jervis were not in the University crew! I thought you were to pull at Henley, Hardy?"

"I was asked to pull, but I couldn't manage the time with the schools coming on, and when the examinations were over, it was too late. The crew were picked and half trained, and none of them have broken down."

"What! every one of them stood putting through the sieve? They must be a rare crew, then," said another.

"You're right," said Diogenes. "Oh! here you are at last," he added, as another man in flannels and knapsack came out of college. "Well, good-by, all, and a pleasant vacation; we must be off, if we are to be in time to see our crew pull over the course to-night:" and the two marched off towards Magdalen bridge.

"By Jove!" remarked a fast youth, in most elaborate toilette, looking after them, "fancy two fellows grinding off to Henley, five miles an hour, in this sun, when they might drop up to the metropolis by train in half the time? Isn't it marvellous?"

"I should like to be going with them," said Tom.

"Well, there's no accounting for tastes. Here's our coach."

"Good-by, then;" and Tom shook hands, and leaving the coach to get packed with portmanteaus, terriers, and undergraduates, he and Hardy walked off towards the High Street.

"So you're not going to-day?" Hardy said.

"No; two or three of my old school-fellows are coming up to stand for scholarships, and I must be here to receive them. But it's very unlucky; I should have liked so to have been at Henley."

"Look, their carriage is already at the door," said Hardy, pointing up High Street, into which they now turned. There were a dozen post-chaises and carriages loading in front of different houses in the street, and amongst them Mr. Winter's old-fashioned travelling-barouche.

"So it is," said Tom; "that's some of uncle's fidgetiness; but he will be sure to dawdle at the last. Come along in."

"Don't you think I had better stay down-stairs? It may seem intrusive."

"No, come along. Why, they asked you to come and see the last of them last night, didn't they?"

Hardy did not require any further urging to induce

him to follow his inclination; so the two went up together. The breakfast things were still on the table, at which sat Miss Winter, in her bonnet, employed in examining the bill, with the assistance of Mary, who leant over her shoulder. She looked up as they entered.

"Oh! I'm so glad you are come. Poor Katie is so bothered, and I can't help her. Do look at the bill; is it all right?"

"Shall I, Katie?"

"Yes, please do. I don't see any thing to object to, except, perhaps, the things I have marked. Do you think we ought to be charged half a crown a day for the kitchen fire?"

"Fire in June! and you have never dined at home once?"

"No, but we have had tea several times."

"It is a regular swindle," said Tom, taking the bill and glancing at it. "Here, Hardy, come and help me cut down this precious total."

They sat down to the bill, the ladies willingly giving place. Mary tripped off to the glass to tie her bonnet.

"Now that is all right!" she said, merrily; "why can't one go on without bills or horrid money?"

"Ah! why can't one?" said Tom, "that would suit most of our complaints. But where's uncle? has he seen the bill?"

"No; papa is in his room; he must not be worried, or the journey will be too much for him."

Here the ladies'-maid arrived, with a message that her father wished to see Miss Winter.

"Leave your money, Katie," said her cousin; "this is gentlemen's business, and Tom and Mr. Hardy will settle it all for us, I am sure."

Tom professed his entire willingness to accept the

charge, delighted at finding himself re-instated in his office of protector at Mary's suggestion. Had the landlord been one of his own tradesmen, or the bill his own bill, he might not have been so well pleased, but, as neither of these was the case, and he had Hardy to back him, he went into the matter with much vigor and discretion, and had the landlord up, made the proper deductions, and got the bill settled and receipted in a few minutes. Then he and Hardy addressed themselves to getting the carriage comfortably packed, and vied with one another in settling and stowing away in the most convenient places the many little odds and ends which naturally accompany young ladies and invalids on their travels; in the course of which employment he managed to snatch a few words here and there with Mary, and satisfied himself that she bore him no ill-will for the events of the previous day.

At last, all was ready for the start, and Tom reported the fact in the sitting-room. "Then I will go and fetch papa," said Miss Winter.

Tom's eyes met Mary's at the moment. He gave a slight shrug with his shoulders, and said, as the door closed after his cousin, "Really I have no patience with Uncle Robert; he leaves poor Katie to do every thing."

"Yes; and how beautifully she does it all, without a word or, I believe, a thought of complaint! I could never be so patient."

"I think it is a pity. If Uncle Robert were obliged to exert himself it would be much better for him. Katie is only spoiling him and wearing herself out."

"Yes, it is very easy for you and me to think and say so. But he is her father; and then he is really an invalid. So she goes on devoting herself to him more and more, and feels she can never do too much for him."

"But if she believed it would be better for him to exert himself? I'm sure it is the truth. Couldn't you try to persuade her?"

"No, indeed; it would only worry her, and be so cruel. But then I am not used to give advice," she added, after a moment's pause, looking demurely at her gloves; "it might do good, perhaps, now, if you were to speak to her."

"You think me so well qualified, I suppose, after the specimen you had yesterday. Thank you; I have had enough of lecturing for the present."

"I am very much obliged to you, really, for what you said to me," said Mary, still looking at her gloves.

The subject was a very distasteful one to Tom. He looked at her for a moment, to see whether she was laughing at him, and then broke it off abruptly,—

"I hope you have enjoyed your visit?"

"Oh, yes, so very much. I shall think of it all the summer."

"Where shall you be all the summer?" asked Tom.

"Not so very far from you. Papa has taken a house only eight miles from Englebourn, and Katie says you live within a day's drive of them."

"And shall you be there all the vacation?"

"Yes, and we hope to get Katie over often. Could not you come and meet her? it would be so pleasant."

"But do you think I might? I don't know your father or mother."

"Oh, yes; papa and mamma are very kind, and will ask anybody I like. Besides, you are a cousin, you know."

"Only up at Oxford, I am afraid."

"Well, now you will see. We are going to have a great archery party next month, and you shall have an invitation."

"Will you write it for me yourself?"

"Very likely; but why?"

"Don't you think I shall value a note in your hand more than —"

"Nonsense; now, remember your lecture — Oh, here are Uncle Robert and Katie."

Mr. Winter was very gracious, and thanked Tom for all his attentions. He had been very pleased, he said, to make his nephew's acquaintance again so pleasantly, and hoped he would come and pass a day or two at Englebourn in the vacation. In his sad state of health he could not do much to entertain a young man, but he could procure him some good fishing and shooting in the neighborhood. Tom assured his uncle that nothing would please him so much as a visit to Englebourn. Perhaps the remembrance of the distance between that parish and the place where Mary was to spend the summer may have added a little to his enthusiasm.

"I should have liked also to have thanked your friend for his hospitality," Mr. Winter went on. "I understood my daughter to say he was here."

"Yes, he was here just now," said Tom; "he must be below, I think."

"What, that good Mr. Hardy?" said Mary, who was looking out of the window; "there he is in the street. He has just helped Hopkins into the rumble, and handed her things to her as if she were a duchess. She has been so cross all the morning, and now she looks quite gracious."

"Then, I think, papa, we had better start."

"Let me give you an arm down-stairs, uncle," said Tom; and so he helped his uncle down to the carriage, the two young ladies following behind, and the landlord standing with obsequious bows at his shop door as if he had never made an overcharge in his life.

While Mr. Winter was making his acknowledgments to Hardy and being helped by him into the most comfortable seat in the carriage, Tom was making tender adieus to the two young ladies behind, and even succeeded in keeping a rose-bud which Mary was carrying when they took their seats. She parted from it half-laughingly, and the post-boy cracked his whip and the barouche went lumbering along High Street. Hardy and Tom watched it until it turned down St. Aldates towards Folly bridge, the latter waving his hand as it disappeared, and then they turned and strolled slowly away side by side in silence. The sight of all the other departures increased the uncomfortable, unsatisfied feeling which that of his own relatives had already produced in Tom's mind.

"Well, it isn't lively stopping up here when everybody is going, is it? What is one to do?"

"Oughtn't you to be looking after your friends who are coming up to try for the scholarships?"

"No, they wont be up till the afternoon by coach."

"Shall we go down the river, then?"

"No, it would be miserable. Hullo, look here, what's up?"

The cause of Tom's astonishment was the appearance of the usual procession of University beadles carrying silver-headed maces, and escorting the vice-chancellor towards St. Mary's.

"Why, the bells are going for service; there must be a University sermon."

"Where's the congregation to come from? Why, half Oxford is off by this time, and those that are left wont want to be hearing sermons."

"Well, I don't know. A good many men seem to be going. I wonder who is to preach."

"I vote we go. It will help to pass the time."

Hardy agreed, and they followed the procession and went up into the gallery of St. Mary's. There was a very fair congregation in the body of the church, as the college staffs had not yet broken up, and even in the gallery the undergraduates mustered in some force. The restless feeling which had brought our hero there seemed to have had a like effect on most of the men who were for one reason or another unable to start on that day.

Tom looked steadily into his cap during the bidding prayer, and sat down composedly afterwards; expecting not to be much interested or benefited, but comforted with the assurance that at any rate it would be almost luncheon time before he would be again thrown on his own resources. But he was mistaken in his expectations, and, before the preacher had been speaking for three minutes, was all attention. The sermon was upon the freedom of the Gospel, the power by which it bursts all bonds and lets the oppressed go free. Its burden was, " Ye shall know the truth, and the truth shall make you free." The preacher dwelt on many sides of these words; the freedom of nations, of societies, of universities, of the conscience of each individual man, were each glanced at in turn; and then reminding his hearers of the end of the academical year, he went on, —

" We have heard it said in the troubles and toils and temptations of the world,* 'Oh, that I could begin life over again! oh, that I could fall asleep, and wake up, twelve, six, three months hence, and find my difficulties solved!' That which we may vainly wish elsewhere by

* This quotation is from the sermon preached by Dr. Stanley before the University on Act Sunday, 1859 (published by J. H. Parker, of Oxford). I hope that the distinguished professor whose words they are will pardon the liberty I have taken in quoting them. No words of my own could have given so vividly what I wanted to say.

a happy Providence is furnished to us by the natural divisions of meeting and parting in this place. To every one of us, old and young, the long vacation on which we are now entering, gives us a breathing space, and time to break the bonds which place and circumstance have woven round us during the year that is past. From all our petty cares, and confusions, and intrigues; from the dust and clatter of this huge machinery amidst which we labor and toil; from whatever cynical contempt of what is generous and devout; from whatever fanciful disregard of what is just and wise; from whatever gall and bitterness is secreted in our best motives; from whatever bonds of unequal dealing in which we have entangled ourselves or others, we are now for a time set free. We stand on the edge of a river which shall for a time at least sweep them away; that ancient river, the river Kishon, the river of fresh thoughts, and fresh scenes and fresh feelings, and fresh hopes; one surely amongst the blessed means whereby God's free and loving grace works out our deliverance, our redemption from evil, and renews the strength of each succeeding year, so that 'we may mount up again as eagles, may run and not be weary, may walk and not faint.'

"And, if turning to the younger part of my hearers, I may still more directly apply this general lesson to them. Is there no one who, in some shape or other, does not feel the bondage of which I have been speaking? He has something on his conscience; he has something on his mind; extravagance, sin, debt, falsehood. Every morning in the first few minutes after waking, it is the first thought that occurs to him; he drives it away in the day; he drives it off by recklessness, which only binds it more and more closely round him. Is there any one who has ever felt, who is at this moment feeling, this grievous burden?

What is the deliverance? How shall he set himself free? In what special way does the redemption of Christ, the free grace of God, present itself to him? There is at least one way clear and simple. He knows it better than any one can tell him. It is those same words which I used with another purpose. 'The truth shall make him free.' It is to tell the truth to his friend, to his parent, to any one, whosoever it be, from whom he is concealing that which he ought to make known. One word of open, frank disclosure — one resolution to act sincerely and honestly by himself and others — one ray of truth let into that dark corner will indeed set the whole man free.

"*Liberavi animam meam.* 'I have delivered my soul.' What a faithful expression is this of the relief, the deliverance effected by one strong effort of will in one moment of time. 'I will arise and go to my father, and will say unto him, Father, I have sinned against Heaven and before thee, and am no more worthy to be called thy son.' So we heard the prodigal's confession this morning. So may the thought well spring up in the minds of any who in the course of this last year have wandered into sin, have found themselves beset with evil habits of wicked idleness, of wretched self-indulgence. Now that you are indeed in the literal sense of the word about to rise and go to your father, now that you will be able to shake off the bondage of bad companionship, now that the whole length of this long absence will roll between you and the past — take a long breath, break off the yoke of your sin, of your fault, of your wrong-doing, of your folly, of your perverseness, of your pride, of your vanity, of your weakness; break it off by truth, break it off by one stout effort, in one steadfast prayer; break it off by innocent and free enjoyment; break it off by honest work. Put your 'hand to the nail and your right hand to the workman's hammer:' strike through the enemy which has ensnared you, pierce and strike him through and through. However powerful he seems 'at your feet he will bow, he will fall, he will lie down; at your feet he will bow and fall, and where he bows, there will he rise up no more. So let all thine enemies perish, O Lord; but let them that love thee be as the sun when he goeth forth in his might.'"

The two friends separated themselves from the crowd in the porch and walked away, side by side, towards their college.

"Well, that wasn't a bad move of ours. It is worth something to hear a man preach that sort of doctrine," said Hardy.

"How does he get to know it all?" said Tom, meditatively.

"All what? I don't see your puzzle."

"Why, all sorts of things that are in a fellow's mind: what he thinks about the first thing in the morning, for instance."

"Pretty much like the rest of us, I take it: by looking at home. You don't suppose that University preachers are unlike you and me."

"Well, I don't know. Now do you think he ever had any thing on his mind that was always coming up and plaguing him, and which he never told to anybody?"

"Yes, I should think so; most of us must have had."

"Have you?"

"Ay, often and often"

"And you think his remedy the right one?"

"The only one. Make a clean breast of it, and the sting is gone. There's plenty more to be done afterwards, of course; but there's no question about step No. 1."

"Did you ever owe a hundred pounds that you couldn't pay?" said Tom, with a sudden effort; and his secret had hardly passed his lips before he felt a relief which surprised himself.

"My dear fellow," said Hardy, stopping in the street, "you don't mean to say you are speaking of yourself?"

"I do though," said Tom, "and it has been on my mind ever since the beginning of Easter term, and has spoilt my temper and every thing — that and something else that you know of. You must have seen me getting more and more ill-tempered, I'm sure. And I have thought of it the first thing in the morning and the last thing at night, and tried to drive the thought away just as he said one did in his sermon. By Jove, I thought he knew all about it, for he looked right at me just when he came to that place."

"But, Brown, how do you mean you owe a hundred pounds? You haven't read much, certainly; but you haven't hunted, or gambled, or tailored much, or gone into any other extravagant folly. You must be dreaming."

"Am I though? Come up to my rooms and I'll tell you all about it: I feel better already, now I've let it out. I'll send over for your commons, and we'll have some lunch."

Hardy followed his friend in much trouble of mind, considering in himself whether with the remainder of his savings he could not make up the sum which Tom had named. Fortunately for both of them a short calculation showed him that he could not, and he gave up the idea of delivering his friend in this summary manner with a sigh. He remained closeted with Tom for an hour, and then came out, looking serious still, but not uncomfortable, and went down to the river. He sculled down to Sandford, bathed in the lasher, and returned in time for chapel. He stayed outside afterwards, and Tom came up to him and seized his arms.

8

"I've done it, old fellow," he said; "look here;" and produced a letter. Hardy glanced at the direction, and saw that it was to his father.

"Come along and post it," said Tom, "and then I shall feel all right."

They walked off quickly to the post-office and dropped the letter into the box.

"There," he said, as it disappeared, "*liberavi animam meam*. I owe the preacher a good turn for that; I've a good mind to write and thank him. Fancy the poor old governor's face to-morrow at breakfast!"

"Well, you seem to take it easy enough now," said Hardy.

"I can't help it. I tell you I haven't felt so jolly this two months. What a fool I was not to have done it before. After all, now I come to think of it, I can pay it myself, at least as soon as I am of age, for I know I've some money, a legacy or something, coming to me then. But that isn't what I care about now."

"I'm very glad, though, that you have the money of your own."

"Yes; but the having told it all is the comfort. Come along, and let's see whether those boys are come. The Old Pig ought to be in by this time, and I want them to dine in Hall. It's only ten months since I came up on it to matriculate, and it seems twenty years. But I'm going to be a boy again for to-night; you'll see if I'm not."

# CHAPTER VI.

### THE LONG VACATION LETTER-BAG.

*June* 24, 184–.

"MY DEAR TOM,— Your letter came to hand this morning, and it has of course given your mother and me much pain. It is not the money that we care about, but that our son should have deliberately undertaken, or pretended to undertake, what he must have known at the time he could not perform himself.

"I have written to my bankers to pay £100 at once to your account at the Oxford Bank. I have also requested my solicitor to go over to Oxford, and he will probably call on you the day after you receive this. You say that this person who holds your note of hand is now in Oxford. You will see him in the presence of my solicitor, to whom you will hand the note when you have recovered it. I shall consider afterwards what further steps will have to be taken in the matter.

"You will not be of age for a year. It will be time enough then to determine whether you will repay the balance of this money out of the legacy to which you will be entitled under your grandfather's will. In the mean time, I shall deduct at the rate of £50 a year from your allowance, and I shall hold you bound in honor to reduce your expenditure by this amount. You are no longer a boy, and one of the first duties which a man owes to his friends and to society is to live within his income.

"I make this advance to you on two conditions. First, that you will never again put your hand to a note or bill in a transaction of this kind. If you have money, lend it or spend it. You may lend or spend foolishly, but that is not the point here; at any rate, you are dealing with what is your own. But in transactions of this kind you are dealing with what is not your own. A gentleman should shrink from the possibility of having to come on others, even on his own father, for the fulfilment of his obligations as he would from a lie. I would sooner see a son of mine in his grave than crawling on through life a slave to wants and habits which he must gratify at other people's expense.

"My second condition is, that you put an end to your acquaintance with these two gentlemen who have led you into this scrape, and have divided the proceeds of your joint note between them. They are both your seniors in standing, you say, and they appear to be familiar with this plan of raising money at the expense of other people. The plain English word for such doings is swindling. What pains me most is that you should have become intimate with young men of this kind. I am not sure that it will not be my duty to lay the whole matter before the authorities of the college. You do not mention their names, and I respect the feeling which has led you not to mention them. I shall know them quite soon enough through my solicitor, who will forward me a copy of the note of hand and signatures in due course.

"Your letter makes general allusion to other matters; and I gather from it that you are dissatisfied with the manner in which you have spent your first year at Oxford. I do not ask for specific confessions, which you seem inclined to offer me; in fact, I would sooner not have them, unless there is any other matter in which you want assistance or advice from me. I know from experience that Oxford is a place full of temptation of all kinds, offered to young men at the most critical time of their lives. Knowing this, I have deliberately accepted the responsibility of sending you there, and I do not repent it. I am glad that you are dissatisfied with your first year. If you had not been, I should have felt much more anxious about your second. Let bygones be bygones between you and me. You know where to go for strength, and to make confessions which no human ear should hear, for no human judgment can weigh the cause. The secret places of a man's heart are for himself and God. Your mother sends her love.

"I am, ever your affectionate father,
"John Brown."

*June* 26*th*, 184–.

"My dear Boy,— I am not sorry that you have taken my last letter as you have done. It is quite right to be sensitive on these points, and it will have done you no harm to have fancied for forty-eight hours that you had in my judgment lost caste as a gentleman. But now I am very glad to be able to ease your mind on this point. You have done a very foolish thing; but it is only the habit, and the getting others to bind themselves, and not the doing it one's self for others, which is disgraceful. You are going to pay honorably for your folly, and will owe me neither thanks nor money in the transaction. I have chosen my own terms for repayment, which you have accepted, and so the financial question is disposed of.

"I have considered what you say as to your companions,— friends I will not call them,— and will promise you not to take any further steps, or to mention the subject to any one. But I must insist on my second condition, that you avoid all further intimacy with them. I do not mean that you are to cut them, or to do any thing that will attract attention. But, no more intimacy.

"And now, my dear boy, as to the rest of your letter. Mine must indeed have failed to express my meaning. God forbid that there should not be the most perfect confidence between us. There is nothing which I desire or value more. I only question whether special confessions will conduce to it. My experience is against them. I almost doubt whether they can be perfectly honest between man and man; and, taking into account the difference of our ages, it seems to me much more likely that we should misunderstand one another. But having said this, I leave it to you to follow your own conscience in the matter. If there is any burden which I can help you to bear, it will be my greatest pleasure, as it is my duty to do it. So now say what you please, or say no more. If you speak, it will be to one who has felt and remembers a young man's trials.

"We hope you will be able to come home to-morrow, or the next day, at latest. Your mother is longing to see you, and I should be glad to have you here for a day or two before the assizes, which are held next week. I should rather like you to accompany me to them, as it will give me the opportunity of introducing you to my brother magistrates from other parts of the county, whom you are not likely to meet elsewhere, and it is a good thing for a young man to know his own county well.

"The cricket club is very flourishing you will be glad to hear, and they have put off their best matches, especially those with the South Hants and Landsdown, till your return; so you are in great request, you see. I am told that the fishing is very good this year, and am promised several days for you in the club water.

"September is a long way off, but there is nothing like being beforehand. I have put your name down for a license: and it is time you should have a good gun of your own; so I have ordered one for you from a man who has lately settled in the county. He was Purdy's foreman, with whom I used to build, and, I can see, understands his business thoroughly. His locks are as good as any I have ever seen. I have told him to make the stock rather longer, and not quite so straight as that of my old double with which you shot last year. I think I remember you criticised my weapon on these points; but there will be time for you to alter the details after you get home, if you disapprove of my orders. It will be more satisfactory if it is built under your own eye. If you continue in the mind for a month's reading with your friend Mr. Hardy, we will arrange it towards the end of the vacation; but would he not come here? From what you say we should very much like to know him. Pray ask him from me whether he will pass the last month of the vacation here coaching you. I should like you to be his first regular pupil. Of course, this will be my affair. And now God bless you, and come home as soon as you can. Your mother sends her best love.

"Ever your most affectionate
"John Brown."


"Englebourn Rectory,
*June 28th*, 184–.

"Dearest Mary, — How good of you to write to me so soon! Your letter has come like a gleam of sunshine. I am in the midst of worries already. Indeed, as you know, I could never quite throw off the fear of what might be happening here, while we were enjoying ourselves at Oxford, and it has all turned out even worse than I expected. I shall never be able to go away again in comfort, I think. And yet, if I had been here, I don't know that I could have done any good. It is so very sad that poor papa is unable to attend to his magistrate's business, and he has been worse than usual, quite laid up in fact, since our return. There is no other magistrate — not even a gentleman in the place, as you know, except the curate, and they will not listen to him, even if he would interfere in their quarrels. But he says he will not meddle with secular matters; and, poor man, I cannot blame him, for it is very sad and wearing to be mixed up in it all.

"But now I must tell you all my troubles. You remember the men whom we saw mowing together just before we went to Oxford. Betty Winburn's son was one of them, and I am afraid the rest are not at all good company for him. When they had finished papa's hay, they went to mow for Farmer Tester. You must remember him, dear, I am sure; the tall, gaunt man, with heavy, thick lips, and a broken nose, and the top of his head quite flat, as if it had been cut off a little above his eyebrows. He is a very miserly man, and a hard master; at least, all the poor people tell me so, and he looks cruel. I have always been afraid of him, and disliked him, for I remember as a child hearing papa complain how troublesome he was in the vestry; and except old Simon, who, I believe, only does it from perverseness, I have never heard anybody speak well of him.

"The first day that the men went to mow for Farmer Tester, he gave them sour beer to drink. You see, dear, they bargain to mow for so much money and their beer. They were very discontented at this, and they lost a good deal of time going to complain to him about it, and they had high words.

"The men said that the beer wasn't fit for pigs, and the farmer said it was quite good enough 'for such as they,' and if they didn't like his beer they might buy their own. In the evening, too, he came down and complained that the mowing was bad, and then there were more high words, for the men are very jealous about their work. However, they went to work as usual the next morning, and all might have gone off, but in the day Farmer Tester found two pigs in his turnip-field which adjoins the common, and had them put in the pound. One of these pigs belonged to Betty Winburn's son, and the other to one of the men who was mowing with him; so, when they came home at night, they found what had happened.

"The constable is our pound-keeper, the little man who amused you so much: he plays the bass-viol in church. When he puts any beasts into the pound he cuts a stick in two, and gives one piece to the person who brings the beasts, and keeps the other himself; and the owner of the beasts has to bring the other end of the stick to him before he can let them out. Therefore, the owner, you see, must go to the person who has pounded his beasts, and make a bargain with him for payment of the damage which has been done, and so get back the other end of the stick, which they call the tally, to produce to the pound-keeper.

"Well, the men went off to the constable's when they heard their pigs were pounded, to find who had the tally, and, when they found it was Farmer Tester, they went in a body to his house, to remonstrate with him, and learn what he set the damages at. The farmer used dreadful language to them, I hear, and said they weren't fit to have pigs, and must pay half a crown for each pig, before they should have the tally; and the men irritated him by telling him that his fences were a shame to the parish, because he was too stingy to have them mended, and that the pigs couldn't have found half a crown's worth of turnips in the whole field, for he never put any manure on it, except what he could get off the road, which ought to belong to the poor. At last the farmer drove them away, saying that he should stop the money out of the price he was to pay for their mowing.

"Then there was very near being a riot in the parish; for some of the men are very reckless people, and they went in the evening, and blew horns, and beat kettles before his house, till the constable, who has behaved very well, persuaded them to go away.

"In the morning one of the pigs had been taken out of the pound; not Betty's son's, I am glad to say, for no doubt it was very wrong of the men to take it out. The farmer was furious, and went with the constable in the morning to find the pig, but they could hear nothing of it anywhere. James Pope, the man to whom it belonged, only laughed at them, and said that he never could keep his pig in himself, because it was grandson to one of the acting pigs that went about to the fairs, and all the pigs of that family took to climbing naturally; so his pig must have climbed out of the pound. This of course was all a story; the men had lifted the pig out of the pound, and then killed it, so that the farmer might not find it, and sold the meat cheap all over the parish. Betty went to the farmer that morning, and paid the half-crown, and got her son's pig out before he came home; but Farmer Tester stopped the other half-crown out of the men's wages, which made matters worse than ever.

"The day that we were in the theatre at Oxford, Farmer Tester was away at one of the markets. He turns his big cattle out to graze on the common, which the poor people say he has no right to do, and in the afternoon a pony of his got into the allotments, and Betty's son caught it, and took it to the constable, and had it put in the pound. The constable tried to persuade him not to do it, but it was of no use; and so, when Farmer Tester came home, he found that his turn had come. I am afraid that he was not sober, for I hear that he behaved dreadfully both to the constable and to Betty's son, and when he found that he could not frighten them, he declared he would have the law of them, if it cost him twenty pounds. So in the morning he went to fetch his lawyer, and when we got home you can fancy what a scene it was.

"You remember how poorly papa was when you left us at Lambourn. By the time we got home he was quite knocked up, and so nervous that he was fit for nothing except to have a quiet cup of tea in his own room. I was sure, as we drove up the street, there was something the matter. The hostler was watching outside the Red Lion, and ran in as soon as we came in sight; and, as we passed the door, out came Farmer Tester, looking very flushed in the face, and carrying his great iron-handled whip, and a person with him, who I found was his lawyer, and they marched after the carriage. Then the constable was standing at his door, too, and he came after us, and there was a group of men outside the rectory gate. We had not been in the house five minutes before the servant came in to say that Farmer Tester and a gentleman wanted to see papa on particular business. Papa sent out word he was very unwell, and that it was not the proper time to come on business; he would see them the next day at twelve o'clock. But they would not go away, and then papa asked me to go out and see them. You can fancy how disagreeable it was; and I was so angry with them for coming, when they knew how nervous papa is after a journey, as well as that I could not have patience to persuade them to leave ; and so at last they made poor papa see them after all. He was lying on a sofa, and quite unfit to cope with a hard, bad man like Farmer Tester, and a fluent, plausible lawyer. They told their story all their own way, and the farmer declared that the man had tempted the pony into the allotments with corn. And the lawyer said that the constable had no right to keep the pony in the pound, and that he was liable to all sorts of punishments. They wanted papa to make an order at once for the pound to be opened, and I think he would have done so, but I asked him in a whisper to send for the constable, and hear what he had to say. The constable was waiting in the kitchen, so he came in in a minute. You can't think how well he behaved; I have quite forgiven him all his obstinacy about the singing. He told the whole story about the pigs, and how Farmer Tester had stopped money out of the men's wages. And when the lawyer tried to frighten him, he answered him quite boldly, that he mightn't know so much about the law, but he knew what was always the custom long before his time at Englebourn about the pound, and if Farmer Tester wanted his beast out, he must bring the tally like another man. Then the lawyer appealed to papa about the law, and said how absurd it was, and that if such a custom were to be upheld, the man who had the tally might charge £100 for the damage. And poor papa looked through his law books, and could find nothing about it all; and while he was doing it Farmer Tester began to abuse the constable, and said he sided with all the good-for-nothing fellows in the parish, and that bad blood would come of it. But the constable quite fired up at that, and told him that it was such as he who made bad blood in the parish, and that poor folks had their rights as well as their betters, and should have them while he was constable. If he got papa's order to open the pound, he supposed he must do it, and 'twas not for him to say what was law, but Harry Winburn had had to get the tally for his pig from Farmer Tester, and what was fair for one was fair for all.

"I was afraid papa would have made the order, but the lawyer said something at last which made him take the other side. So he settled that the farmer should pay five shillings for the tally, which was what he had taken from Betty, and had stopped out of the wages, and that was the only order he would make, and the lawyer might do what he pleased about it. The constable seemed satisfied with this, and undertook to take the money down to Harry Winburn, for Farmer Tester declared he would sooner let the pony starve than go himself. And so papa got rid of them after an hour and more of this talk. The lawyer and Farmer Tester went away grumbling and very angry to the Red Lion. I was very anxious to hear how the matter ended; so I sent after the constable to ask him to come back and see me when he had settled it all, and about nine o'clock he came. He had had a very hard job to get Harry Winburn to take the money, and give up the tally. The men said that if Farmer Tester could make them pay half a crown for a pig in his turnips, which were no bigger than radishes, he ought to pay ten shillings at least for his pony trampling down their corn, which was half grown; and I couldn't help thinking this seemed very reasonable. In the end, however, the constable had persuaded them to take the money, and so the pony was let out.

"I told him how pleased I was at the way he had behaved, but the little man didn't seem quite satisfied himself. He should have liked to have given the lawyer a piece more of his mind, he said, only he was no scholar; 'but I've a got all the feelin's of a man, miss, though I med'nt have the ways o' bringin' on 'em out.' You see I am quite coming round to your opinion about him. But when I said that I hoped all the trouble was over, he shook his head, and he seems to think that the men will not forget it, and that some of the wild ones will be trying to pay Farmer Tester out in the winter nights, and I could see he was very anxious about Harry Winburn; so I promised him to go and see Betty.

"I went down to her cottage yesterday, and found her very low, poor old soul, about her son. She has had a bad attack again, and I am afraid her heart is not right. She will not live long if she has much to make her anxious, and how is that to be avoided? For her son's courting is all going wrong, she can see, though he will not tell her any thing about it; but he gets more moody and restless, she says, and don't take a pride in any thing, not even in his flowers or his allotment; and he takes to going about, more and more every day, with these men, who will be sure to lead him into trouble.

"After I left her, I walked up to the Hawk's Lynch, to see whether the view and the air would not do me good; and it did do me a great deal of good, dear, and I thought of you, and when I should see your bright face and hear your happy laugh again. The village looked so pretty and peaceful, I could hardly believe, while I was up there, that there were all these miserable quarrels and heart-burnings going on in it. I suppose they go on everywhere, but one can't help feeling as if there was something specially hard in those which come under one's own eyes, and touch one's self. And then they are so frivolous, and every thing might go on so comfortably if people would only be reasonable. I ought to have been a man, I am sure, and then I might, perhaps, be able to do more, and should have more influence. If poor papa were only well and strong!

"But, dear, I shall tire you with all these long histories and complainings. I have run on till I have no room left for any thing else; but you can't think what a comfort it is to me to write it all to you, for I have no one to tell it to. I feel so much better, and more cheerful since I sat down to write this. You must give my dear love to uncle and aunt, and let me hear from you again whenever you have time. If you could come over again and stay for a few days it would be very kind; but I must not press it, as there is nothing to attract you here, only we might talk over all that we did and saw at Oxford.

"Ever, dearest Mary, your very affectionate cousin,
"KATIE.

"P.S. — I should like to have the pattern of the jacket you wore the last day at Oxford. Could you cut it out in thin paper, and send it in your next?"

*July —, 184–.*

"MY DEAR BROWN, — I was very glad to see your hand, and to hear such flourishing accounts of your vacation doings. You wont get any like announcement out of me, for cricket has not yet come so far west as this, at least not to settle. We have a few pioneers and squatters in the villages; but, I am sorry to say, nothing yet like matches between the elevens of districts. Neighbors we have none, except the rector; so I have plenty of spare time, some of which I feel greatly disposed to devote to you; and I hope you wont find me too tedious to read.

"It is very kind of your father to wish that you should be my first pupil, and to propose that I should spend the last month of this vacation with you in Berkshire. But I do not like to give up a whole month. My father is getting old and infirm, and I can see that it would be a great trial to him, although he urges it, and is always telling me not to let him keep me at home. What do you say to meeting me half-way? I mean, that you should come here for half of the time, and then that I should return with you for the last fortnight of the vacation. This I could manage perfectly.

"But you cannot in any case be my first pupil; for, not to mention that I have been, as you know, teaching for some years, I have a pupil here at this minute. You are not likely to guess who it is, though you know him well enough, — perhaps I should say too well, — so, in a word, it is Blake. I had not been at home three days before I got a letter from him, asking me to take him, and putting it in such a way that I couldn't refuse. I would sooner not have had him, as I had already got out of taking a reading party with some trouble, and felt inclined to enjoy myself here in dignified idleness till next term. But what can you do when a man puts it to you as a great personal favor, etc., etc.? So I wrote to accept. You may imagine my disgust a day or two afterwards, at getting a letter from an uncle of his, some official person in London apparently, treating the whole matter in a *business* point of view, and me as if I were a training groom. He is good enough to suggest a stimulant to me in the shape of extra pay and his future patronage in the event of his nephew's taking a first in Michaelmas term. If I had received this letter before, I think it would have turned the scale, and I should have refused. But the thing was done, and Blake isn't fairly responsible for his relative's views. " So here he has been for a fortnight. He took a lodging in the village at first; but of course my dear old father's ideas of hospitality were shocked at this, and here he is, our inmate.

"He reads fiercely by fits and starts. A feeling of personal hatred against the examiners seems to urge him on more than any other motive; but this will not be strong enough to keep him to regular work, and without regular work he wont do, notwithstanding all his cleverness, and he is a marvellously clever fellow. So the first thing I have to do is to get him steadily to the collar, and how to do it is a pretty particular puzzle. For he hasn't a grain of enthusiasm in his composition, nor any power, as far as I can see, of throwing himself into the times and scenes of which he is reading. The philosophy of Greece and the history of Rome are matters of perfect indifference to him — to be got up by catch-words and dates for examination, and nothing more. I don't think he would care a straw if Socrates had never lived, or Hannibal had destroyed Rome. The greatest names and deeds of the Old World are just so many dead counters to him — the Jewish just as much as the rest. I tried him with the story of the attempt of Antiochus Epiphanes to conquer the Jews, and the glorious rising of all that was living in the Holy Land under the Maccabees. Not a bit of it; I couldn't get a spark out of him. He wouldn't even read the story, because it is in the Apocrypha, and so, as he said, the d——d examiners couldn't ask him any thing about it in the schools.

"Then his sense of duty is quite undeveloped. He has no notion of going on doing any thing disagreeable because he ought. So here I am at fault again. Ambition he has in abundance; in fact, so strongly, that very likely it may in the end pull him through, and make him work hard enough for his Oxford purposes at any rate. But it wants repressing rather than encouragement, and I certainly sha'n't appeal to it.

"You will begin to think I dislike him and want to get

rid of him, but it isn't the case. You know what a good temper he has, and how remarkably well he talks; so he makes himself very pleasant, and my father evidently enjoys his company; and then to be in constant intercourse with a subtle intellect like his, is pleasantly exciting, and keeps one alive and at high pressure, though one can't help always wishing that it had a little heat in it. You would be immensely amused if you could drop in on us.

"I think I have told you, or you must have seen it for yourself, that my father's principles are true blue, as becomes a sailor of the time of the great war, while his instincts and practice are liberal in the extreme. Our rector, on the contrary, is liberal in principles, but an aristocrat of the aristocrats in instinct and practice. They are always ready enough therefore to do battle, and Blake delights in the war, and fans it and takes part in it as a sort of free lance, laying little logical pit-falls for the combatants alternately, with that deferential manner of his. He gets some sort of intellectual pleasure, I suppose, out of seeing where they *ought* to tumble in; for tumble in they don't, but clear his pit-falls in their stride, — at least my father does, — quite innocent of having neglected to distribute his middle term; and the rector, if he has some inkling of these traps, brushes them aside, and disdains to spend powder on any one but his old adversary and friend. I employ myself in trying to come down ruthlessly on Blake himself; and so we spend our evenings after dinner, which comes off at the primitive hour of five. We used to dine at three, but my father has conformed now to college hours. If the rector does not come, instead of argumentative talk, we get stories out of my father. In the mornings we bathe and boat and read. So, you see, he and I have plenty of one

another's company, and it is certainly odd that we get on
so well with so very few points of sympathy. But, luckily,
besides his good temper and cleverness, he has plenty of
humor. On the whole, I think we shall rub through the
two months which he is to spend here without getting to
hate one another, though there is little chance of our becoming friends. Besides putting some history and science
into him (scholarship he does not need), I shall be satisfied if I can make him give up his use of the pronoun
'you' before he goes. In talking of the corn laws, or
foreign policy, or India, or any other political subject,
however interesting, he never will identify himself as an
Englishman; and '*you* do this,' or '*you* expect that,' is
forever in his mouth, speaking of his own countrymen.
I believe if the French were to land to-morrow on Port-
land, he would comment on our attempts to dislodge
them as if he had no concern with the business, except as
a looker-on.

"You will think all this a rather slow return for your
jolly, gossiping letter, full of cricket, archery, fishing, and
I know not what pleasant goings-on. But what is one to
do? one can only write about what is one's subject of interest for the time being, and Blake stands in that relation to me just now. I should prefer it otherwise, but *si
on n'a pas ce qu'on aime il faut aimer ce qu'on a.* I have
no incident to relate; these parts get on without incidents
somehow, and without society. I wish there were some,
particularly ladies' society. I break the tenth command-
ment constantly, thinking of Commemoration, and that
you are within a ride of Miss Winter and her cousin.
When you see them next, pray present my respectful
compliments. It is a sort of consolation to think that one
may cross their fancy for a moment and be remembered

as part of a picture which gives them pleasure. With which piece of sentiment I may as well shut up. Don't you forget my message now, and—
"Believe me, ever yours most truly,
"John Hardy.

"P.S. I mean to speak to Blake, when I get a chance, of that wretched debt which you have paid, unless you object. I should think better of him if he seemed more uncomfortable about his affairs. After all he may be more so than I think, for he is very reserved on such subjects."

"Englebourn Rectory,
"*July*, 184–.

"Dearest Mary,—I send the coachman with this note, in order that you may not be anxious about me. I have just returned from poor Betty Winburn's cottage to write it. She is very, very ill, and I do not think can last out more than a day or two; and she seems to cling to me so that I cannot have the heart to leave her. Indeed, if I could make up my mind to do it, I should never get her poor, white eager face out of my head all day, so that I should be very bad company and quite out of place at your party, making everybody melancholy and uncomfortable who came near me. So, dear, I am not coming. Of course, it is a great disappointment. I had set my heart on being with you, and enjoying it all thoroughly; and even at breakfast this morning knew of nothing to hinder me. My dress is actually lying on the bed at this minute, and it looks very pretty, especially the jacket like yours, which I and Hopkins have managed to make up from the pattern you sent, though you forgot the sleeves, which made it rather hard to do.  Ah, well! it is of no use to think of how pleasant things would have been which one cannot have.  You must write me an account of how it all went off, dear; or perhaps you can manage to get over here before long to tell me.

"I must now go back to poor Betty.  She is such a faithful, patient old thing, and has been such a good woman all her life that there is nothing painful in being by her now, and one feels sure that it will be much happier and better for her to be at rest.  If she could only feel comfortable about her son I am sure she would think so herself.  Oh, I forgot to say that her attack was brought on by the shock of hearing that he had been summoned for an assault.  Farmer Tester's son, a young man of about his own age, has, it seems, been of late waylaying Simon's daughter and making love to her.  It is so very hard to make out the truth in matters of this kind.  Hopkins says she is a dressed-up little minx who runs after all the young men in the parish; but really, from what I see and hear from other persons, I think she is a good girl enough. Even Betty, who looks on her as the cause of most of her own trouble, has never said a word to make me think that she is at all a light person, or more fond of admiration than any other good-looking girl in the parish.

"But those Testers are a very wicked set.  You cannot think what a misfortune it is in a place like this to have these rich families with estates of their own, in which the young men begin to think themselves beyond the common farmers.  They ape the gentlemen, and give themselves great airs, but of course no gentleman will associate with them, as they are quite uneducated; and the consequence is that they live a great deal at home, and give themselves up to all kinds of wickedness.  This young Tester is one of these. His father is a very bad old man, and does a great deal of harm here; and the son is following in his steps, and is quite as bad, or worse. So you see I shall not easily believe that Harry Winburn has been much in the wrong. However, all I know of it at present is that young Tester was beaten by Harry yesterday evening in the village street, and that they came to papa at once for a summons.

"Oh, here is the coachman ready to start; so I must conclude, dear, and go back to my patient. I shall often think of you during the day. I am sure you will have a charming party. With best love to all, believe me, ever, dearest,

"Your most affectionate<br>
"KATIE.

"P.S.—I am very glad that uncle and aunt take to Tom, and that he is staying with you for some days. You will find him very useful in making the party go off well, I am sure."

# CHAPTER VII.

### AMUSEMENTS AT BARTON MANOR.

"A LETTER, miss, from Englebourn," said a footman, coming up to Mary with the note given at the end of the last chapter on a waiter. She took it and tore it open; and, while she is reading it, the reader may be introduced to the place and company in which we find her. The scene is a large old-fashioned square brick house, backed by fine trees, in the tops of which the rooks live, and the jackdaws and starlings in the many holes which time has worn in the old trunks; but they are all away on this fine summer morning, seeking their meal and enjoying themselves in the neighboring fields. In front of the house is a pretty flower-garden, separated by a haw-haw from a large pasture, sloping southwards gently down to a brook, which glides along through water-cress and willow beds to join the Kennet. The beasts have all been driven off, and on the upper part of the field, nearest the house, two men are fixing up a third pair of targets on the rich short grass. A large tent is pitched near the archery-ground, to hold quivers and bow-cases, and luncheon, and to shelter lookers-on from the midday sun. Beyond the brook a pleasant, well-timbered country lies, with high chalk-downs for an horizon, ending in Marlborough hill, faint and blue in the west. This is the place which Mary's father has taken for the summer and autumn, and where she is fast becoming the pet of the neighborhood.

It will not perhaps surprise readers to find that our

hero has managed to find his way to Barton Manor in the second week of the vacation, and, having made the most of his opportunities, is acknowledged as a cousin by Mr. and Mrs. Porter. Their boys are at home for the holidays, and Mr. Porter's great wish is that they should get used to the country in their summer holidays. And as they have spent most of their childhood and boyhood in London, to which he has been tied pretty closely hitherto, this is a great opportunity. The boys only wanted a preceptor, and Tom presented himself at the right moment, and soon became the hero of Charley and Neddy Porter. He taught them to throw flies and bait crawfish nets, to bat fowl, and ferret for rabbits, and to saddle and ride their ponies, besides getting up games of cricket in the spare evenings, which kept him away from Mr. Porter's dinner-table. This last piece of self-denial, as he considered it, quite won over that gentleman, who agreed with his wife that Tom was just the sort of companion they would like for the boys, and so the house was thrown open to him.

The boys were always clamoring for him when he was away, and making their mother write off to press him to come again; which he, being a very good-natured young man, and particularly fond of boys, was ready enough to do. So this was the third visit he had paid in a month.

Mr. and Mrs. Brown wondered a little that he should be so very fond of the young Porters, who were good boys enough, but very much like other boys of thirteen and fifteen, of whom there were several in the neighborhood. He had indeed just mentioned an elder sister, but so casually that their attention had not been drawn to the fact, which had almost slipped out of their memories. On the other hand, Tom seemed so completely to identify himself with the boys and their pursuits, that it never occurred

to their father and mother, who were doatingly fond of
them, that, after all, they might not be the only attraction.
Mary seemed to take very little notice of him, and went on
with her own pursuits much as usual. It was true that she
liked keeping the score at cricket, and coming to look at
them fishing or rabbiting in her walks; but all that was
very natural. It is a curious and merciful dispensation
of Providence that most fathers and mothers seem never
to be capable of remembering their own experience, and
will probably go on till the end of time thinking of their
sons of twenty and daughters of sixteen or seventeen as
mere children, who may be allowed to run about together
as much as they please. And, where it is otherwise, the
results are not very different, for there are certain mysterious ways of holding intercourse implanted in the youth
of both sexes, against which no vigilance can avail.

So on this, her great fête day, Tom had been helping
Mary all the morning in dressing the rooms with flowers,
and arranging all the details — where people were to sit
at the cold dinner; how to find the proper number of
seats; how the dining-room was to be cleared in time for
dancing when the dew began to fall. In all which matters there were many obvious occasions for those *petits
soins* which are much valued by persons in like situations;
and Tom was not sorry that the boys had voted the whole
preparations a bore, and had gone off to the brook to
gropple in the bank for crawfish till the shooting began.
The arrival of the note had been the first *contre-temps* of
the morning, and they were now expecting guests to arrive every minute.

"What is the matter? No bad news, I hope," he said,
seeing her vexed expression.

"Why, Katie can't come. I declare I could sit down

and cry. I sha'n't enjoy the party a bit now, and I wish it were all over."

"I am sure Katie would be very unhappy if she thought you were going to spoil your day's pleasure on her account."

"Yes, I know she would; but it is so provoking when I had looked forward so to having her."

"You have never told me why she cannot come; she was quite full of it all when I saw her a few days back."

"Oh, there is a poor old woman in the village dying who is a great friend of Katie's. Here is her letter; let me see," she said, glancing over it to see that there was nothing in it which she did not wish him to read, "you may read it, if you like."

Tom began reading. "Betty Winburn," he said, when he came to the name, "what, poor dear old Betty! why, I've known her ever since I was born. She used to live in our parish, and I haven't seen her this eight years nearly. And her boy Harry, I wonder what has become of him?"

"You will see if you read on," said Mary; and so he read to the end, and then folded it up and returned it.

"So poor old Betty is dying. Well, she was always a good soul, and very kind to me when I was a boy. I should like to see her once again, and perhaps I might be able to do something for her son."

"Why should we not ride over to Englebourn to-morrow? They will be glad to get us out of the way while the house is being straightened."

"I should like it of all things, if it can be managed."

"Oh, I will manage it somehow, for I must go and see that dear Katie. I do feel so ashamed of myself when I think of all the good she is doing, and I do nothing but put flowers about, and play the piano. Isn't she an angel now?"

"Of course she is."

"Yes; but I wont have that sort of matter-of-course acquiescence. Now, do you really mean that Katie is as good as an angel?"

"As seriously as if I saw the wings growing out of her shoulders, and dewdrops hanging on them."

"You deserve to have some things not at all like wings growing out of your head. How is it that you never see when I don't want you to talk your nonsense?"

"How am I to talk sense about angels? I don't know any thing about them."

"You know what I mean, perfectly. I say that dear Katie is an angel, and I mean that I don't know any thing in her — no, not one single thing — which I should like to have changed. If the angels are all as good as she —"

"*If!* why I shall begin to doubt your orthodoxy."

"You don't know what I was going to say."

"It doesn't matter what you were going to say. You couldn't have brought that sentence round to an orthodox conclusion. Oh, please don't look angry, now. Yes, I quite see what you mean. You can think of Katie just as she is now in heaven, without being shocked."

Mary paused for a moment before she answered, as if she were rather taken by surprise at this way of putting her meaning, and then said seriously, —

"Indeed, I can. I think we should all be perfectly happy if we were all as good as she is."

"But she is not very happy herself, I am afraid."

"Of course not; how can she be, when all the people about her are so troublesome and selfish?"

"I can't fancy an angel the least like Uncle Robert; can you?"

"I wont talk about angels any more. You have made me feel quite as if I had been saying something wicked."

"Now really, it is too hard that you should lay the blame on me, when you began the subject yourself. You ought at least to let me say what I have to say about angels."

"Why, you said you knew nothing about them half a minute ago."

"But I may have my notions like other people. You have your notions. Katie is your angel."

"Well, then, what are your notions?"

"Katie is rather too dark for my idea of an angel. I can't fancy a dark angel."

"Why, how can you call Katie dark?"

"I only say she is too dark for my idea of an angel."

"Well, go on."

"Then, she is rather too grave."

"Too grave for an angel!"

"For my idea of an angel — one doesn't want one's angel to be like one's self, and I am so grave, you know."

"Yes, very. Then your angel is to be a laughing angel. A laughing angel, and yet very sensible; never talking nonsense?"

"Oh, I didn't say that."

"But you said he wasn't to be like you."

"*He!* who in the world do you mean by *he?*"

"Why, your angel, of course."

"My angel! You don't really suppose that my angel is to be a man?"

"I have no time to think about it. Look, they are putting those targets quite crooked. You are responsible for the targets; we must go and get them straight."

They walked across the ground towards the targets, and Tom settled them according to his notions of opposites.

"After all, archery is slow work," he said, when the targets were settled satisfactorily. "I don't believe anybody really enjoys it."

"Now that is because you men haven't it all to yourselves. You are jealous of any sort of game in which we can join. I believe you are afraid of being beaten."

"On the contrary, that is its only recommendation, that you can join in it."

"Well, I think that ought to be recommendation enough. But I believe it is much harder than most of your games. You can't shoot half as well as you play cricket; can you?"

"No, because I never practise. It isn't exciting to be walking up and down between two targets, and doing the same thing over and over again. Why, you don't find it so yourself. You hardly ever shoot."

"Indeed I do, though, constantly."

"Why, I have scarcely ever seen you shooting."

"That is because you are away with the boys all day."

"Oh, I am never too far to know what is going on. I'm sure you have never practised for more than a quarter of an hour any day that I have been here."

"Well, perhaps I may not have. But I tell you I am very fond of it."

Here the two boys came up from the brook, Neddy with his Scotch cap full of cray-fish.

"Why, you wretched boys, where you been? You are not fit to be seen," said Mary, shaking the arrows at them, which she was carrying in her hand. "Go and dress directly, or you will be late. I think I heard a carriage drive up just now."

"Oh, there's plenty of time. Look what whackers,

Cousin Tom," said Charley, holding out one of his prizes by its back towards Tom, while the indignant cray-fish flapped its tail and worked about with its claws in the hopes of getting hold of something to pinch.

"I don't believe those boys have been dry for two hours together in daylight since you first came here," said Mary to Tom.

"Well, and they're all the better for it, I'm sure," said Tom.

"Yes, that we are," said Charley.

"I say, Charley," said Tom, "your sister says she is very fond of shooting."

"Ay, and so she is. And isn't she a good shot too? I believe she would beat you at fifty yards."

"There now, you see, you need not have been so unbelieving," said Mary.

"Will you give her a shot at your new hat, Cousin Tom?" said Neddy.

"Yes, Neddy, that I will;" and he added to Mary, "I will bet you a pair of gloves you do not hit it in three shots."

"Very well," said Mary, "at thirty yards?"

"No, no! fifty yards was the named distance."

"No, fifty yards is too far. Why, your hat is not bigger than the gold."

"Well, I don't mind splitting the difference; we will say forty."

"Very well—three shots at forty yards."

"Yes; here, Charley, run and hang my hat on that target." The boys rushed off with the hat—a new white one—and hung it with a bit of string over the centre of one of the targets, and then, stepping a little aside, stood, clapping their hands, shouting to Mary to take good aim.

"You must string my bow," she said, handing it to him

as she buckled on her guard. "Now, do you repent? I am going to do my best, mind, if I do shoot."

"I scorn repentance: do your worst," said Tom, stringing the bow and handing it back to her. "And now I will hold your arrows; here is the forty yards."

Mary came to the place which he had stepped, her eyes full of fun and mischief; and he saw at once that she knew what she was about as she took her position and drew the first arrow. It missed the hat by some three inches only, and the boys clapped and shouted.

"Too near to be pleasant," said Tom, handing the second arrow. "I see you can shoot."

"Well, I will let you off still."

"Gloves and all?"

"No, of course you must pay the gloves."

"Shoot away then. Ah, that will do," he cried, as the second arrow struck considerably above the hat, "I shall get my gloves yet," and he handed the third arrow. They were too intent on the business in hand to observe that Mr. and Mrs. Porter and several guests were already on the hand bridge which crossed the haw-haw.

Mary drew her third arrow, paused a moment, loosed it, and this time with fatal aim.

The boys rushed to the target, towards which Mary and Tom also hurried, Mr. and Mrs. Porter and the newcomers following more quietly.

"Oh, look here—what fun," said Charley, as Tom came up, holding up the hat spiked on the arrow which he had drawn out of the target.

"What a wicked shot," he said, taking the hat and turning to Mary. "Look here, you have actually gone through three places—through crown, and side, and brim."

Mary began to feel quite sorry at her own success, and looked at the wounded hat sorrowfully.

"Hullo, look here—here's papa and mamma and some people, and we aint dressed! Come along, Neddy," and the boys made away towards the back premises, while Mary and Tom, turning round found themselves in the presence of Mr. and Mrs. Porter, Mr. Brown, and two or three other guests.

## CHAPTER VIII.

### BEHIND THE SCENES.

Mr. and Mrs. Brown had a long way to drive home that evening, including some eight miles of very indifferent chalky road over the downs, which separate the Vale of Kennet from the Vale of White Horse. Mr. Brown was an early man, and careful of his horses, who responded to his care by being always well up to much more work than they were ever put to. The drive to Barton Manor and back in a day was a rare event in their lives. Their master, taking this fact into consideration, was bent on giving them plenty of time for the return journey, and had ordered his groom to be ready to start by eight o'clock; but, that they might not disturb the rest by their early departure, he had sent the carriage to the village inn instead of to the Porters' stables.

At the appointed time, therefore, and when the evening's amusements were just beginning at the manor house, Mr. Brown sought out his wife; and, after a few words of leave-taking to their host and hostess, the two slipped quietly away, and walked down the village. The carriage was standing before the inn all ready for them, with the hostler and Mr. Brown's groom at the horses' heads. The carriage was a high phaeton having a roomy front seat with a hood to it, specially devised by Mr. Brown with a view to his wife's comfort, and that he might with a good conscience enjoy at the same time the pleasures of her society and of driving his own horses. When once in her place Mrs. Brown was as comfortable as she would have been in the most luxurious barouche with C springs, but the ascent was certainly rather a drawback. The pleasure of sitting by her husband and of receiving his assiduous help in the preliminary climb, however, more than compensated to Mrs. Brown for this little inconvenience.

Mr. Brown helped her up as usual, and arranged a plaid carefully over her knees, the weather being too hot for the apron. He then proceeded to walk round the horses, patting them, examining the bits, and making inquiries as to how they had fed: and, having satisfied himself on these points, and feed the hostler, took the reins, seated himself by his wife, and started at a steady pace towards the hills at the back of Barton village.

For a minute or two neither spoke, Mr. Brown being engrossed with his horses and she with her thoughts. Presently, however, he turned to her, and, having ascertained that she was quite comfortable, went on,—

"Well, my dear, what do you think of them?".

"Oh, I think they are agreeable people," answered Mrs. Brown; "but one can scarcely judge from seeing them to-day. It is too far for a drive; we shall not be home till midnight."

"But I am very glad we came. After all they are connections through poor Robert, and he seems anxious that they should start well in the county. Why, he has actually written twice, you know about our coming to-day. We must try to show them some civility."

"It is impossible to come so far often," Mrs. Brown persisted.

"It is too far for ordinary visiting. What do you say to asking them to come and spend a day or two with us?"

"Certainly, my dear, if you wish it," answered Mrs. Brown, but without much cordiality in her voice.

"Yes, I should like it; and it will please Robert so much. We might have him and Katie over to meet them, don't you think?"

"Let me see," said Mrs. Brown, with much more alacrity, "Mr. and Mrs. Porter will have the best bedroom and dressing-room; Robert must have the south room, and Katie the chintz. Yes, that will do; I can manage it very well."

"And their daughter; you have forgotten her."

"Well, you see, dear, there is no more room."

"Why, there is the dressing-room, next to the south room, with a bed in it. I'm sure nobody can want a better room."

"You know, John, that Robert cannot sleep if there is the least noise. I could never put any one into his dressing-room; there is only a single door between the rooms, and, even if they made no noise, the fancy that some one was sleeping there would keep him awake all night."

"Plague take his fancies! Robert has given way to them till he is fit for nothing. But you can put him in the chintz room, and give the two girls the south bedroom and dressing-room."

"What, put Robert in a room which looks north? My dear John, what can you be thinking about?"

Mr. Brown uttered an impatient grunt, and, as a vent to his feelings more decorous on the whole than abusing his brother-in-law, drew his whip more smartly than usual across the backs of his horses. The exertion of muscle necessary to reduce those astonished animals to their accustomed steady trot restored his temper, and he returned to the charge,—

"I suppose we must manage it on the second floor,

then, unless you could get a bed run up in the school-room."

"No, dear; I really should not like to do that — it would be so very inconvenient. We are always wanting the room for workwomen or servants; besides, I keep my account books and other things there."

"Then I'm afraid it must be on the second floor. Some of the children must be moved. The girl seems a nice girl with no nonsense about her, and wont mind sleeping up there. Or, why not put Katie up-stairs?"

"Indeed, I should not think of it. Katie is a dear good girl, and I will not put any one over her head."

"Nor I, dear. On the contrary, I was asking you to put her over another person's head," said Mr. Brown, laughing at his own joke. This unusual reluctance on the part of his wife to assist in carrying out any hospitable plans of his began to strike him; so, not being an adept at concealing his thoughts, or gaining his point by any attack except a direct one, after driving on for a minute in silence he turned suddenly on his wife, and said, —

"Why, Lizzie, you seem not to want to ask the girl."

"Well, John, I do not see the need of it at all."

"No, and you don't want to ask her."

"If you must know, then, I do not."

"Don't you like her?"

"I do not know her well enough either to like or dislike."

"Then, why not ask her, and see what she is like? But the truth is, Lizzie, you have taken a prejudice against her."

"Well, John, I think she is a thoughtless girl, and extravagant; not the sort of girl, in fact, that I should wish to be much here."

"Thoughtless and extravagant!" said Mr. Brown, looking grave; "how you women can be so sharp on one another! Her dress seemed to me simple and pretty, and her manners very lady-like and pleasing."

"You seem to have quite forgotten about Tom's hat," said Mrs. Brown.

"Tom's white hat — so I had," said Mr. Brown, and he relapsed into a low laugh at the remembrance of the scene. "I call that *his* extravagance, and not hers."

"It was a new hat, and a very expensive one, which he had bought for the vacation, and it is quite spoilt."

"Well, my dear; really, if Tom will let girls shoot at his hats, he must take the consequences. He must wear it with the holes, or buy another."

"How can he afford another, John? You know how poor he is."

Mr. Brown drove on for several minutes without speaking. He knew perfectly well what his wife was coming to now, and, after weighing in his mind the alternatives of accepting battle or making sail and changing the subject altogether, said, —

"You know, my dear, he has brought it on himself. A headlong, generous sort of youngster, like Tom, must be taught early that he can't have his cake and eat his cake. If he likes to lend his money, he must find out that he hasn't it to spend."

"Yes, dear, I quite agree with you. But £50 a year is a great deal to make him pay."

"Not a bit too much, Lizzie. His allowance is quite enough without it to keep him like a gentleman. Besides, after all, he gets it in meal or in malt; I have just paid £25 for his gun."

"I know how kind and liberal you are to him; only I am so afraid of his getting into debt."

"I wonder what men would do, if they hadn't some soft-hearted woman always ready to take their parts and pull them out of scrapes," said Mr. Brown. "Well, dear, how much do you want to give the boy?"

"Twenty-five pounds, just for this year. But out of my own allowance, John."

"Nonsense!" replied Mr. Brown; "you want your allowance for yourself and the children."

"Indeed, dear John, I would sooner not do it at all then, if I may not do it out of my own money."

"Well, have it your own way. I believe you would always look well dressed, if you never bought another gown. Then, to go back to what we were talking about just now — you will find a room for the girl, somehow?"

"Yes, dear, certainly, as I see you are bent on it."

"I think it would be scarcely civil not to ask her, especially if Katie comes. And I own I think her very pretty, and have taken a great fancy to her."

"Isn't it odd that Tom should never have said any thing about her to us? He has talked of all the rest, till I knew them quite well before I went there."

"No; it seems to me the most natural thing in the world."

"Yes, dear, very natural. But I can't help wishing he had talked about her more; I should think it less dangerous."

"Oh, you think Master Tom is in love with her, eh?" said Mr. Brown, laughing.

"More unlikely things have happened. You take it very easily, John."

"Well, we have all been boys and girls, Lizzie. The world hasn't altered much, I suppose, since I used to get up at five on winter mornings, to ride some twenty miles to cover, on the chance of meeting a young lady on a gray pony. I remember how my poor dear old father used to wonder at it, when our hounds met close by, in a better country. I'm afraid I forgot to tell him what a pretty creature 'Gipsey' was, and how well she was ridden."

"But Tom is only twenty, and he must go into a profession."

"Yes, yes; much too young, I know — too young for any thing serious. We had better see them together, and then, if there is any thing in it, we can keep them apart. There cannot be much the matter yet."

"Well, dear, if you are satisfied, I am sure I am."

And so the conversation turned on other subjects, and Mr. and Mrs. Brown enjoyed their moonlight drive home through the delicious summer night, and were quite sorry when the groom got down from the hind-seat to open their own gates at half-past twelve.

About the same time, the festivities at Barton Manor were coming to a close. There had been cold dinner in the tent at six, after the great match of the day; and, after dinner, the announcement of the scores, and the distribution of prizes to the winners. A certain amount of toasts and speechifying followed, which the ladies sat through with the most exemplary appearance of being amused. When their healths had been proposed and acknowledged, they retired, and were soon followed by the younger portion of the male sex; and, while the J. P.'s and clergymen sat quietly at their wine, which Mr. Porter took care should be remarkably good, and their wives went in to look over the house and have tea, their sons and daughters split up into groups, and some shot handicaps, and some walked about and flirted, and some played at bowls or lawn billiards. And soon the band appeared again from the servants' hall, mightily refreshed, and dancing began on the grass, and in due time was transferred to the tent, when the grass got damp with the night dew, and then to the hall of the house, when the lighting of the tent began to fail. And then there came a supper, extemporized out of the remains of the dinner; after which papas and mammas began to look at their watches, and remonstrate with daughters, coming up with sparkling eyes and hair a little shaken out of place, and pleading for "just one more dance." "You have been going on ever since one o'clock," remonstrated the parents; "And are ready to go on till one the next day," replied the children. By degrees, however, the frequent sound of wheels were heard, and the dancers got thinner and thinner, till, for the last half-hour, some half-dozen couples of young people danced an interminable reel, while Mr. and Mrs. Porter, and a few of the most good-natured matrons of the neighborhood looked on. Soon after midnight the band struck; no amount of negus could get any thing more out of them but "God save the Queen," which they accordingly played and departed; and then came the final cloaking and driving off of the last guests. Tom and Mary saw the last of them into their carriage at the hall-door, and lingered a moment in the porch.

"What a lovely night!" said Mary. "How I hate going to bed!"

"It is a dreadful bore," answered Tom; "but here is the butler waiting to shut up; we must go in."

"I wonder where papa and mamma are."

"Oh, they are only seeing things put a little to rights. Let us sit here till they come; they must pass by to get to their rooms."

So the two sat down on some hall chairs.

"Oh, dear! I wish it were all coming over again to-morrow," said Tom, leaning back, and looking up at the ceiling. "By the way, remember I owe you a pair of gloves: what color shall they be?"

"Any color you like. I can't bear to think of it. I felt so dreadfully ashamed when they all came up, and your mother looked so grave; I am sure she was very angry."

"Poor mother, she was thinking of my hat with three arrow holes in it."

"Well, I am very sorry, because I wanted them to like me."

"And so they will; I should like to know who can help it."

"Now, I wont have any of your nonsensical compliments. Do you think they enjoyed the day?"

"Yes, I am sure they did. My father said he had never liked an archery meeting so much."

"But they went away so early."

"They had a very long drive, you know. Let me see," he said, feeling in his breast-pocket, "mother left me a note, and I have never looked at it till now." He took a slip of paper out and read it, and his face fell.

"What is it?" said Mary, leaning forward.

"Oh, nothing; only I must go to-morrow morning."

"There, I was sure she was angry."

"No, no; it was written this morning before she came here. I can tell by the paper."

"But she will not let you stay here a day, you see."

"I have been here a good deal, considering all things. I should like never to go away."

"Perhaps papa might find a place for you, if you asked him. Which should you like, — to be tutor to the boys, or gamekeeper?"

"On the whole, I should prefer the tutorship at present; you take so much interest in the boys."

11*

"Yes, because they have no one to look after them now in the holidays. But, when you come as tutor, I shall wash my hands of them."

"Then I shall decline the situation."

"How are you going home to-morrow?"

"I shall ride round by Englebourn. They wish me to go round and see Katie and Uncle Robert. You talked about riding over there yourself this morning."

"I should like it so much. But how can we manage it? I can't ride back by myself."

"Couldn't you stay and sleep there?"

"I will ask mamma. No, I am afraid it can hardly be managed;" and so saying, Mary leant back in her chair, and began to pull to pieces some flowers she held in her hand.

"Don't pull them to pieces; give them to me," said Tom. "I have kept the rosebud you gave me at Oxford, folded up in — "

"Which you took, you mean to say. No, I wont give you any of them — or, let me see — yes, here is a sprig of lavender; you may have that."

"Thank you. But why lavender?"

"Lavender stands for sincerity. It will remind you of the lecture you gave me."

"I wish you would forget that. But you know what flowers mean, then? Do give me a lecture: you owe me one. What do those flowers mean which you will not give me, — the piece of heather, for instance?"

"Heather signifies constancy."

"And the carnations?"

"Jealousy."

"And the heliotrope?"

"Oh, never mind the heliotrope."

"But it is such a favorite of mine. Do tell me what it means?"

"*Je vous aime,*" said Mary, with a laugh, and a slight

blush; "it is all nonsense. Oh, here's mamma at last," and she jumped up and went to meet her mother, who came out of the drawing-room, candle in hand.

"My dear Mary, I thought you were gone to bed," said Mrs. Porter, looking from one to the other, seriously.

"Oh, I'm not the least tired, and I couldn't go without wishing you and papa good-night, and thanking you for all the trouble you have taken."

"Indeed, we ought all to thank you," said Tom; "everybody said it was the pleasantest party they had ever been at."

"I am very glad it went off well," said Mrs. Porter, gravely; "and now, Mary, you must go to bed."

"I am afraid I must leave you to-morrow morning," said Tom.

"Yes; Mrs. Brown said they expect you at home to-morrow."

"I am to ride round by Uncle Robert's; would you like one of the boys to go with me?"

"O dear mamma, could not Charley and I ride over to Englebourn? I do so long to see Katie."

"No, dear; it is much too far for you. We will drive over in a few days' time."

And, so saying, Mrs. Porter wished Tom good-night, and led off her daughter.

Tom went slowly up-stairs to his room, and, after packing his portmanteau for the carrier to take in the morning, threw up his window and leant out into the night, and watched the light clouds swimming over the moon, and the silver mist folding the water meadows and willows in its soft, cool mantle. His thoughts were such as will occur to any reader who has passed the witching age of twenty; and the scent of the heliotrope-bed, in the flower-garden below, seemed to rise very strongly on the night air.

## CHAPTER IX.

#### A CRISIS.

In the forenoon of the following day Tom rode slowly along the street of Englebourn towards the rectory gate. He had left Barton soon after breakfast, without having been able to exchange a word with Mary except in the presence of her mother, and yet he had felt more anxious than ever before at least to say good-by to her without witnesses. With this view he had been up early, and had whistled a tune in the hall, and held a loud conversation with the boys, who appeared half-dressed in the gallery above, while he brushed the dilapidated white hat, to let all whom it might concern know that he was on the move. Then he had walked up and down the garden in full view of the windows till the bell rang for prayers. He was in the breakfast-room before the bell had done ringing, and Mrs. Porter, followed by her daughter, entered at the same moment. He could not help fancying that the conversation at breakfast was a little constrained, and particularly remarked that nothing was said by the heads of the family when the boys vociferously bewailed his approaching departure, and tried to get him to name some day for his return before their holidays ended. Instead of encouraging the idea, Mrs. Porter reminded Neddy and Charley that they had only ten days more, and had not yet looked at the work they had to do for their tutor in the holidays. Immediately after breakfast Mrs. Porter wished him good-by herself very kindly, but (he could not help thinking) without that air of near relationship which he had flattered himself was well established between himself and all the members of the Porter family; and then she had added, "Now, Mary, you must say good-by; I want you to come and help me with some work this morning." He had scarcely looked at her all the morning, and now one shake of the hand and she was spirited away in a moment, and he was left standing, dissatisfied and uncomfortable, with a sense of incompleteness in his mind, and as if he had had a thread in his life suddenly broken off which he could not tell how to get joined again.

However, there was nothing for it but to get off. He had no excuse for delay, and had a long ride before him; so he and the boys went round to the stable. On their passage through the garden the idea of picking a nosegay and sending it to her by one of the boys came into his head. He gathered the flowers, but then thought better of it, and threw them away. What right, after all, had he to be sending flowers to her—above all, flowers to which they had attached a meaning, jokingly it was true, but still a meaning? No, he had no right to do it; it would not be fair to her, or her father and mother, after the kind way in which they had all received him. So he threw away the flowers, and mounted and rode off, watched by the boys, who waved their straw hats as he looked back just before coming to a turn in the road which would take him out of sight of the Manor House. He rode along at a foot's pace for some time, thinking over the events of the past week; and then, beginning to feel purposeless, and somewhat melancholy, urged his horse into a smart trot along the waste land which skirted the road. But, go what pace he would, it mattered not; he could not leave his thoughts behind. So he pulled up again after a mile or so, slackened his reins, and, leaving his horse to pick his own way along the road, betook himself to the serious consideration of his position.

The more he thought of it the more discontented he became, and the day clouded over as if to suit his temper. He felt as if within the last twenty-four hours he had been somehow unwarrantably interfered with. His mother and Mrs. Porter had both been planning something about him, he felt sure. If they had any thing to say, why couldn't they say it out to him? But what could there be to say? Couldn't he and Mary be trusted together without making fools of themselves? He did not stop to analyze his feelings towards her, or to consider whether it was very prudent or desirable for her that they should be thrown so constantly and unreservedly together. He was too much taken up with what he chose to consider his own wrongs for any such consideration. "Why can't they let me alone?" was the question which he asked himself perpetually, and it seemed to him the most reasonable one in the world, and that no satisfactory answer was possible to it, except that he ought to be, and should be, let alone. And so at last he rode along Englebourn Street, convinced that what he had to do before all other things just now was to assert himself properly, and show every one, even his own mother, that he was no longer a boy to be managed according to any one's fancies except his own.

He rode straight to the stables and loosed the girths of his horse and gave particular directions about grooming and feeding him, and stayed in the stall for some minutes rubbing his ears and fondling him. The antagonism which possessed him for the moment against mankind perhaps made him appreciate the value of his relations with a well-trained beast. Then he went round to the house and inquired for his uncle. He had not been in Englebourn for some years, and the servant did not know him, and answered that Mr. Winter was not out of his room and never saw strangers till the afternoon. Where was Miss Winter then? She was down the village at Widow Winburn's, and he couldn't tell when she would be back, the man said. The contents of Katie's note of the day before had gone out of his head, but the mention of Betty's name recalled them, and with them something of the kindly feeling which he had had on hearing of her illness. So, saying he would call later to see his uncle, he started again to find the widow's cottage, and his cousin.

The servant had directed him to the last house in the village, but, when he got outside the gate, there were houses in two directions. He looked about for some one from whom to inquire further, and his eye fell upon our old acquaintance, the constable, coming out of his door with a parcel under his arm.

The little man was in a brown study, and did not notice Tom's first address. He was, in fact, anxiously thinking over his old friend's illness and her son's trouble; and was on his way to Farmer Grove's, having luckily the excuse of taking a coat to be tried on, in the hopes of getting him to interfere and patch up the quarrel between young Tester and Harry.

Tom's first salute had been friendly enough; no one knew better how to speak to the poor, amongst whom he had lived all his life, than he. But, not getting any answer, and being in a touchy state of mind, he was put out, and shouted, —

"Hullo, my man, can't you hear me?"

"Ees, I beant dunch," replied the constable, turning and looking at his questioner.

"I thought you were, for I spoke loud enough before. Which is Mrs. Winburn's cottage?"

"The furdest house down ther," he said, pointing, "'tis

in my way if you've a mind to come." Tom accepted the offer and walked along by the constable.

"Mrs. Winburn is ill, isn't she?" he asked, after looking his guide over.

"Ees, her be — terreble bad," said the constable.

"What is the matter with her, do you know?"

"Zummat o' fits, I hears. Her've had em this six year, on and off."

"I suppose it's dangerous. I mean, she isn't likely to get well?"

"'Tis in the Lord's hands," replied the constable, "but her's that bad wi' pain, at times, 'twould be a mussy if 'twould plaase he to tak her out on't."

"Perhaps she mightn't think so," said Tom, superciliously; he was not in the mind to agree with any one. The constable looked at him solemnly for a moment and then said, —

"Her's been a God-fearin' woman from her youth up, and her's had a deal o' trouble. Thaay as the Lord loveth he chasteneth, and 'tisn't such as thaay as is afeard to go afore him."

"Well, I never found that having troubles made people a bit more anxious to get 'out on't,' as you call it," said Tom.

"It don't seem to me as you can 'a had much o' trouble to judge by," said the constable, who was beginning to be nettled by Tom's manner.

"How can you tell that?"

"Leastways 'twould be whoam-made, then," persisted the constable, "and ther's a sight o' odds atween whoam-made troubles and thaay as the Lord sends."

"So there may be; but I may have seen both sorts for any thing you can tell."

"Nay, nay; the Lord's troubles leaves his marks."

"And you don't see any of *them* in my face, eh?"

The constable jerked his head after his own peculiar fashion, but declined to reply directly to this interrogatory. He parried it by one of his own.

"In the doctorin' line, make so bould?"

"No," said Tom. "You don't seem to have such very good eyes, after all."

"Oh, I seed you wasn't old enough to be doin' for yourself, like; but I thought you med ha' been a 'sistant, or summat."

"Well, then, you're just mistaken," said Tom, considerably disgusted at being taken for a country doctor's assistant.

"I ax your pardon," said the constable. "But if you beant in the doctorin' line, what be gwine to Widow Winburn's for, make so bould?"

"That's my look-out, I suppose," said Tom, almost angrily. "That's the house, isn't it?" and he pointed to the cottage already described at the corner of Englebourn Copse.

"Ees."

"Good-day, then."

"Good-day," muttered the constable, not at all satisfied with this abrupt close of the conversation, but too unready to prolong it. He went on his own way slowly, looking back often, till he saw the door open; after which he seemed better satisfied, and ambled out of sight.

"The old snuffler!" thought Tom, as he strode up to the cottage door — "a ranter, I'll be bound, with his 'Lord's troubles,' and 'Lord's hands,' and 'Lord's marks.' I hope Uncle Robert hasn't many such in the parish."

He knocked at the cottage door, and in a few seconds it opened gently, and Katie slipped out with her finger on her lips. She made a slight gesture of surprise at seeing him, and held out her hand.

"Hush!" she said, "she is asleep. You are not in a hurry?"

"No, not particularly," he answered, abruptly; for there was something in her voice and manner which jarred with his humor.

"Hush!" she said again, "you must not speak so loud. We can sit down here, and talk quietly. I shall hear if she moves."

So he sat down opposite to her in the little porch of the cottage. She left the door ajar, so that she might catch the least movement of her patient, and then turned to him with a bright smile, and said,—

"Well, I am so glad to see you! What good wind blows you here?"

"No particularly good wind, that I know of. Mary showed me your letter yesterday, and mother wished me to come round here on my way home; and so here I am."

"And how did the party go off? I long to hear about it."

"Very well; half the county were there, and it was all very well done."

"And how did dear Mary look?"

"Oh, just as usual. But now, Katie, why didn't you come? Mary and all of us were so disappointed."

"I thought you read my letter."

"Yes, so I did."

"Then you know the reason."

"I don't call it a reason. Really, you have no right to shut yourself up from every thing. You will be getting moped to death."

"But do I look moped?" she said; and he looked at

her, and couldn't help admitting to himself, reluctantly, that she did not. So he re-opened fire from another point.

"You will wear yourself out, nursing every old woman in the parish."

"But I don't nurse every old woman."

"Why, there is no one here but you to-day now," he said, with a motion of his head towards the cottage.

"No, because I have let the regular nurse go home for a few hours. Besides, this is a special case. You don't know what a dear old soul Betty is."

"Yes, I do; I remember her ever since I was a child."

"Ah, I forgot; I have often heard her talk of you. Then you ought not to be surprised at any thing I may do for her."

"She is a good, kind old woman, I know. But still I must say, Katie, you ought to think of your friends and relations a little, and what you owe to society."

"Indeed, I do think of my friends and relations very much, and I should have liked, of all things, to have been with you yesterday. You ought to be pitying me, instead of scolding me."

"My dear Katie, you know I didn't mean to scold you; and nobody admires the way you give yourself up to visiting, and all that sort of thing, more than I; only you ought to have a little pleasure sometimes. People have a right to think of themselves and their own happiness a little."

"Perhaps I don't find visiting, and all that sort of thing, as you call it, so very miserable. But now, Tom, you saw in my letter that poor Betty's son has got into trouble?"

"Yes; and that is what brought on her attack, you said"

"I believe so. She was in a sad state about him all yesterday, — so painfully eager and anxious. She is better to-day; but still I think it would do her good if you would see her, and say you will be a friend to her son. Would you mind?"

"It was just what I wished to do yesterday. I will do all I can for him, I'm sure. I always liked him as a boy; you can tell her that. But I don't feel, somehow, to-day, at least, as if I could do any good by seeing her."

"Oh, why not?"

"I don't think I'm in the right humor. Is she very ill?"

"Yes, very ill indeed; I don't think she can recover."

"Well, you see, Katie, I'm not used to death-beds. I shouldn't say the right sort of thing."

"How do you mean — the right sort of thing?"

"Oh, you know. I couldn't talk to her about her soul. I'm not fit for it, and it isn't my place."

"No, indeed, it isn't. But you can remind her of old times, and say a kind word about her son."

"Very well, if you don't think I shall do any harm."

"I'm sure it will comfort her. And now tell me about yesterday."

They sat talking for some time in the same low tone, and Tom began to forget his causes of quarrel with the world, and gave an account of the archery party from his own point of view. Katie saw, with a woman's quickness, that he avoided mentioning Mary, and smiled to herself, and drew her own conclusions.

At last, there was a slight movement in the cottage, and, laying her hand on his arm, she got up quickly and went in. In a few minutes she came to the door again.

"How is she?" asked Tom.

"Oh, much the same; but she has waked without pain, which is a great blessing. Now, are you ready?"

"Yes; but you must go with me."

"Come in, then." She turned, and he followed into the cottage.

Betty's bed had been moved into the kitchen, for the sake of light and air. He glanced at the corner where it stood with almost a feeling of awe, as he followed his cousin on tip-toe. It was all he could do to recognize the pale, drawn face which lay on the coarse pillow. The rush of old memories which the sight called up, and the thought of the suffering of his poor old friend, touched him deeply.

Katie went to the bed-side, and stooping down, smoothed the pillow, and placed her hand for a moment on the forehead of her patient. Then she looked up, and beckoned to him, and said, in her low, clear voice, —

"Betty, here is an old friend come to see you; my cousin, Squire Brown's son. You remember him quite a little boy."

The old woman moved her head towards the voice and smiled, but gave no further sign of recognition. Tom stole across the floor, and sat down by the bed-side.

"Oh, yes, Betty," he said, leaning towards her and speaking softly, "you must remember me. Master Tom, — who used to come to your cottage on baking days for hot bread, you know."

"To be sure, I minds un, bless his little heart," said the old woman faintly. "Hev he come to see poor Betty? Do'ee let un com, and lift un up so as I med see un. My sight be getting dimlike."

"Here he is, Betty," said Tom, taking her hand — a hard-working hand, lying there with the skin all puckered from long and daily acquaintance with the washing-tub — "I'm Master Tom."

"Ah, dearee me," she said, slowly, looking at him with lustreless eyes. "Well, you be growed into a fine young gentleman, surely. And how's the Squire, and Madam Brown, and all the fam'ly?"

"Oh, very well, Betty, — they will be so sorry to hear of your illness."

"But there aint no hot bread for un. 'Tis ill to bake wi' no fuz bushes, and bakers' stuff is poor for hungry folk."

"I'm within three months as old as your Harry, you know," said Tom, trying to lead her back to the object of his visit.

"Harry," she repeated, and then collecting herself went on, "our Harry? where is he? They haven't sent un to prison, and his mother a dyin'?"

"Oh, no, Betty; he will be here directly. I came to ask whether there is any thing I can do for you."

"You'll stand by un, poor buoy — our Harry, as you used to play wi' when you was little — 'twas they as aggravated un so as he couldn't abear it, afore ever he'd a struck a fly."

"Yes, Betty; I will see that he has fair play. Don't trouble about that; it will be all right. You must be quite quiet, and not trouble yourself about any thing, that you may get well and about again."

"Nay, nay, Master Tom. I be gwine whoam; ees, I be gwine whoam to my maester, Harry's father — I knows I be — and you'll stand by un when I be gone; and Squire Brown'll say a good word for un to the magistrates?"

"Yes, Betty, that he will. But you must cheer up, and you'll get better yet; don't be afraid."

"I beant afeard, Master Tom: no, bless you, I beant

afeard but what the Lord'll be mussiful to a poor lone woman like me, as has had a sore time of it since my maester died, wi' a hungry boy like our Harry to kep, back and belly; and the rheumatics terrible bad all winter time."

"I'm sure, Betty, you have done your duty by him, and every one else."

"Dwontee speak o' doin's, Master Tom. 'Tis no doin's o' owrn as'll make any odds where I be gwine."

Tom did not know what to answer; so he pressed her hand and said,—

"Well, Betty, I am very glad I have seen you once more; I sha'n't forget it. Harry sha'n't want a friend while I live."

"The Lord bless you, Master Tom, for that word," said the dying woman, returning the pressure, as her eyes filled with tears. Katie, who had been watching her carefully from the other side of the bed, made him a sign to go.

"Good-by, Betty," he said; "I wont forget, you may be sure; God bless you;" and then, disengaging his hand gently, went out again into the porch, where he sat down to wait for his cousin.

In a few minutes the nurse returned, and Katie came out of the cottage soon afterwards.

"Now I will walk up home with you," she said. "You must come in and see papa. Well, I'm sure, you must be glad you went in. Was not I right?"

"Yes, indeed; I wish I could have said something more to comfort her."

"You couldn't have said more. It was just what she wanted."

"But where is her son? I ought to see him before I go."

"He has gone to the doctor's for some medicine. He will be back soon."

"Well, I must see him; and I should like to do something for him at once. I'm not very flush of money, but I must give you something for him. You'll take it; I shouldn't like to offer it to him."

"I hardly think he wants money; they are well off now. He earns good wages, and Betty has done her washing up to this week."

"Yes, but he will be fined, I suppose, for this assault; and then, if she should die, there will be the funeral expenses."

"Very well; as you please," she said; and Tom proceeded to hand over to her all his ready money, except a shilling or two. After satisfying his mind thus he looked at her, and said,—

"Do you know, Katie, I don't think I ever saw you so happy and in such spirits?"

"There now! And yet you began talking to me as if I were looking sad enough to turn all the beer in the parish sour."

"Well, so you ought to be, according to Cocker, spending all your time in sick-rooms."

"According to who?"

"According to Cocker."

"Who is Cocker?"

"Oh, I don't know; some old fellow who wrote the rules of arithmetic, I believe; it's only a bit of slang. But, I repeat, you have a right to be sad, and it's taking an unfair advantage of your relations to look as pleasant as you do."

Katie laughed; "You ought not to say so, at any rate," she said, "for you look all the pleasanter for your visit to a sick-room."

"Did I look very unpleasant before?"

"Well, I don't think you were in a very good humor."

"No, I was in a very bad humor, and talking to you and poor old Betty has set me right, I think. But you said hers was a special case. It must be very sad work in general."

"Only when one sees people in great pain, or when they are wicked, and quarrelling, or complaining about nothing; then I do get very low sometimes. But even then it is much better than keeping to one's self. Any thing is better than thinking of one's self, and one's own troubles."

"I dare say you are right," said Tom, recalling his morning's meditations, "especially when one's troubles are home-made. Look, here's an old fellow who gave me a lecture on that subject before I saw you this morning, and took me for the apothecary's boy."

They were almost opposite David's door, at which he stood with a piece of work in his hand. He had seen Miss Winter from his look-out window, and had descended from his board in hopes of hearing news.

Katie returned his respectful and anxious salute, and said, "She is no worse, David. We left her quite out of pain and very quiet."

"Ah, 'tis to be hoped as she'll hev a peaceful time on't now, poor soul," said David; "I've a been to Farmer Grove's, and I hopes as he'll do summat about Harry."

"I'm glad to hear it," said Miss Winter, "and my cousin here, who knew Harry very well when they were little boys together, has promised to help him. This is Harry's best friend," she said to Tom, "who has done more than any one to keep him right."

David seemed a little embarrassed, and began jerking his head about when his acquaintance of the morning, whom he had scarcely noticed before, was introduced by Miss Winter as "my cousin."

"I wish to do all I can for him," said Tom, "and I'm very glad to have made your acquaintance. You must let me know whenever I can help;" and he took out a card and handed it to David, who looked at it, and then said,—

"And I be to write to you, sir, then, if Harry gets into trouble?"

"Yes, but we must keep him out of trouble, even home-made ones, which don't leave good marks, you know," said Tom.

"And thaay be nine out o' ten o' aal as comes to a man, sir," said David, "as I've a told Harry scores o' times."

"That seems to be your text, David," said Tom, laughing.

"Ah, and 'tis a good un too, sir. Ax Miss Winter else. 'Tis a sight better to hev the Lord's troubles while you be about it, for thaay as hasn't makes wus for theirselves out o' nothin'. Dwon't em, miss?"

"Yes; you know that I agree with you, David."

"Good-by, then," said Tom, holding out his hand, "and mind you let me hear from you."

"What a queer old bird, with his whole wisdom of man packed up small for ready use, like a quack doctor," he said, as soon as they were out of hearing.

"Indeed, he isn't the least like a quack doctor. I don't know a better man in the parish, though he is rather obstinate, like all the rest of them."

"I didn't mean to say any thing against him, I assure you," said Tom; "on the contrary I think him a fine old fellow. But I didn't think so this morning, when he showed me the way to Betty's cottage." The fact was that Tom saw all things and persons with quite a different pair of eyes from those which he had been provided with when he arrived in Englebourn that morning. He even made allowances for old Mr. Winter, who was in his usual querulous state at luncheon, though perhaps it would have been difficult in the whole neighborhood to find a more pertinent comment on and illustration of the constable's text than the poor old man furnished, with his complaints about his own health and all he had to do and think of, and everybody about him. It did strike Tom, however, as very wonderful how such a character as Katie's could have grown up under the shade of, and in constant contact with, such an one as her father's. He wished his uncle good-by soon after luncheon, and he and Katie started again down the village — she to return to her nursing and he on his way home. He led his horse by the bridle and walked by her side down the street. She pointed to the Hawk's Lynch as they walked along, and said, "You should ride up there; it is scarcely out of your way. Mary and I used to walk there every day when she was here, and she was so fond of it."

At the cottage they found Harry Winburn. He came out, and the two young men shook hands, and looked one another over, and exchanged a few shy sentences. Tom managed with difficulty to say the little he had to say, but tried to make up for it by a hearty manner. It was not the time or place for any unnecessary talk; so in a few minutes he was mounted and riding up the slope towards the heath. "I should say he must be half a stone lighter than I," he thought, "and not quite so tall; but he looked as hard as iron, and tough as whipcord. What a No. 7 he'd make in a heavy crew! Poor fellow, he seems dreadfully cut up. I hope I shall be able to be of use to him. Now for this place which Katie showed me from the village street."

He pressed his horse up the steep side of the Hawk's Lynch. The exhilaration of the scramble, and the sense of power, and of some slight risk, which he felt as he helped on the gallant beast with hand and knee and heel, and the loose turf and stones flew from his hoofs and rolled down the hill behind him, made his eyes kindle and his pulse beat quicker as he reached the top and pulled up under the Scotch firs. "This was her favorite walk, then. No wonder. What an air, and what a view!" He jumped off his horse, slipped the bridle over his arm and let him pick away at the short grass and tufts of heath as he himself first stood, and then sat, and looked out over the scene which she had so often looked over. She might have sat on the very spot he was sitting on; she must have taken in the same expanse of wood and meadow, village and park, and dreamy, distant hill. Her presence seemed to fill the air round him. A rush of new thoughts and feelings swam through his brain and carried him, a willing piece of drift-man, along with them. He gave himself up to the stream, and revelled in them. His eye traced back the road along which he had ridden in the morning, and rested on the Barton woods, just visible in the distance, on this side of the point where all outline except that of the horizon began to be lost. The flickering July air seemed to beat in a pulse of purple glory over the spot. The soft wind which blew straight from Barton seemed laden with her name, and whispered it in the firs over his head. Every nerve in his body was bounding with new life, and he could sit still no longer. He rose, sprang on his horse, and, with a shout of joy, turned from the vale and rushed away on to the heath, northwards, towards his home behind the chalk hills. He had ridden into Englebourn in the morning an almost unconscious dabbler by the margin of the great stream; he rode from the Hawk's Lynch in the afternoon over head and ears, and twenty, a hundred, ay, unnumbered fathoms below that, deep, consciously, and triumphantly in love.

But at what a pace, and in what a form! Love, at least in his first access, must be as blind a horseman as he is an archer. The heath was rough with peat-cutting and turf-cutting, and many a deep-rutted farm road and tracks of heather and furze. Over them and through them went horse and man—horse rising seven, and man twenty off, a well-matched pair in age for a wild ride—headlong towards the north, till a blind rut somewhat deeper than usual put an end to their career, and sent the good horse staggering forward some thirty feet on to his nose and knees, and Tom over his shoulder, on to his back in the heather.

"Well, it's lucky it's no worse," thought our hero, as he picked himself up and anxiously examined the horse, who stood trembling and looking wildly puzzled at the whole proceeding; "I hope he hasn't overreached. What will the governor say? His knees are all right. Poor old boy," he said, patting him, "no wonder you look astonished. You're not in love. Come along; we wont make fools of ourselves any more. What is it?—

"'A true love forsaken a new love may get,
But a neck that's once broken can never be set.'

What stuff; one may get a neck set for any thing I know; but a new love — blasphemy!"

The rest of the ride passed off soberly enough, except in Tom's brain, wherein were built up in gorgeous succession castles such as we have all built, I suppose, before now. And with the castles were built up side by side good honest resolves to be worthy of her, and win her and worship her with body, and mind, and soul. And, as a first instalment away to the winds went all the selfish morning thoughts; and he rode down the northern slope of the chalk hills a dutiful and affectionate son, at peace with Mrs. Porter, and honoring her for her care of the treasure which he was seeking, and in good time for dinner.

"Well, dear," said Mrs. Brown to her husband when they were alone that night, "did you ever see Tom in such spirits, and so gentle and affectionate? Dear boy; there can be nothing the matter."

"Didn't I tell you so?" replied Mr. Brown; "you women have always got some nonsense in your heads as soon as your boys have a hair on their chin or your girls begin to put up their back hair."

"Well, John, say what you will, I'm sure Mary Porter is a very sweet, taking girl, and —"

"I am quite of the same opinion," said Mr. Brown, "and am very glad you have written to ask them here."

And so the worthy couple went happily to bed.

# CHAPTER X.

### BROWN PATRONUS.

On a Saturday afternoon in August, a few weeks after his eventful ride, Tom returned to Englebourn Rectory, to stay over Sunday and attend Betty Winburn's funeral. He was strangely attracted to Harry by the remembrance of their old boyish rivalry; by the story which he had heard from his cousin, of the unwavering perseverance with which the young peasant clung to and pursued his suit for Simon's daughter; but, more than all, by the feeling of gratitude with which he remembered the effect his visit to Betty's sick-room had had on him, on the day of his ride from Barton Manor. On that day he knew that he had ridden into Englebourn in a miserable mental fog, and had ridden out of it in sunshine, which had lasted through the intervening weeks. Somehow or another he had got set straight then and there, turned into the right road and out of the wrong one, at what he very naturally believed to be the most critical moment of his life.

Without stopping to weigh accurately the respective merits of the several persons whom he had come in contact with on that day, he credited them all with a large amount of gratitude and good-will, and Harry with his mother's share as well as his own. So he had been longing to *do* something for him ever since; the more he rejoiced in and gave himself up to his own new sensations, the more did his gratitude become as it were a burden to him, and yet no opportunity offered of letting off some of it in action. The magistrates, taking into consideration the dangerous state of his mother, had let Harry off with a reprimand for his assault, so there was nothing to be done there. He wrote to Katie, offering more money for the Winburns, but she declined, adding, however, to her note by way of postscript, that he might give it to her clothing club, or coal club. Then came the news of Betty's death, and an intimation from Katie that she thought Harry would be much gratified if he would attend the funeral. He jumped at the suggestion. All Englebourn, from the Hawk's Lynch to the Rectory, was hallowed ground to him. The idea of getting back there, so much nearer to Barton Manor, filled him with joy which he tried in vain to repress when he thought of the main object of his visit.

He arrived in time to go and shake hands with Harry before dinner, and though scarcely a word passed between them, he saw with delight that he had evidently given pleasure to the mourner. Then he had a charming long evening with Katie, walking in the garden with her between dinner and tea, and after tea discoursing in low tones over her work-table, while Mr. Winter benevolently slept in his arm-chair. Their discourse branched into many paths, but managed always somehow to end in the sayings, beliefs, and perfections of the young lady of Barton Manor. Tom wondered how it had happened so when he got to his own room, as he fancied he had not betrayed himself in the least. He had determined to keep resolutely on his guard, and to make a confidant of no living soul till he was twenty-one; and though sorely tempted to break his resolution in favor of Katie, had restrained himself. He might have spared himself all the trouble, but that he did not know, being unversed in the ways of women, and all unaware of the subtlety and quickness of their intuitions in all matters connected with the heart. Poor, dear, stolid, dim-sighted mankind, how they do see through us and walk round us!

The funeral on the Sunday afternoon between churches had touched him much, being the first he had ever attended. He walked next behind the chief mourner, the few friends, amongst whom David was conspicuous, yielding place to him. He stood beside him in church, and at the open grave, and made the responses as firmly as he could, and pressed his shoulder against his, when he felt the strong frame of the son trembling with the weight and burden of his resolutely suppressed agony. When they parted at the cottage door, to which Tom accompanied the mourner and his old and tried friend David, though nothing but a look and a grasp of the hand passed between them, he felt that they were bound by a new and invisible bond; and as he walked back up the village and past the churchyard, where the children were playing about on the graves, stopping every now and then to watch the sexton as he stamped down and filled in the mould on the last-made one, beside which he had himself stood as a mourner, and heard the bells beginning to chime for the afternoon service, resolved within himself that he would be a true and helpful friend to the widow's son. On this subject he could talk freely to Katie, and did so that evening, expounding how much one in his position could do for a young laboring man if he really was bent upon it, and building up grand castles for Harry, the foundations of which rested on his own determination to benefit and patronize him. Katie listened half doubtingly at first, but was soon led away by his confidence, and poured out the tea in the full belief that, with Tom's powerful aid, all would go well. After which they took to reading the Christian Year together, and branched into discussions on profane poetry, which Katie considered scarcely proper for the evening, but which, nevertheless, being of such rare occurrence with her, she had not the heart to stop.

The next morning Tom was to return home, and after breakfast began the subject of his plans for Harry again. When Katie produced a small paper packet, and handed it to him, saying,—

"Here is your money again!"

"What money?"

"The money you left with me for Harry Winburn. I thought at the time that most probably he would not take it."

"But are you sure he doesn't want it? Did you try hard to get him to take it?" said Tom, holding out his hand reluctantly for the money.

"Not myself. I couldn't offer him money myself, of course; but I sent it by David, and begged him to do all he could to persuade him to take it."

"Well, and why wouldn't he?"

"Oh, he said the club-money which was coming in was more than enough to pay for the funeral, and for himself he didn't want it."

"How provoking! I wonder if old David really did his best to get him to take it?"

"Yes, I am sure he did. But you ought to be very glad to find some independence in a poor man."

"Bother his independence. I don't like to feel that it costs me nothing but talk—I want to pay."

"Ah, Tom, if you knew the poor as well as I do, you wouldn't say so. I am afraid there are not two other men in the parish who would have refused your money. The fear of undermining their independence takes away all my pleasure in giving."

"Undermining! Why, Katie, I am sure I have heard you mourn over their stubbornness and unreasonableness."

"Oh, yes; they are often provokingly stubborn and unreasonable, and yet not independent about money, or any thing they can get out of you. Besides, I acknowledge that I have become wiser of late; I used to like to see them dependent, and cringing to me, but now I dread it."

"But you would like David to give in about the singing, wouldn't you?"

"Yes, if he would give in, I should be very proud. I have learnt a great deal from him; I used positively to dislike him, but now that I know him, I think him the best man in the parish. If he ever does give in, and I think he will, it will be worth any thing, just because he is so independent."

"That's all very well, but what am I to do to show Harry Winburn that I mean to be his friend, if he wont take money?"

"You have come over to his mother's funeral—he will think more of that than of all the money you could give him; and you can show sympathy for him in a great many ways."

"Well, I must try. By the way, about his love affair; is the young lady at home? I have never seen her, you know."

"No, she is away with an aunt, looking out for a place. I have persuaded her to get one, and leave home again for the present. Her father is quite well now, and she is not wanted."

"Well, it seems I can't do any good with her, then, but could not I go and talk to her father about Harry? I might help him in that way."

"You must be very careful, Simon is such an odd-tempered old man."

"Oh, I'm not afraid; he and I are great chums, and a little soft soap will go a long way with him. Fancy if I could get him this very morning to 'sanction Harry's suit,' as the phrase is; what should you thing of me?"

"I should think very highly of your powers of persuasion."

Not the least daunted by his cousin's misgivings, Tom started in quest of Simon, and found him at work in front of the greenhouse, surrounded by many small pots and heaps of finely sifted mould, and absorbed in his occupation.

Simon was a rough, stolid Berkshire rustic, somewhat of a tyrant in the bosom of his family, an unmanageable servant, a cross-grained acquaintance; as a citizen, stiff-necked and a grumbler, who thought that nothing ever went right in the parish; but, withal, a thorough honest worker, and when allowed to go his own way,—and no other way would he go, as his mistress had long since discovered,—there was no man who earned his daily bread more honestly. He took a pride in his work, and the rectory garden was always trim and well kept, and the beds bright with flowers from early spring till late autumn.

He was absorbed in what he was about, and Tom came up close to him without attracting the least sign of recognition, so he stopped, and opened the conversation.

"Good-day, Simon; it's a pleasure to see a garden looking so gay as yours."

Simon looked up from his work, and, when he saw who it was, touched his battered old hat, and answered,—

"Mornin', sir. Ees, you finds me allus in blume."

"Indeed I do, Simon; but how do you manage it? I should like to tell my father's gardener."

"'Tis no use to tell un if a hevn't found out for hisself; 'tis nothing but lookin' a bit forrard and farmyard stuff as does it."

"Well, there's plenty of farmyard stuff at home, and yet, somehow, we never look half so bright as you do."

"May be as your gardener just takes and hits it auver the top o' the ground, and lets it lie. That's no kinder good, that beant — 'tis the roots as wants the stuff; and you med jist as well take and put a round o' beef agin my back bwone as hit the stuff auver the ground, and never see as it gets to the roots o' the plants."

"No, I don't think it can be that," said Tom, laughing; "our gardener seems always to be digging his manure in, but somehow he can't make it come out in flowers as you do."

"Ther' be mwore waays o' killin' a cat besides choking on un wi' cream," said Simon, chuckling in his turn.

"That's true, Simon," said Tom; "the fact is, a gardener must know his business as well as you to be always in bloom, eh?"

"That's about it, sir," said Simon, on whom the flattery was beginning to tell.

Tom saw this, and thought he might now feel his way a little further with the old man.

"I'm over on a sad errand," he said; "I've been to poor Widow Winburn's funeral — she was an old friend of yours, I think?"

"Ees; I minds her long afore she wur married," said Simon, turning to his pots again.

"She wasn't an old woman, after all," said Tom.

"Sixty-two year old cum Michaelmas," said Simon.

"Well, she ought to have been a strong woman for another ten years at least; why, you must be older than she by some years, Simon, and you can do a good day's work yet with any man."

Simon went on with his potting without replying, except by a carefully measured grunt, sufficient to show that he had heard the remark, and was not much impressed by it.

Tom saw that he must change his attack, so, after watching Simon for a minute, he began again.

"I wonder why it is that the men of your time of life are so much stronger than the young ones in constitution. Now, I don't believe there are three young men in Englebourn who would have got over that fall you had at Farmer Groves' so quick as you have; most young men would have been crippled for life by it."

"Zo 'em would, the young wosbirds. I dwon't make no account on 'em," said Simon.

"And you don't feel any the worse for it, Simon?"

"Narra mossel," replied Simon; but presently he seemed to recollect something, and added, "I wunt saay but what I feels it at times when I've got to stoop about much."

"Ah, I'm sorry to hear that, Simon. Then you oughtn't to have so much stooping to do; potting, and that sort of thing, is the work for you, I should think, and just giving an eye to every thing about the place. Anybody could do the digging and setting out cabbages, and your time is only wasted at it." Tom had now found the old man's weak point.

"Ees, sir, and so I tells miss," he said; "but wi' nothin' but a bit o' glass no bigger 'n a cowcumber frame, 'tis all as a man can do to keep a few plants alive droo' the winter."

"Of course," said Tom, looking round at the very respectable greenhouse which Simon had contemptuously likened to a cucumber-frame, "you ought to have at least another house as big as this for forcing."

"Master aint pleased, he aint," said Simon, "if he dwont get his things, his spring wegebatles, and his strawberries, as early as though we'd a got forcin pits, and glass like other folk. 'Tis a year and mwore since he promised as I sh'd hev glass along that ther' wall, but 'tis no nigher comin' as I can see. I be to spake to miss about it now he says, and when I spakes to her, 'tis, 'O Simon, we must wait till the 'spensary's 'stablished,' or, 'O Simon, last winter wur a werry tryin' wun, and the sick club's terrible bad off for funds,'—and so we gwoes on, and med gwo on for aught as I can see, so long as ther's a body sick or bad off in all the parish. And that'll be allus. For what wi' miss' wisitin' on 'em, and sendin' on 'em dinners, and a'al the doctor's stuff as is served out o' the 'spensary — wy, 'tis enough to keep 'em bad a'al ther' lives. Ther aint no credit in gettin' well. Ther wur no sich a caddle about sick folk when I wur a buoy."

Simon had never been known to make such a long speech before, and Tom augured well for his negotiation.

"Well, Simon," he said, "I've been talking to my cousin, and I think she will do what you want now. The dispensary is set up, and the people are very healthy. How much glass should you want now along that wall?"

"A matter o' twenty fit or so," said Simon.

"I think that can be managed," said Tom, "I'll speak to my cousin about it, and then you would have plenty to do in the houses, and you'd want a regular man under you."

"Ees; t'would take two on us reg'lar to kep things as should be."

"And you ought to have somebody who knows what he is about. Can you think of any one who would do, Simon?"

"Ther's a young chap as works for Squire Wurley. I've heard as he wants to better hisself."

"But he isn't an Englebourn man. Isn't there any one in the parish?"

"Ne'er a one as I knows on."

"What do you think of Harry Winburn — he seems a good hand with flowers?" The words had scarcely passed his lips when Tom saw that he had made a mistake. Old Simon retired into himself at once, and a cunning, distrustful look came over his face. There was no doing anything with him. Even the new forcing-house had lost its attractions for him, and Tom, after some further ineffectual attempts to bring him round, returned to the house somewhat crest-fallen.

"Well, how have you succeeded?" said Katie, looking up from her work, as he came in and sat down near her table. Tom shook his head.

"I'm afraid I've made a regular hash of it," he said. "I thought at first I had quite come round the old savage by praising the garden, and promising that you would let him have a new house."

"You don't mean to say you did that!" said Katie, stopping her work.

"Indeed, but I did, though. I was drawn on, you know. I saw it was the right card to play, so I couldn't help it."

"O Tom! how could you do so? We don't want another house the least in the world; it is only Simon's vanity. He wants to beat the gardener at the Grange at the flower-shows. Every penny will have to come out of what papa allows me for the parish."

"Don't be afraid, Katie, you wont have to spend a penny. Of course I reserved a condition. The new house was to be put up if he would take Harry as under-gardener."

"What did he say to that?"

"Well, he said nothing. I never came across such an old Turk. How you have spoiled him. If he isn't pleased, he wont take the trouble to answer you a word. I was very near telling him a piece of my mind. But he looked all the more. I believe he would poison Harry if he came here. What can have made him hate him so?"

"He is jealous of him. Mary and I were so foolish as to praise poor Betty's flowers before Simon, and he has never forgiven it. I think, too, that he suspects, somehow, that we talked about getting Harry here. I ought to have told you, but I quite forgot it."

"Well, it can't be helped. I don't think I can do any good in that quarter, so now I shall be off to the Grange, to see what I can do there."

"How do you mean?"

"Why, Harry is afraid of being turned out of his cottage. I saw how it worried him, thinking about it; so I shall go to the Grange, and say a good word for him. Wurley can't refuse, if I offer to pay the rent myself—it's only six pounds a year. Of course I shan't tell Harry; and he will pay it all the same; but it may make all the difference with Wurley, who is a regular screw."

"Do you know Mr. Wurley?"

"Yes, just to speak to. He knows all about me, and he will be very glad to be civil."

"No doubt he will; but I don't like your going to his house. You don't know what a bad man he is. Nobody but men on the turf, and that sort of people, go there now; and I believe he thinks of nothing but gambling and game preserving."

"Oh, yes, I know all about him. The county people are beginning to look shy at him, so he'll be all the more likely to do what I ask him."

"But you wont get intimate with him?"

"You needn't be afraid of that."

"It is a sad house to go to; I hope it wont do you any harm."

"Ah, Katie!" said Tom, with a smile, not altogether cheerful, "I don't think you need be anxious about that. When one has been a year at Oxford, there isn't much snow left to soil; so now I am off. I must give myself plenty of time to cook Wurley."

"Well, I suppose I must not hinder you," said Katie. "I do hope you will succeed in some of your kind plans for Harry."

"I shall do my best; and it is a great thing to have somebody besides one's self to think about, and try to help—some poor person—don't you think so, even for a man?"

"Of course I do. I am sure you can't be happy without it, any more than I. We shouldn't be our mother's children if we could be."

"Well, good-by, dear; you can't think how I enjoy these glimpses of you and your work. You must give my love to Uncle Robert."

And so they bade one another adieu, lovingly, after the manner of cousins, and Tom rode away with a very soft place in his heart for his Cousin Katie. It was not the least the same sort of passionate feeling of worship with which he regarded Mary. The two feelings could lie side by side in his heart with plenty of room to spare. In fact, his heart had been getting so big in the last few weeks, that it seemed capable of taking in the whole of mankind, not to mention woman. Still, on the whole, it may be safely asserted, that, had matters been in at all a more forward state, and could she have seen exactly what was passing in his mind, Mary would probably have objected to the kind of affection which he felt for his cousin at this particular time. The joke about cousinly love is probably as old, and certainly as true, as Solomon's proverbs. However, as matters stood, it could be no concern of Mary what his feelings were towards Katie, or any other person.

Tom rode in at the lodge gate of the Grange soon after eleven o'clock, and walked his horse slowly through the park, admiring the splendid timber, and thinking how he should break his request to the owner of the place. But his thoughts were interrupted by the proceedings of the rabbits, which were out by hundreds all along the sides of the plantations, and round the great trees. A few of the nearest just deigned to notice him by scampering to their holes under the roots of the antlered oaks, into which some of them popped with a disdainful kick of their hind legs, while others turned round, sat up, and looked at him. As he neared the house, he passed a keeper's cottage, and was saluted by the barking of dogs from the neighboring kennel; and the young pheasants ran about round some twenty hen-coops, which were arranged along opposite the door where the keeper's children were playing. The pleasure of watching the beasts and birds kept him from arranging his thoughts, and he reached the hall-door without having formed the plan of his campaign.

A footman answered the bell, who doubted whether his master was down, but thought he would see the gentleman if he would send in his name. Whereupon Tom handed in his card; and in a few minutes, a rakish-looking stableboy came round for his horse, and the butler appeared, with his master's compliments, and a request that he would step into the breakfast-room. Tom followed this portly personage through the large, handsome hall, on the walls of which hung a buff coat or two and some old-fashioned arms, and large paintings of dead game and fruit — through a drawing-room, the furniture of which was all covered up in melancholy cases — into the breakfast-parlor, where the owner of the mansion was seated at table in a lounging jacket. He was a man of forty, or thereabouts, who would have been handsome, but for the animal look about his face. His cheeks were beginning to fall into chops, his full lips had a liquorish look about them, and bags were beginning to form under his light blue eyes. His hands were very white and delicate, and shook a little as he poured out his tea; and he was full and stout in body, with small shoulders, and thin arms and legs; in short, the last man whom Tom would have chosen as bow in a pair oar. The only part of him which showed strength were his dark whiskers, which were abundant, and elaborately oiled and curled. The room was light and pleasant, with two windows looking over the park, and furnished luxuriously, in the most modern style, with all manner of easy-chairs and sofas. A glazed case or two of well-bound books showed that some former owner had cared for such things; but the doors had, probably, never been opened in the present reign. The master, and his usual visitors, found sufficient food for the mind in the Racing Calendar, Boxiana, the Adventures of Corinthian Tom, and *Bell's Life*, which lay on a side table; or in the pictures and prints of racers, opera dancers, and steeple-chases, which hung in profusion on the walls. The breakfast-table was beautifully appointed, in the matter of China and plate; and delicate little rolls, neat pats of butter in ice, and two silver hot dishes containing curry and broiled salmon, and a plate of fruit, piled in tempting profusion, appealed, apparently in vain, to the appetite of the lord of the feast.

"Mr. Brown, sir," said the butler, ushering in our hero to his master's presence.

"Ah, Brown, I'm very glad to see you here," said Mr.

Wurley, standing up and holding out his hand. "Have any breakfast?"

"Thank you, no; I have breakfasted," said Tom, somewhat astonished at the intimacy of the greeting; but it was his cue to do the friendly thing, so he shook the proffered hand, which felt very limp, and sat down by the table, looking pleasant.

"Ridden from home this morning?" said Mr. Wurley, picking over daintily some of the curry to which he had helped himself.

"No; I was at my uncle's, at Englebourn, last night. It is very little out of the way, so I thought I would just call on my road home."

"Quite right. I'm very glad you came without ceremony. People about here are so d—d full of ceremony. It don't suit me all that humbug. But I wish you'd just pick a bit."

"Thank you. Then I will eat some fruit," said Tom, helping himself to some of the freshly picked grapes; "how very fine these are!"

"Yes, I'm open to back my houses against the field for twenty miles round. This curry isn't fit for a pig. Take it out, and tell the cook so." The butler solemnly obeyed, while his master went on with one of the frequent oaths with which he garnished his conversation. "You're right, they can't spoil the fruit. They're a set of skulking devils, are servants. They think of nothing but stuffing themselves, and how they can cheat you most, and do the least work." Saying which, he helped himself to some fruit; and the two eat their grapes for a short time in silence. But even fruit seemed to pall quickly on him, and he pushed away his plate. The butler came back with a silver tray, with soda water, and a small decanter of brandy, and long glasses on it.

14*

"Wont you have something after your ride?" said the host to Tom; "some soda water, with a dash of bingo clears one's head in the morning."

"No, thank you," said Tom, smiling; "it's bad for training."

"Ah, you Oxford men are all for training," said his host, drinking greedily of the foaming mixture which the butler handed to him. "A glass of bitter ale is what you take, eh? I know. Get some ale for Mr. Brown."

Tom felt that it would be uncivil to refuse this orthodox offer, and took his beer accordingly, after which his host produced a box of Hudson's Regalias, and proposed to look at the stables. So they lighted their cigars, and went out. Mr. Wurley had taken of late to the turf, and they inspected several young horses which were entered for country stakes. Tom thought them weedy-looking animals, but patiently listened to their praises and pedigrees, upon which his host was eloquent enough; and rubbing up his latest readings in *Bell's Life*, and the racing talk which he had been in the habit of hearing in Drysdale's rooms, managed to hold his own, and asked, with a grave face, about the price of the Coronation colt for the next Derby, and whether Scott's lot was not the right thing to stand on for the St. Leger, thereby raising himself considerably in his host's eyes. There were no hunters in the stable, at which Tom expressed his surprise. In reply, Mr. Wurley abused the country, and declared that it was not worth riding across, the fact being that he had lost his nerve, and that the reception which he was beginning to meet with in the field, if he came out by chance, was of the coldest.

From the stables they strolled to the keeper's cottage, where Mr. Wurley called for some buckwheat and Indian corn, and began feeding the young pheasants, which were running about almost like barn-door fowls close to them.

"We've had a good season for the young birds," he said; "my fellow knows that part of his business, d—n him, and don't lose many. You had better bring your gun over in October; we shall have a week in the covers early in the month."

"Thank you, I shall be very glad," said Tom; "but you don't shoot these birds?"

"Shoot 'em! what the devil should I do with them?"

"Why, they're so tame I thought you just kept them about the house for breeding. I don't care so much for pheasant shooting; I like a good walk after a snipe, or creeping along to get a wild duck, much better. There's some sport in it, or even in partridge shooting with a couple of good dogs, now—"

"You're quite wrong. There's nothing like a good dry ride in a cover with lots of game, and a fellow behind to load for you."

"Well, I must say, I prefer the open."

"You've no covers over your way, have you?"

"Not many."

"I thought so. You wait till you've had a good day in my covers, and you wont care a d—n for quartering all day over wet turnips. Besides, this sort of thing pays. They talk about pheasants costing a guinea a head on one's table. It's d—d stuff; at any rate, mine don't cost *me* much. In fact, I say it pays, and I can prove it."

"But you feed your pheasants?"

"Yes, just round the house for a few weeks, and I sow a little buckwheat in the covers. But they have to keep themselves pretty much, I can tell you."

"Don't the farmers object?"

"Yes, d—n them; they're never satisfied. But they

don't grumble to *me* ; they know better. There are a dozen fellows ready to take any farm that's given up, and they know it. Just get a beggar to put a hundred or two into the ground, and he wont quit hold in a hurry. Will you play a game at billiards?"

The turn which their conversation had taken hitherto had offered no opening to Tom for introducing the object of his visit, and he felt less and less inclined to come to the point. He looked his host over and over again, and the more he looked the less he fancied asking any thing like a favor of him. However, as it had to be done, he thought he couldn't do better than fall into his ways for a few hours, and watch for a chance. The man seemed good-natured in his way; and all his belongings — the fine park and house, and gardens and stables — were not without their effect on his young guest. It is not given to many men of twice his age to separate a man from his possessions, and look at him apart from them. So he yielded easily enough, and they went to billiards in a fine room opening out of the hall; and Tom, who was very fond of the game, soon forgot every thing in the pleasure of playing on such a table.

It was not a bad match. Mr. Wurley understood the game far better than his guest, and could give him advice as to what side to put on and how to play for cannons. This he did in a patronizing way, but his hand was unsteady and his nerve bad. Tom's good eye and steady hand, and the practice he had had at the St. Ambrose pool-table, gave him considerable advantage in the hazards. And so they played on, Mr. Wurley condescending to bet only half a crown a game, at first giving ten points, and then five, at which latter odds Tom managed to be two games ahead when the butler announced lunch at two o'clock.

"I think I must order my horse," said Tom, putting on his coat.

"No, d——n it, you must give me my revenge. I'm always five points better after lunch, and after dinner I could give you fifteen points. Why shouldn't you stop and dine and sleep? I expect some men to dinner."

"Thank you, I must get home to-day."

"I should like you to taste my mutton; I never kill it under five years old. You don't get that every day."

Tom, however, was proof against the mutton; but consented to stay till towards the hour when the other guests were expected, finding that his host had a decided objection to being left alone. So after lunch, at which Mr. Wurley drank the better part of a bottle of old sherry to steady his nerves, they returned again to billiards and Hudson's Regalias.

They played on for another hour; and though Mr. Wurley's hand was certainly steadier, the luck remained with Tom. He was now getting rather tired of playing, and wanted to be leaving, and he began to remember the object of his visit again. But Mr. Wurley was nettled at being beaten by a boy, as he counted his opponent, and wouldn't hear of leaving off. So Tom played on carelessly game after game, and was soon again only two games ahead. Mr. Wurley's temper was recovering, and now Tom protested that he must go. Just one game more his host urged, and Tom consented. Wouldn't he play for a sovereign? No. So they played double or quits; and after a sharp struggle Mr. Wurley won the game, at which he was highly elated, and talked again grandly of the odds he could give after dinner.

Tom felt that it was now or never, and so as he put on his coat, he said, —

"Well, I'm much obliged to you for a very pleasant day, Mr. Wurley."

"I hope you'll come over again, and stay and sleep. I shall always be glad to see you. It is so cursed hard to keep somebody always going in the country."

"Thank you; I should like to come again. But now I want to ask a favor of you before I go."

"Eh, well, what is it?" said Mr. Wurley, whose face and manner became suddenly any thing but encouraging.

"There's that cottage of yours, the one at the corner of Englebourn Copse, next the village."

"The woodman's house, I know," said Mr. Wurley.

"The tenant is dead, and I want you to let it to a friend of mine; I'll take care the rent is paid."

Mr. Wurley pricked up his ears at this announcement. He gave a sharp look at Tom; and then bent over the table, made a stroke, and said, "Ah, I heard the old woman was dead. Who's your friend, then?"

"Well, I mean her son," said Tom, a little embarrassed; "he's an active young fellow, and will make a good tenant, I'm sure."

"I dare say," said Mr. Wurley, with a leer; "and I suppose there's a sister to keep house for him, eh?"

"No, but he wants to get married."

"Wants to get married, eh?" said Mr. Wurley, with another leer and oath. "You're right; that's a deal safer kind of thing for you."

"Yes," said Tom, resolutely disregarding the insinuation which he could not help feeling was intended; "it will keep him steady, and if he can get the cottage it might make all the difference. There wouldn't be much trouble about the marriage then, I dare say."

"You'll find it a devilish long way. You're quite right,

mind you, not to get them settled close at home; but Englebourn is too far, I should say."

"What does it matter to me?"

"Oh, you're tired of her! I see. Perhaps it wont be too far, then."

"Tired of her! who do you mean?"

"Ha, ha!" said Mr. Wurley, looking up from the table over which he was leaning, for he went on knocking the balls about; "devilish well acted. But you needn't try to come the old soldier over me. D——n it, I'm not such a fool as that."

"I don't know what you mean by coming the old soldier. I only asked you to let the cottage, and I will be responsible for the rent. I'll pay in advance if you like."

"Yes, you want me to let the cottage for you to put in this girl."

"I beg your pardon," said Tom, interrupting him, and scarcely able to keep his temper, "I told you it was for this young Winburn."

"Of course you told me so. Ha, ha!"

"And you don't believe me?"

"Come now, all's fair in love and war. But, d——n it, you needn't be mealy-mouthed with me. You don't mind his living there; he's away at work all day, eh? and his wife stays at home."

"Mr. Wurley, I give you my honor I never saw the girl in my life that I know of, and I don't know that she will marry him."

"What did you talk about your friend for, then?" said Mr. Wurley, stopping and staring at Tom, curiosity beginning to mingle with his look of cunning unbelief.

"Because I meant just what I said."

"And the friend, then?"

"I have told you several times that this young Winburn is the man."

"What, *your friend?*"

"Yes, my friend," said Tom; and he felt himself getting red at having to call Harry his friend in such company. Mr. Wurley looked at him for a few moments, and then took his leg off the billiard table, and came round to Tom with the sort of patronizing air with which he had lectured him on billiards.

"I say, Brown, I'll give you a piece of advice," he said. "You're a young fellow, and haven't seen any thing of the world. Oxford's all very well, but it isn't the world. Now I tell you, a young fellow can't do himself greater harm than getting into low company and talking as you have been talking. D—n it, man, it might ruin you in the county! That sort of radical stuff wont do, you know, calling a farm laborer your friend."

Tom chafed at this advice from a man who he well knew was notoriously in the habit of entertaining at his house, and living familiarly with, betting men, and trainers, and all the riff-raff of the turf. But he restrained himself by a considerable effort, and instead of retorting, as he felt inclined to do, said, with an attempt to laugh it off, "Thank you, I don't think there's much fear of my turning radical. But will you let me the cottage?"

"My agent manages all that. We talked about pulling it down. The cottage is in my preserves, and I don't mean to have some poaching fellow there to be sneaking out at night after my pheasants."

"But his grandfather and great-grandfather lived there."

"I dare say, but it's my cottage."

"But surely, that gives him a claim to it."

"D—n it! it's my cottage. You're not going to tell me I mayn't do what I like with it, I suppose?"

"I only said that his family, having lived there so long, gives him a claim."

"A claim to what? These are some more of your cursed radical notions. I think they might teach you something better at Oxford."

Tom was now perfectly cool, but withal in such a tremendous fury of excitement that he forgot the interests of his client altogether.

"I came here, sir," he said, very quietly and slowly, "not to request your advice on my own account, or your opinion on the studies of Oxford, valuable as no doubt they are: I came to ask you to let this cottage to me, and I wish to have your answer."

"I'll be d—d if I do; there's my answer."

"Very well," said Tom; "then I have only to wish you good-morning. I am sorry to have wasted a day in the company of a man who sets up for a country gentleman with the tongue of a Thames bargee, and the heart of a Jew pawnbroker."

Mr. Wurley rushed to the bell and rang it furiously. "By —!" he almost screamed, shaking his fist at Tom, "I'll have you horsewhipped out of my house;" and then poured forth a flood of uncomplimentary slang, ending in another pull at the bell, and "By — I'll have you horsewhipped out of my house."

"You had better try it on — you and your flunkies together," said Tom, taking a cigar-case out of his pocket and lighting up, the most defiant and exasperating action he could think of on the spur of the moment. "Here's one of them, so I'll leave you to give him his orders, and wait five minutes in the hall, where there's more room." And so, leaving the footman gaping at his lord, he turned on his heel, with the air of Bernardo del Carpio after he had bearded King Alphonso, and walked into the hall.

He heard men running to and fro, and doors banging, as he stood there looking at the old buff-coats, and rather thirsting for a fight. Presently a door opened, and the portly butler shuffled in, looking considerably embarrassed, and said, —

"Please, sir, to go out quiet, else he'll be having one of his fits."

"Your master, you mean?"

"Yes, sir," said the butler, nodding; "D. T., sir. After one of his rages the black dog comes, and it's hawful work; so I hope you'll go, sir."

"Very well; of course I'll go. I don't want to give him a fit." Saying which, Tom walked out of the hall-door, and leisurely round to the stables, where he found already signs of commotion. Without regarding them, he got his horse saddled and bridled, and after looking him over carefully, and patting him, and feeling his girths, in the yard, in the presence of a cluster of retainers of one sort or another, who were gathering from the house and offices, and looking sorely puzzled whether to commence hostilities or not, mounted and walked quietly out.

After his anger had been a little cooled by the fresh air of the wild country at the back of the Hawk's Lynch, which he struck into on his way home soon after leaving the park, it suddenly occurred to him that, however satisfactory to himself the results of his encounter with this unjust landlord might seem, they would probably prove any thing but agreeable to the would-be tenant, Harry Winburn. In fact, as he meditated on the matter, it became clear to him that in the course of one morning he had probably exasperated old Simon against his aspirant son-in-law, and put a serious spoke in Harry's love-wheel on the one hand; while on the other, he had insured his speedy expulsion from his cottage, if not the demolition of that building. Whereupon he became somewhat low under the conviction that his friendship, which was to work such wonders for the said Harry, and deliver him out of all his troubles, had as yet only made his whole look-out in the world very much darker and more dusty. In short, as yet he had managed to do considerably less than nothing for his friend, and he felt very small before he got home that evening. He was far, however, from being prepared for the serious way in which his father looked upon his day's proceedings. Mr. Brown was sitting by himself after dinner when his son turned up, and had to drink several extra glasses of port to keep himself decently composed, while Tom narrated the events of the day in the intervals of his attacks on the dinner, which was brought back for him. When the servant had cleared away, Mr. Brown proceeded to comment on the history in a most decided manner.

Tom was wrong to go to the Grange in the first instance; and this part of the homily was amplified by a discourse on the corruption of the turf in general, and the special curse of small country races in particular, which such men as Wurley supported, and which, but for them, would cease. Racing, which used to be the pastime of great people, who could well afford to spend a few thousands a year on their pleasure, had now mostly fallen into the hands of the very worst and lowest men of all classes, most of whom would not scruple, as Mr. Brown strongly put it, to steal a copper out of a blind beggar's hat. If he must go, at any rate he might have done his errand and come away, instead of staying there all day accepting the man's hospitality. Mr. Brown himself really should be much embarrassed to know what to do if the man should happen to attend the next sessions or assizes. But, above all, having accepted his hospitality, to turn round at the end and insult the man in his own house! This seemed to Brown *père* a monstrous and astounding performance.

This new way of putting matters took Tom entirely by surprise. He attempted a defence, but in vain. His father admitted that it would be a hard case if Harry were turned out of his cottage, but wholly refused to listen to Tom's endeavors to prove that a tenant in such a case had any claim or right as against his landlord. A weekly tenant was a weekly tenant, and no succession of weeks' holding could make him any thing more. Tom found himself rushing into a line of argument which astonished himself and sounded wild, but in which he felt sure there was some truth, and which, therefore, he would not abandon, though his father was evidently annoyed, and called it mere mischievous sentiment. Each was more moved than he would have liked to own; each in his own heart felt aggrieved, and blamed the other for not understanding him. But though obstinate on the general question, upon the point of his conduct in leaving the Grange, Tom was fairly brought to shame, and gave in at last, and expressed his sorrow, though he could not help maintaining that if his father could have heard what took place, and seen the man's manner, he would scarcely blame him for what he had said and done. Having once owned himself in the wrong, however, there was nothing for it but to write an apology, the composition of which was as disagreeable a task as had ever fallen to his lot.

## CHAPTER XI.

Μηδὲν ἄγαν.

HAS any person, of any nation or language, found out and given to the world any occupation, work, diversion, or pursuit, more subtlely dangerous to the susceptible youth of both sexes than that of nutting in pairs? If so, who? where? what? A few years later in life, perhaps district-visiting, and attending schools together, may in certain instances be more fatal; but in the first bright days of youth, a day's nutting against the world—a day in autumn, warm enough to make sitting in sheltered nooks in the woods, where the sunshine can get very pleasant, and yet not too warm to make exercise uncomfortable— two young people who have been thrown much together, one of whom is conscious of the state of his feelings towards the other, and is, moreover, aware that his hours are numbered, that in a few days at furthest they will be separated for many months, that persons in authority on both sides are beginning to suspect something (as is apparent from the difficulty they have had in getting away together at all on this same afternoon)—here is a conjunction of persons and circumstances, if ever there was one in the world, which is surely likely to end in a catastrophe. Indeed, so obvious to the meanest capacity is the danger of the situation that, as Tom had, in his own mind, stated his character for resolution with his private self on the keeping of his secret till after he was of age, it is hard to conceive how he can have been foolish enough to get himself into a hazel copse alone with Miss Mary on the earliest day he could manage it after the arrival of the Porters, on their visit to Mr. and Mrs. Brown. That is to say, it would be hard to conceive if it didn't just happen to be the most natural thing in the world.

For the first twenty-four hours after their meeting in the home of his father, the two young people, and Tom in particular, felt very uncomfortable. Mary, being a young lady of very high spirits, and, as readers may probably have discovered, much given to that kind of conversation which borders as nearly upon what men commonly call chaff as a well-bred girl can venture on, was annoyed to find herself quite at fault in all her attempts to get her old antagonist of Commemoration to show fight. She felt in a moment how changed his manner was, and thought it by no means changed for the better. As for Tom, he felt foolish and shy at first to an extent which drove him half wild; his words stuck in his throat, and he took to blushing again like a boy of fourteen. In fact, he got so angry with himself that he rather avoided her actual presence, though she was scarcely a moment out of his sight. Mr. Brown made the most of his son's retreat, devoted himself most gallantly to Mary, and was completely captivated by the first night of their arrival, and triumphed over his wife when they were alone at the groundlessness of her suspicions. But she was by no means so satisfied on the subject as her husband.

In a day or two, however, he began to take heart of grace, and to find himself oftener at Mary's side, with something to say, and more to look. But now she, in her turn, began to be embarrassed, for all attempts to re-establish their old footing failed; and the difficulty of finding a satisfactory new one remained to be solved—so for the present, though neither of them found it quite satisfactory, they took refuge in the presence of a third party, and attached themselves to Katie, talking at one another through her. Nothing could exceed Katie's judiciousness as a medium of communication, and through her a better understanding began to establish itself, and the visit which both of them had been looking forward to so eagerly, seemed likely, after all, to be as pleasant in fact as it had been in anticipation. As they became more at ease, the vigilance of Mrs. Brown and Mrs. Porter seemed likely to revive. But in a country house there must be plenty of chances for young folk who mean it to be together, and so they found and made use of their opportunities, giving at the same time as little cause to their natural guardians as possible for any serious interference. The families got on, on the whole, so well together that the visit was prolonged from the original four or five days to a fortnight; and this time of grace was drawing to a close when the event happened which made the visit memorable to our hero.

On the morning in question, Mr. Brown arranged at breakfast that he and his wife should drive Mr. and Mrs. Porter to make calls on several of the neighbors. Tom declared his intention of taking a long day after the partridges, and the young ladies were to go and make a sketch of the house from a point which Katie had chosen. Accordingly, directly after luncheon the carriage came round, and the elders departed, and the young ladies started together, carrying their sketching apparatus with them.

It was probably a bad day for scent, for they had not been gone a quarter of an hour when Tom came home, deposited his gun, and followed on their steps. He found them sitting under the lee of a high bank, sufficiently intent on their drawings, but neither surprised nor sorry to find that he had altered his mind and come back to interrupt them. So he lay down near them, and talked of Oxford and Englebourn, and so from one thing to another, till he got upon the subject of nutting, and the sylvan beauties of a neighboring wood. Mary was getting on badly with her drawing, and jumped at the idea of a ramble in the wood; but Katie was obdurate, and resisted all their solicitations to move. She suggested, however, that they might go, and as Tom declared that they should not be out of call, and would be back in half an hour at furthest, Mary consented, and they left the sketcher, and strolled together out of the fields, and into the road, and so through a gate into the wood. It was a pleasant oak wood. The wild flowers were over, but the great masses of ferns, four or five feet high, made a grand carpet round the stems of the forest monarchs, and a fitting couch, for here and there one of them, which had been lately felled, and lay in fallen majesty, with bare shrouded trunk awaiting the sawyers. Further on the hazel underwood stood thickly on each side of the green rides, down which they sauntered side by side. Tom talked of the beauty of the wood in spring-time, and the glorious succession of coloring pale yellow, and deep blue and white, and purple, which the primroses, and hyacinths, and starwert, and fox-gloves gave each in their turn in the early year, and mourned over their absence. But Mary preferred autumn, and would not agree with him. She was enthusiastic for ferns and heather. He gathered some sprigs of the latter for her, from a little sandy patch which they passed, and some more for his own button-hole; and then they engaged in the absorbing pursuit of nutting, and the talk almost ceased. He caught the higher branches, and bent them down to her, and watched her as she gathered them, and wondered at the ease and grace of all her movements, and the unconscious beauty of her attitudes. Soon she became more enterprising herself, and made little excursions into the copse, surmounting briers, and passing through tangled places like a Naiad, before he could be there to help her. And so they went on, along the rides and through the copse, forgetting Katie and time, till they were brought up by the fence on the further side of the wood. The ditch was on the outside, and on the inside a bank with a hedge on the top, full of tempting hazel bushes. She clapped her hands at the sight, and declining his help, stepped lightly up the bank, and began gathering. He turned away for a moment, jumped up the bank himself, and followed her example.

He was standing up in the hedge, and reaching after a tempting cluster of nuts, when he heard a short, sharp cry of pain behind him, which made him spring backwards, and nearly miss his footing as he came to the ground. Recovering himself, and turning round, he saw Mary lying at the foot of the bank, writhing in pain.

He was at her side in an instant, and dreadfully alarmed.

"Good heavens! what has happened?" he said.

"My ankle!" she cried; and the effort of speaking brought the sudden flush of pain to her brow.

"Oh! what can I do?"

"The boot! the boot!" she said, leaning forward to unlace it, and then sinking back against the bank. "It is so painful! I hope I sha'n't faint."

Poor Tom could only clasp his hands as he knelt by her, and repeat, "Oh, what can I do — what can I do?"

His utter bewilderment presently roused Mary, and her natural high courage was beginning to master the pain.

"Have you a knife?"

"Yes — here," he said, pulling one out of his pocket, and opening it; "here it is."

"Please cut the lace."

Tom with beating heart and trembling hand, cut the lace, and then looked up at her.

"Oh, be quick — cut it again; don't be afraid."

He cut it again; and without taking hold of the foot, gently pulled out the ends of the lace.

She again leaned forward, and tried to take off the boot. But the pain was too great, and she sank back, and put her hand up to her flushed face.

"May I try? — perhaps I could do it."

"Yes, pray do. Oh, I can't bear the pain!" she added, next moment; and Tom felt ready to hang himself for having been the cause of it.

"You must cut the boot off, please."

"But perhaps I may cut you. Do you really mean it?"

"Yes, really. There, take care. How your hand shakes. You will never do for a doctor."

His hand did shake certainly. He had cut a little hole in the stocking; but, under the circumstances, we need not wonder — the situation was new and trying. Urged on by her, he cut and cut away, and, at last, off came the boot, and her beautiful little foot lay on the green turf. She was much relieved at once, but still in great pain; and now he began to recover his head.

"The ankle should be bound up; may I try?"

"Oh, yes; but what with?"

Tom dived into his shooting-coat pocket, and produced one of the large many-colored neck-wrappers which were fashionable at Oxford in those days.

"How lucky," he said, as he tore it into strips. "I think this will do. Now, you'll stop me, wont you, if I hurt, or don't do it right?"

"Don't be afraid; I'm much better. Bind it tight — tighter than that."

He wound the strips as tenderly as he could round her foot and ankle, with hands all alive with nerves, and wondering more and more at her courage, as she kept urging him to draw the bandage tighter yet. Then, still under her direction, he fastened and pinned down the ends; and as he was rather neat with his fingers, from the practice of tying flies and splicing rods and bats, produced, on the whole, a creditable sort of bandage. Then he looked up at her, the perspiration standing on his forehead, as if he had been pulling a race, and said, —

"Will that do? I'm afraid it's very awkward."

"Oh, no; thank you so much! But I'm so sorry you have torn your handkerchief."

Tom made no answer to this remark, except by a look. What could he say, but that he would gladly have torn his skin off for the same purpose, if it would have been of any use; but this speech did not seem quite the thing for the moment.

"But how do you feel? Is it very painful?" he asked.

"Rather. But don't look so anxious. Indeed, it is very bearable. But what are we to do now?"

He thought for a moment, and said, with something like a sigh, —

"Shall I run home, and bring the servants and a sofa, or something to carry you on?"

"No, I shouldn't like to be left here alone."

His face brightened again.

"How near is the nearest cottage?" she asked.

"There's none nearer than the one which we passed on the road, on the other side of the wood, you know."

"Then I must try to get there. You must help me up."

He sprang to his feet and stooped over her, doubting

how to begin helping her. He had never felt so shy in his life. He held out his hands.

"I think you must put your arm round me," she said, after looking at him for a moment. Her woman's instinct was satisfied with the look. He lifted her on to her feet.

"Now, let me lean on your arm. There, I dare say I shall manage to hobble along well enough;" and she made a brave attempt to walk. But the moment the injured foot touched the ground, she stopped with a catch of her breath, and a shiver, which went through Tom like a knife; and the flush came back into her face, and she would have fallen had he not again put his arm round her waist, and held her up. "I am better again now," she said, after a second or two.

"But Mary, dear Mary, don't try to walk again, for my sake. I can't bear it."

"But what am I to do?" she said. "I must get back somehow."

"Will you let me carry you?"

She looked in his face again, and then dropped her eyes, and hesitated.

"I wouldn't offer, dear, if there were any other way. But you mustn't walk; indeed, you must not; you may lame yourself for life."

He spoke very quietly, with his eyes fixed on the ground, though his heart was beating so that he feared she would hear it.

"Very well," she said; "but I'm very heavy."

So he lifted her gently, and stepped off down the ride, carrying his whole world in his arms, in an indescribable flutter of joy and triumph and fear. He had gone some forty yards or so, when he staggered, and stopped for a moment.

"Oh, pray put me down — pray do! You'll hurt yourself. I'm too heavy."

For the credit of muscular Christianity, one must say, that it was not her weight, but the tumult in his own inner man which made her bearer totter. Nevertheless, if one is wholly unused to the exercise, the carrying a healthy young English girl weighing hard on eight stone, is as much as most men can conveniently manage.

"I'll just put you down for a moment," he said. "Now take care of the foot;" and he stooped, and placed her tenderly against one of the oaks which bordered the ride, standing by her side without looking at her. Neither of them spoke for a minute. Then he asked, still looking away down the ride, "How is the foot?"

"Oh, pretty well," she answered, cheerfully. "Now, leave me here, and go for help. It is absurd of me to mind being left; and you mustn't carry me any more."

He turned, and their eyes met for a moment, but that was enough.

"Are you ready?" he said.

"Yes; but take care. Don't go far. Stop directly you feel tired."

Then he lifted her again, and this time carried her without faltering, till they came to a hillock covered with soft grass. Here they rested again; and so by easy stages he carried her through the wood, and out into the road, to the nearest cottage, neither of them speaking.

An old woman came to the door in answer to his kick, and went off into ejaculations of pity and wonder in the broadest Berkshire, at seeing Master Tom and his burden. But he pushed into the house and cut her short with, —

"Now, Mrs. Pike, don't talk, that's a dear good woman, but bustle about, and bring that arm-chair here, and the other low one, with a pillow on it, for the young lady's foot to rest on."

The old woman obeyed his injunctions, except as to talking; and while she placed the chairs and shook up the pillow, descanted on the sovereign virtues of some green oil and opodeldoc, which was as good as a charm for sprains and bruises.

Mary gave him one grateful look as he lowered her tenderly and reluctantly into the chair, and then spoke cheerfully to Mrs. Pike, who was foraging in a cupboard, to find if there was any of her famous specific in the bottom of the bottle. As he stood up, and thought what to do next, he heard the sound of distant wheels, and looking through the window saw the carriage coming homewards. It was a sorrowful sight to him.

"Now, Mrs. Pike," he said, "never mind the oil. Here's the carriage coming; just step out and stop it."

The old dame scuttled out into the road. The carriage was within one hundred yards. He leaned over the rough arm-chair in which she was leaning back, looked once more into her eyes; and then, stooping forwards, kissed her lips, and the next moment was by the side of Mrs. Pike, signalling the coachman to stop.

In the bustle which followed he stood aside, and watched Mary with his heart in his mouth. She never looked at him, but there was no anger, but only a dreamy look in her sweet face, which seemed to him a thousand times more beautiful than ever before. Then to avoid inquiries and to realize all that had passed in the last wonderful three hours, he slipped away while they were getting her into the carriage, and wandered back into the wood, pausing at each of their halting-places. At last, he reached the scene of the accident, and here his cup of happiness was likely to brim over, for he found the mangled little boot and the cut lace, and securing the precious prize, hurried back home, to be in time for dinner.

Mary did not come down, but Katie, the only person of whom he dared to inquire, assured him that she was doing famously. The dinner was very embarrassing, and he had the greatest difficulty in answering the searching inquiries of his mother and Mrs. Porter, as to how, when, where, and in whose presence the accident had happened. As soon as the ladies rose, he left his father and Mr. Porter over their old port and politics, and went out in the twilight into the garden, burdened with the weight of sweet thought. He felt that he had something to do — to set himself quite right with Mary; he must speak somehow, that night, if possible, or he should not be comfortable or at peace with his conscience. There were lights in her room. He guessed by the shadows that she was lying on a couch by the open window, round which the other ladies were flitting. Presently lights appeared in the drawing-room, and as the shutters were being closed he saw his mother and Mrs. Porter come in, and sit down near the fire. Listening intently, he heard Katie talking in a low voice in the room above, and saw her head against the light as she sat down close to the window, probably at the head of the couch where Mary was lying. Should he call to her? If he did how could he say what he wanted to say through her?

A happy thought struck him. He turned to the flower-beds, hunted about, and gathered a bunch of heliotrope, hurried up to his room, took the sprig of heather out of his shooting-coat, tied them together, caught up a reel and line from his table, and went into the room over Mary's. He threw the window open, and leaning out said gently,

"Katie." No answer. He repeated the name louder. No answer still, and leaning out yet further he saw that the window had been shut. He lowered the bunch of flowers, and swinging it backwards and forwards made it strike the window below — once, twice; at the third stroke he heard the window open.

"Katie," he whispered again, "is that you?"

"Yes, where are you? What is this?"

"For her," he said in the same whisper. Katie untied the flowers, and he waited a few moments, and then again called her name, and she answered.

"Has she the flowers?"

"Yes, and she sends you her love, and says you are to go down to the drawing-room;" and with that the window closed, and he went down with a lightened conscience into the drawing-room, and after joining in the talk by the fire for a few minutes, took a book, and sat down at the further side of the table. Whether he ever knew what the book was may be fairly questioned, but to all appearances he was deep in the perusal of it till the tea and Katie arrived, and the gentlemen from the dining-room. Then he tried to join in the conversation again, but, on the whole, life was a burden to him that night till he could get fairly away to his own room, and commune with himself, gazing at the yellow harvest moon with his elbows on the window-sill.

The ankle got well very quickly, and Mary was soon going about with a gold-headed stick which had belonged to Mr. Brown's father, and a limp which Tom thought the most beautiful movement he had ever seen. But though she was about again, by no amount of patient vigilance could he now get the chance of speaking to her alone. But he consoled himself with the thought that she must understand him; if he had spoken, he couldn't have made himself clearer.

And now the Porters' visit was all but over, and Katie and her father left for Englebourn. The Porters were to follow the next day, and promised to drive round and stop at the Rectory for lunch. Tom petitioned for a seat in their carriage to Englebourn. He had been devoting himself to Mrs. Porter ever since the accident, and had told her a good deal about his own early life. His account of his early friendship for Betty and her son, and the renewal of it on the day he left Barton Manor, had interested her, and she was moreover not insensible to his assiduous and respectful attentions to herself, which had of late been quite marked: she was touched, too, at his anxiety to hear all about her boys, and how they were going on at school. So on the whole Tom was in high favor with her, and she most graciously assented to his occupying the fourth seat in their barouche. She was not without her suspicions of the real state of the case with him, but his behavior had been so discreet that she had no immediate fears, and after all, if any thing should come of it some years hence, her daughter might do worse. In the mean time she would see plenty of society in London; where Mr. Porter's vocations kept him during the greater part of the year.

They reached Englebourn after a pleasant long morning's drive; and Tom stole a glance at Mary, and felt that she understood him, as he pointed out the Hawk's Lynch and the clump of Scotch firs to her mother; and told how you might see Barton from the top of it, and how he loved the place, and the old trees, and the view.

Katie was at the door ready to receive them, and carried off Mary and Mrs. Porter to her own room. Tom walked round the garden with Mr. Porter, and then sat in the drawing-room, and felt melancholy. He roused himself, however, when the ladies came down and luncheon was announced. Mary was full of her reminiscences of the Englebourn people, and especially of poor Mrs. Winburn and her son, in whom she had begun to take a deep interest, perhaps from overhearing some of Tom's talk to her mother. So Harry's story was canvassed again, and Katie told them how he had been turned out of his cottage, and how anxious she was as to what would come of it.

"And is he going to marry your gardener's daughter after all?" asked Mrs. Porter.

"I am afraid there is not much chance of it," said Katie; "I cannot make Martha out."

"Is she at home, Katie?" asked Mary; "I should like to see her again. I took a great fancy to see her when I was here."

"Yes, she is at the lodge. We will walk there after luncheon."

So it was settled that the carriage should pick them up at the lodge; and soon after luncheon, while the horses were being put to, the whole party started for the lodge after saying good-by to Mr. Winter, who retired to his room much fatigued by his unwonted hospitality.

Old Simon's wife answered their knock at the lodge door, and they all entered, and Mrs. Porter paid her compliments on the cleanliness of the room.

Then Mary said, "Is your daughter at home, Mrs. Gibbons?"

"Ees, miss, someweres handy," replied Mrs. Gibbons; "her hav'n't been gone out not dree minutes."

"I should like so much to say good-by to her," said

Mary. "We shall be leaving Barton soon, and I shall not see her again till next summer."

"Lor bless'ee, miss, 'tis werry good ov ee," said the old dame very proud; "do'ee set down then while I gives her a call." And with that she hurried out of the door which led through the back kitchen into the little yard behind the lodge, and the next moment they heard her calling out, —

"Patty, Patty, whar bist got to? Come in, and see the gentle-folk."

The name which the old woman was calling out made Tom start.

"I thought you said her name was Martha," said Mrs. Porter.

"Patty is short for Martha in Berkshire," said Katie, laughing.

"And Patty is such a pretty name, I wonder you don't call her Patty," said Mary.

"We had a housemaid of the same name a year or two ago, and it made such a confusion — and when one once gets used to a name it is so hard to change — so she has always been called Martha."

"Well, I'm all for Patty; don't you think so?" said Mary, turning to Tom.

The sudden introduction of a name which he had such reasons for remembering, the memories and fears which it called up, above all, the bewilderment which he felt at hearing it tossed about and canvassed by Mary in his presence, as if there were nothing more in it than in any other name, confused him so that he floundered and blundered in his attempt to answer, and at last gave it up altogether. She was surprised, and looked at him inquiringly. His eyes fell before hers, and he turned away to the window, and looked at the carriage, which had just drawn up at the lodge door. He had scarcely time to think how foolish he was to be so moved, when he heard the back-kitchen door opened again, and the old woman and her daughter come in. He turned round sharply, and there on the floor of the room, courtesying to the ladies, stood the ex-barmaid of the Choughs. His first impulse was to hurry away, she was looking down, and he might not be recognized; his next to stand his ground, and take whatever might come. Mary went up to her and took her hand, saying that she could not go away without coming to see her. Patty looked up to answer, and glancing round the room caught sight of him.

He stepped forward, and then stopped and tried to speak, but no words would come. Patty looked at him, dropped Mary's hand, blushed up to the roots of her hair as she looked timidly round at the wondering spectators, and, putting her hands to her face, ran out of the back-door again.

"Lawk a massy! what ever can ha' cum to our Patty?" said Mrs. Gibbons, following her out.

"I think we had better go," said Mr. Porter, giving his arm to his daughter, and leading her to the door. "Good-by, Katie; shall we see you again at Barton?"

"I don't know, uncle," Katie answered, following with Mrs. Porter, in a state of sad bewilderment.

Tom, with his brain swimming, got out a few stammering farewell words, which Mr. and Mrs. Porter received with marked coldness as they stepped into their carriage. Mary's face was flushed and uneasy, but at her he scarcely dared to steal a look, and to her was quite unable to speak a word.

Then the carriage drove off, and he turned, and found

Katie standing at his side, her eyes full of serious wonder. His fell before them.

"My dear Tom," she said, "what is all this? I thought you had never seen Martha?"

"So I thought — I didn't know — I can't talk now — I'll explain all to you — don't think very badly of me, Katie — God bless you!" with which words he strode away, while she looked after him with increasing wonder and then turned and went into the lodge.

He hastened away from the Rectory and down the village street, taking the road home mechanically, but otherwise wholly unconscious of roads and men. David, who was very anxious to speak to him about Harry, stood at his door making signs to him to stop in vain, and then gave chase, calling out after him, till he saw that all attempts to attract his notice were useless, and so ambled back to his shop-board much troubled in mind.

The first object which recalled Tom at all to himself was the little white cottage looking out of Englebourn Copse towards the village, in which he had sat by poor Betty's death-bed. The garden was already getting wild and tangled, and the house seemed to be uninhabited. He stopped for a moment and looked at it with bitter searchings of heart. Here was the place where he had taken such a good turn as he had fondly hoped, in connection with the then inmates of which he had made the strongest good resolutions he had ever made in his life perhaps. What was the good of his trying to befriend anybody; his friendship turned to a blight; whatever he had as yet tried to do for Harry had only injured him, and now how did they stand? Could they ever be friends again after that day's discovery? To do him justice, the probable ruin of all his own prospects, the sudden coldness of Mr.

and Mrs. Porter's looks, and Mary's averted face, were not the things he thought on first, and did not trouble him most. He thought of Harry, and shuddered at the wrong he had done him as he looked at his deserted home. The door opened and a figure appeared. It was Mr. Wurley's agent, the lawyer who had been employed by Farmer Tester in his contest with Harry and his mates about the pound. The man of law saluted him with a smirk of scarcely concealed triumph, and then turned into the house again and shut the door, as if he did not consider further communication necessary or safe. Tom turned with a muttered imprecation on him and his master, and hurried away along the lane which led to the heath. The Hawk's Lynch lay above him, and he climbed the side mechanically and sat himself again on the old spot.

He sat for some time looking over the landscape, graven on his mind as it was by his former visit, and bitterly, oh, how bitterly! did the remembrance of that visit, and of the exultation and triumph which then filled him, and carried him away over the heath with a shout towards his home, come back on him. He could look out from his watch-tower no longer, and lay down with his face between his hands on the turf, and groaned as he lay.

But his good angel seemed to haunt the place, and soon the cold fit began to pass away, and better and more hopeful thoughts to return. After all, what had he done since his last visit to that place to be ashamed of? Nothing. His attempts to do Harry service, unlucky as they had proved, had been honest. Had he become less worthy of the love which had first consciously mastered him there some four weeks ago? No; he felt, on the contrary, that it had already raised him, and purified him, and made a man of him.

But this last discovery, how could he ever get over that? Well, after all, the facts were just the same before, only now they had come out. It was right that they should have come out; better for him and for every one that they should be known and faced. He was ready to face them, to abide any consequences that they might now bring in their train. His heart was right towards Mary, towards Patty, towards Harry, that he felt sure of. And if so, why should he despair of either his love or his friendship coming to a bad end?

And so he sat up again, and looked out bravely towards Barton, and began to consider what was to be done. His eyes rested on the Rectory. That was the first place to begin with. He must set himself right with Katie; let her know the whole story. Through her he could reach all the rest, and do whatever must be done to clear the ground and start fresh again.

At first he thought of returning to her at once, and rose to go down to Englebourn. But any thing like retracing his steps was utterly distasteful to him just then. Before him he saw light, dim enough as yet, but still a dawning; towards that he would press, leaving every thing behind him to take care of itself. So he turned northwards, and struck across the heath at his best pace. The violent exercise almost finished his cure, and his thoughts became clearer and more hopeful as he neared home. He arrived there as the household were going to bed, and found a letter waiting for him. It was from Hardy, saying that Blake had left him, and he was now thinking of returning to Oxford, and would come for his long-talked-of visit to Berkshire, if Tom was still at home and in the mind to receive him.

Never was a letter more opportune. Here was the

tried friend on whom he could rely for help and advice and sympathy. Who knew all the facts, too, from beginning to end. His father and mother were delighted to hear that they should now see the friend of whom he had spoken so much; so he went up-stairs, and wrote an answer, which set Hardy to work packing his portmanteau in the far west, and brought him speedily to the side of his friend under the lee of the Berkshire hills.

# CHAPTER XII.

#### SECOND YEAR.

For some days after his return home — in fact, until his friend's arrival, he was thoroughly beaten down and wretched, notwithstanding his efforts to look hopefully forward, and keep up his spirits. His usual occupations were utterly distasteful to him; and, instead of occupying himself, he sat brooding over his late misfortune, and hopelessly puzzling his head as to what he could do to set matters right. The conviction in which he always landed was that there was nothing to be done, and that he was a desolate and blighted being, deserted of gods and men. Hardy's presence and company soon shook him out of this maudlin nightmare state, and he began to recover as soon as he had his old sheet-anchor friend to hold on to and consult with. Their consultations were held chiefly in the intervals of woodcraft, in which they spent most of the hours between breakfast and dinner. Hardy did not take out a certificate, and wouldn't shoot without one; so, as the best autumn exercise, they selected a tough old pollard elm, infinitely ugly, with knotted and twisted roots, curiously difficult to get at and cut through, which had been long marked as a blot by Mr. Brown, and condemned to be felled as soon as there was nothing more pressing for his men to do. But there was always something of more importance; so that the cross-grained old tree might have remained until this day, had not Hardy and Tom pitched on him as a foeman worthy of their axes. They shovelled and picked and hewed away with great energy. The woodman who visited them occasionally, and who, on examining their first efforts, had remarked that the severed roots looked a little "as tho' the dogs had been a gnawin' at 'em," began to hold them in respect, and to tender his advice with some deference. By the time the tree was felled and shrouded, Tom was in a convalescent state.

Their occupation had naturally led to discussions on the advantages of emigration, the delights of clearing one's own estate, building one's own house, and getting away from conventional life with a few tried friends. Of course, the pictures which were painted included foregrounds with beautiful children playing about the clearing, and graceful women, wives of the happy squatters, flitting in and out of the log-houses and sheds, clothed and occupied after the manner of our ideal grandmothers; with the health and strength of Amazons, the refinement of high-bred ladies, and wondrous skill in all domestic works, confections, and contrivances. The log-houses would also contain fascinating select libraries, continually reinforced from home, sufficient to keep all dwellers in the happy clearing in communion with all the highest minds of their own and former generations. Wondrous games in the neighboring forest, dear old home customs established and taking root in the wilderness, with ultimate dainty flower-gardens, conservatories, and piano-fortes—a millennium on a small scale, with universal education, competence, prosperity, and equal rights! Such castle-building, as an accompaniment to the hard exercise of woodcraft, worked wonders for Tom in the next week, and may be safely recommended to parties in like evil case with him.

But more practical discussions were not neglected, and it was agreed that they should make a day at Englebourn together before their return to Oxford, Hardy undertaking to invade the Rectory with the view of re-establishing his friend's character there.

Tom wrote a letter to Katie to prepare her for a visit. The day after the ancient elm was fairly disposed of they started early for Englebourn, and separated at the entrance to the village — Hardy proceeding to the Rectory to fulfil his mission, which he felt to be rather an embarrassing one, and Tom to look after the constable, or whoever else could give him information about Harry.

He arrived at the Red Lion, their appointed trysting-place, before Hardy, and spent a restless half-hour in the porch and bar waiting for his return. At last Hardy came, and Tom hurried him into the inn's best room, where bread and cheese and ale awaited them, and, as soon as the hostess could be got out of the room, began impatiently, —

"Well; you have seen her?"

"Yes; I have come straight here from the Rectory."

"And is it all right, eh? Had she got my letter?"

"Yes, she had had your letter."

"And you think she is satisfied?"

"Satisfied? No, you can't expect her to be satisfied."

"I mean, is she satisfied that it isn't so bad after all as it looked the other day? What does Katie think of me?"

"I think she is still very fond of you, but that she has been puzzled and outraged by this discovery, and cannot get over it all at once."

"Why didn't you tell her the whole story from beginning to end?"

"I tried to do so as well as I could."

"Oh, but I can see you haven't done it. She doesn't really understand how it is."

"Perhaps not; but you must remember it is an awkward subject to be talking about to a young woman. I would sooner stand another fellowship examination than go through it again."

"Thank you, old fellow," said Tom, laying his hand on Hardy's shoulder; "I feel that I'm unreasonable and impatient; but you can excuse it; you know that I don't mean it."

"Don't say another word; I only wish I could have done more for you."

"But what do you suppose Katie thinks of me?"

"Why, you see, it sums itself up in this: she sees that you have been making serious love to Patty, and have turned the poor girl's head, more or less, and that now you are in love with somebody else. Why, put it how we will, we can't get out of that. There are the facts, pure and simple, and she wouldn't be half a woman if she didn't resent it."

"But it's hard lines, too, isn't it, old fellow? No, I wont say that; I deserve it all, and much worse. But you think I may come round all right?"

"Yes, all in good time. I hope there's no danger in any other quarter?"

"Goodness knows! There's the rub, you see. She will go back to town disgusted with me; I sha'n't see her again, and she wont hear of me for I don't know how long; and she will be meeting heaps of men. Has Katie been over to Barton?"

"Yes; she was there last week, just before they left."

"Well, what happened?"

"She wouldn't say much; but I gathered that they are very well."

"Oh, yes, bother it, of course they are very well. But didn't she talk to Katie about what happened last week?"

"Of course she did. What else should they talk about?"

"But you don't know what they said?"

"No; but you may depend on it that Miss Winter will be your friend. My dear fellow, there is nothing for it but time."

"Well, I suppose not," said Tom, with a groan. "Do you think I should call and see Katie?"

"No; I think better not."

"Well, then, we may as well get back," said Tom, who was not sorry for his friend's decision. So they paid their bill, and started for home, taking Hawk's Lynch on the way, that Hardy might see the view.

"And what did you find out about young Winburn?" he said, as they passed down the street.

"Oh, no good," said Tom; "he was turned out, as I thought, and has gone to live with an old woman up on the heath here, who is no better than she should be; and none of the farmers will employ him."

"You didn't see him, I suppose?"

"No; he is away with some of the heath people, hawking besoms and chairs about the country. They make them when there is no harvest work, and loaf about into Oxfordshire and Buckinghamshire, and other counties, selling them."

"No good will come of that sort of life, I'm afraid."

"No; but what is he to do?"

"I called at the lodge as I came away, and saw Patty and her mother. It's all right in that quarter. The old woman doesn't seem to think any thing of it; and Patty is a good girl, and will make Harry Winburn, or anybody else, a capital wife. Here's your locket and the letters; so now that's all over."

"Did she seem to mind giving them up?"

"Not very much. No, you are lucky there. She will get over it."

"But you told her that I am her friend for life, and that she is to let me know if I can ever do any thing for her?"

"Yes; and now I hope this is the last job of the kind I shall ever have to do for you."

"But what bad luck it has been! If I had only seen her before, or known who she was, nothing of all this would have happened."

To which Hardy made no reply; and the subject was not alluded to again in their walk home.

A day or two afterwards they returned to Oxford — Hardy to begin his work as fellow and assistant-tutor of the college, and Tom to see whether he could not make a better hand of his second year than he had of his first. He began with a much better chance of doing so, for he was thoroughly humbled. The discovery that he was not altogether such a hero as he had fancied himself, had dawned upon him very distinctly by the end of his first year, and the events of the long vacation had confirmed the impression, and pretty well taken all the conceit out of him for the time. The impotency of his own will, even when he was bent on doing the right thing, his want of insight and foresight in whatever matter he took in hand, the unruliness of his tempers and passions just at the moments when it behoved him to have them most thoroughly in hand and under control, were a set of disagreeable facts which had been driven well home to him. The results, being even such as we have seen, he did not much repine at, for he felt he had deserved them; and there was a sort of grim satisfaction, dreary as the prospect was, in facing them, and taking his punishment like a man. This was what he had felt at the first blush on the Hawk's Lynch;

and, as he thought over matters again by his fire, with his oak sported, on the first evening of term, he was still in the same mind. This was clearly what he had to do now. How to do it was the only question.

At first he was inclined to try to set himself right with the Porters and the Englebourn circle, by writing further explanations and confessions to Katie. But, on trying his hand at a letter, he found that he could not trust himself. The temptation of putting every thing in the best point of view for himself was too great; so he gave up the attempt, and merely wrote a few lines to David, to remind him that he was always ready and anxious to do all he could for his friend, Harry Winburn, and to beg that he might have news of any thing which happened to him, and how he was getting on. He did not allude to what had lately happened, for he did not know whether the facts had become known, and was in no hurry to open the subject himself.

Having finished his letter, he turned again to his meditations over the fire, and, considering that he had some little right to reward resolution, took off the safety valve, and allowed the thoughts to bubble up freely which were always underlying all others that passed through his brain, and making constant low, delicious, but just now somewhat melancholy, music in his head and heart. He gave himself up to thinking of Mary, and their walk in the wood, and the sprained ankle, and all the sayings and doings of that eventful autumn day. And then he opened his desk and examined certain treasures therein concealed, including a withered rosebud, a sprig of heather, a cut boot-lace, and a scrap or two of writing. Having gone through some extravagant forms of worship, not necessary to be specified, he put them away. Would it ever all come right?

He made his solitary tea, and sat down again to consider the point. But the point would not be considered alone. He began to feel more strongly what he had had several hints of already, that there was a curiously close connection between his own love story and that of Harry Winburn and Patty — that he couldn't separate them, even in his thoughts. Old Simon's tumble, which had recalled his daughter from Oxford at so critical a moment for him; Mary's visit to Englebourn at this very time; the curious yet natural series of little accidents which had kept him in ignorance of Patty's identity until the final catastrophe—then again, the way in which Harry Winburn and his mother had come across him on the very day of his leaving Barton; the fellowship of a common mourning which had seemed to bind them together so closely, and this last discovery which he could not help fearing must turn Harry into a bitter enemy, when he heard the truth, as he must, sooner or later,—as all these things passed before him, he gave in to a sort of superstitious feeling that his own fate hung in some way or another upon that of Harry Winburn. If he helped on his suit, he was helping on his own; but whether he helped on his own or not, was, after all, not that which was uppermost in his thoughts. He was much changed in this respect since he last sat in those rooms, just after his first days with her. Since then an angel had met him, and had "touched the chord of self, which, trembling," was passing "in music out of sight."

The thought of Harry and his trials enabled him to indulge in some good honest indignation, for which there was no room in his own case. That the prospects in life of such a man should be in the power, to a great extent, of such people as Squire Wurley and Farmer Tester; that, because he happened to be poor, he should be turned out of the cottage where his family had lived for a hundred years, at a week's notice, through the caprice of a drunken gambler; that, because he had stood up for his rights, and had thereby offended the worst farmer in the parish, he should be a marked man, and unable to get work — these things appeared so monstrous to him, and made him so angry, that he was obliged to get up and stamp about the room. And from the particular case he very soon got to generalizations.

Questions which had before now puzzled him gained a new significance every minute, and became real to him. Why a few men should be rich, and all the rest poor; above all, why he should be one of the few? Why the mere possession of property should give a man power over all his neighbors? Why poor men who were ready and willing to work should only be allowed to work, as a sort of favor, and should after all get the merest tithe of what their labor produced, and be tossed aside as soon as their work was done, or no longer required? These, and other such problems, rose up before him, crude and sharp, asking to be solved. Feeling himself quite unable to give any but one answer to them, that he was getting out of his depth, and that the whole business was in a muddle, he had recourse to his old method when in difficulties, and, putting on his cap, started off to Hardy's rooms to talk the matter over, and see whether he could not get some light on it from that quarter.

He returned in an hour or so, somewhat less troubled in his mind, inasmuch as he had found his friend in pretty much the same state as himself. But one step he had gained. Under his arm he carried certain books from Hardy's scanty library, the perusal of which he hoped, at least, might enable him, sooner or later, to feel that he had got on to some sort of firm ground. At any rate, Hardy had advised him to read them; so, without more ado, he drew his chair to the table and began to look into them.

This glimpse of the manner in which Tom spent the first evening of his second year at Oxford, will enable intelligent readers to understand why, though he took to reading far more kindly and earnestly than he had ever done before, he made no great advance in the proper studies of the place. Not that he wholly neglected these, for Hardy kept him pretty well up to the collar, and he passed his little-go creditably, and was fairly placed at the college examinations. In some of the books which he had to get up for lectures he was really interested. The politics of Athens, the struggle between the Roman plebs and patricians, Mons Sacer, and the Agrarian Laws — these began to have a new meaning to him, but chiefly because they bore more or less on the great Harry Winburn problem; which problem, indeed, for him had now fairly swelled into the condition-of-England problem, and was becoming every day more and more urgent and importunate, shaking many old beliefs, and leading him whither he knew not.

This very matter of leading was a sore trial to him. The further he got on his new road the more he felt the want of guidance—the guidance of some man; for that of books he soon found to be bewildering. His college tutor, whom he consulted, only deprecated the waste of time; but, on finding it impossible to dissuade him, at last recommended the economic works of that day as the proper well-springs of truth on such matters. To them Tom accordingly went, and read with the docility and faith of youth, bent on learning, and feeling itself in the presence of men who had, or assumed, the right of speaking with authority.

And they spoke to him with authority, and he read on,

believing much and hoping more; but somehow they did not really satisfy him, though they silenced him for the time. It was not the fault of the books, most of which laid down clearly enough that what they professed to teach was the science of man's material interests, and the laws of the making and employment of capital. But this escaped him in his eagerness, and he wandered up and down their pages in search of quite another science, and of laws with which they did not meddle. Nevertheless, here and there they seemed to touch upon what he was in search of. He was much fascinated, for instance, by the doctrine of "the greatest happiness of the greatest number," and for its sake swallowed for a time, though not without wry faces the dogmas, that self-interest is the true pivot of all social action, that population has a perpetual tendency to outstrip the means of living, and that to establish a preventive check on population is the duty of all good citizens. And so he lived on for some time in a dreary, uncomfortable state, fearing for the future of his country, and with little hope about his own. But, when he came to take stock of his newly acquired knowledge, to weigh it and measure it, and found it to consist of a sort of hazy conviction that society would be all right and ready for the millennium, when every man could do what he liked, and nobody could interfere with him, and there should be a law against marriage, the result was more than he could stand. He roused himself, and shook himself, and began to think, "Well, these my present teachers are very clever men, and well-meaning men, too. I see all that; but, if their teaching is only to land me here, why it was scarcely worth while going through so much to get so little."

Casting about still for guidance, Grey occurred to him. Grey was in residence as a bachelor, attending divinity lectures, and preparing for ordination. He was still working hard at the night-school, and Tom had been there once or twice to help him when the curate was away. In short, he was in very good books with Grey, who had got the better of his shyness with him. He saw that Tom was changed and sobered, and in his heart hoped some day to wean him from the pursuits of the body, to which he was still fearfully addicted, and to bring him into the fold. This hope was not altogether unfounded; for, notwithstanding the strong bias against them which Tom had brought with him from school, he was now at times much attracted by many of the high church doctrines, and the men who professed them. Such men as Grey he saw did really believe something, and were in earnest about carrying their beliefs into action. The party might and did comprise many others of the weakest sort, who believed and were in earnest about nothing, but who liked to be peculiar. Nevertheless, while he saw it laying hold of many of the best men of his time, it is not to be wondered at that he was drawn towards it. Some help might lie in these men if he could only get at it!

So he propounded his doubts and studies, and their results, to Grey. But it was a failure. Grey felt no difficulty, or very little, in the whole matter; but Tom found that it was because he believed the world to belong to the devil. "*Laissez faire*," "buying cheap and selling dear," Grey held might be good enough laws for the world—very probably were. The laws of the Church were "self-sacrifice," and "bearing one another's burdens;" her children should come out from the regions where the other's laws were acknowledged.

Tom listened, was dazzled at first, and thought he was getting on the right track; but very soon he found that Grey's specific was not of the least use to him! It was no good to tell him of the rules of a society to which he felt that he neither belonged, nor wished to belong, for clearly it could not be the Church of England. He was an outsider! Grey would probably admit it to be so, if he asked him. He had no longing to be any thing else, *if* the Church meant an exclusive body, which took no care of any but its own people, and had nothing to say to the great world in which he and most people had to live, and buying and selling, and hiring and working, had to go on. The close corporation might have very good laws, but they were nothing to him. What he wanted to know about was the law which this great world—the devil's world, as Grey called it—was ruled by, or rather ought to be ruled by. Perhaps, after all, Bentham and the others, whose books he had been reading, might be right! At any rate, it was clear that they had in their thoughts the same world that he had—the world which included himself and Harry Winburn, and all laborers and squires and farmers. So he turned to them again, not hopefully, but more inclined to listen to them than he had been before he had spoken to Grey.

Hardy was so fully occupied with college lectures and private pupils, that Tom had scruples about taking up much of his spare time in the evenings. Nevertheless, as Grey had broken down, and there was nobody else on whose judgment he could rely who would listen to him, whenever he had a chance he would propound some of his puzzles to his old friend. In some respects he got little help, for Hardy was almost as much at sea as he himself on such subjects as "value," and "wages," and the "laws of supply and demand." But there was an indomitable belief in him that all men's intercourse with one another, and not merely that of Churchmen, must be founded on the principle of "doing as they would be done by," and not on "buying cheap and selling dear," and that these never could or would be reconciled with one another, or mean the same thing, twist them how you would. This faith of his friend's comforted Tom greatly, and he was never tired of bringing it out; but at times he had his doubts whether Grey might not be right — whether, after all, that and the like maxims and principles were meant to be the laws of the kingdoms of this world. He wanted some corroborative evidence on the subject from an impartial and competent witness, and at last hit upon what he wanted. For, one evening, on entering Hardy's rooms, he found him on the last pages of a book, which he shut with an air of triumph on recognizing his visitor. Taking it up, he thrust it into Tom's hands, and slapping him on the shoulder, said, "There, my boy, that's what we want, or pretty near it at any rate. Now, don't say a word, but go back to your rooms, and swallow it whole and digest it, and then come back and tell me what you think of it."

"But I want to talk to you."

"I can't talk; I have spent the better part of two days over that book, and have no end of papers to look over. There; get back to your rooms, and do what I tell you, or sit down here and hold your tongue."

So Tom sat down and held his tongue, and was soon deep in Carlyle's Past and Present. How he did revel in it — in the humor, the power, the pathos, but above all in the root and branch denunciations of many of the doctrines in which he had been so lately voluntarily and wearily chaining himself! The chains went snapping off one after another, and in his exultation he kept spouting out passage after passage in a song of triumph, "Enlightened egoism never so luminous is not the rule by which man's life can be led — *laissez faire,* supply and demand, cash payment for the sole nexus, and so forth, were not, are not, and never will be, a practical law of union for a society of men," etc., etc., until Hardy fairly got up and turned him out, and he retired with his new-found treasure to his own rooms.

He had scarcely ever in his life been so moved by a book before. He laughed over it, and cried over it, and began half a dozen letters to the author to thank him which he fortunately tore up. He almost forgot Mary for several hours during his first enthusiasm. He had no notion how he had been mastered and oppressed before. He felt as the crew of a small fishing-smack, who are being towed away by an enemy's cruiser, might feel on seeing a frigate with the Union Jack flying, bearing down and opening fire on their captor; or as a small boy at school, who is being fagged against rules by the right of the strongest, feels when he sees his big brother coming round the corner. The help which he had found was just what he wanted. There was no narrowing of the ground here, no appeal to men as members of any exclusive body whatever to separate themselves and come out of the devil's world; but to men as men, to every man as a man, to the weakest and meanest as well as to the strongest and most noble, telling them that the world is God's world, that every one of them has a work in it, and bidding them find their work and set about it.

The strong tinge of sadness which ran through the whole book, and its unsparing denunciations of the established order of things, suited his own unsettled and restless frame of mind. So he gave himself up to his new bondage, and rejoiced in it as though he had found at last what he was seeking for; and, by the time that long vacation came round again, to which we are compelled to hurry him, he was filled full of a set of contradictory notions and beliefs which were destined to astonish and perplex the mind of that worthy J. P. for the county of Berks, Brown the elder, whatever other effect they might have on society at large.

Readers must not suppose, however, that our hero had given up his old pursuits; on the contrary, he continued to boat and cricket and spar with as much vigor as ever. His perplexities also made him a little more silent at his pastimes than he used to be. But, as we have already seen him thus employed, and know the ways of the animal in such matters, it is needless to repeat. What we want to do is to follow him into new fields of thought and action, and mark, if it may be, how he develops, and gets himself educated in one way and another; and this plunge into the great sea of social, political, and economical questions is the noticeable fact (so far as any is noticeable) of his second year's residence.

During the year he had only very meagre accounts of matters at Englebourn. Katie, indeed, had come round sufficiently to write to him, but she scarcely alluded to her cousin. He only knew that Mary had come out in London, and was much admired, and that the Porters had not taken Barton again, but were going abroad for the autumn and winter. The accounts of Harry were bad; he was still living at Daddy Collins', nobody knew how, and working gang-work occasionally with the outlaws of the heath.

The only fact of importance in the neighborhood had been the death of Squire Wurley, which happened suddenly in the spring. A distant cousin had succeeded him, a young man of Tom's own age.

He was also in residence at Oxford, and Tom knew him. They were not very congenial; so he was much astonished when young Wurley, on his return to college after his relative's funeral, rather sought him out, and seemed to wish to know more of him. The end of it was an invitation to Tom to come to the Grange, and spend a week or so at the beginning of the long vacation. There was to be a party of Oxford men, and nobody else there; and they meant to enjoy themselves thoroughly, Wurley said.

Tom felt much embarrassed how to act, and, after some hesitation, told his inviter of his last visit to the mansion in question, thinking that a knowledge of the circumstances might change his mind. But he found that young Wurley knew the facts already; and in fact, he couldn't help suspecting that his quarrel with the late owner had something to say to his present invitation. However, it did not lie in his mouth to be curious on the subject; and so he accepted the invitation gladly, much delighted at the notion of beginning his vacation so near Englebourn, and having the run of the Grange fishing, which was justly celebrated.

# CHAPTER XIII.

### THE RIVER SIDE.

So, from Henley, Tom went home just to see his father and mother, and pick up his fishing gear, and then started for the Grange. On his road thither, he more than once almost made up his mind to go round by Englebourn, get his first interview with Katie over, and find out how the world was really going with Harry and his sweetheart, of whom he had had such meagre intelligence of late. But, for some reason or another, when it came to taking the turn to Englebourn, he passed it by, and, contenting himself for the time with a distant view of the village and the Hawk's Lynch, drove straight to the Grange.

He had not expected to feel very comfortable at first in the house which he had left the previous autumn in so strange a manner, and he was not disappointed. The rooms reminded him unpleasantly of his passage of arms with the late master, and the grave and portly butler was somewhat embarrassed in his reception of him; while the footman, who carried off his portmanteau, did it with a grin which put him out. The set of men whom he found there were not of his sort. They were young Londoners, and he a thorough countryman. But the sight of the stream, by which he took a hasty stroll before dinner, made up for every thing, and filled him with pleasurable anticipations. He thought he had never seen a sweeter bit of water.

The dinner to which the party of young gentlemen sat

down was most undeniable. The host talked a little too
much, perhaps, under all the circumstances, of *my* wine,
*my* plate, *my* mutton, etc., provoking the thought of how
long they had been his. But he was bent on hospitality
after his fashion, and his guests were not disposed to criticise much.

The old butler did not condescend to wait, but brought
in a magnum of claret after dinner, carefully nursing it as
if it were a baby, and placing it patronizingly before his
young master. Before they adjourned to the billiard-room, which they did direct, they had disposed of several
of the same; but the followers were brought in by a footman, the butler being employed in discussing a bottle of
an older vintage with the steward in the still-room. Then
came pool, pool, pool, soda-water and brandy, and cigars,
into the short hours; but Tom stole away early, having
an eye to his morning's fishing, and not feeling much at
home with his companions.

He was out soon after sunrise the next morning. He
never wanted to be called when there was a trout-stream
within reach; and his fishing instinct told him that, in
these sultry dog-days, there would be little chance of sport
when the sun was well up. So he let himself gently out
of the hall-door — paused a moment on the steps to fill
his chest with the fresh morning air, as he glanced at the
weather-cock over the stables — and then set to work to
put his tackle together on the lawn, humming a tune to
himself as he selected an insinuating red hackle and alder
fly from his well-worn book, and tied them on to his cast.
Then he slung his creel over his shoulder, picked up his
rod, and started for the water.

As he passed the gates of the stable-yard, the keeper
came out — a sturdy, bullet-headed fellow, in a velveteen

coat, and cord breeches and gaiters — and touched his hat. Tom returned the salute, and wished him good-morning.

"Mornin', sir; you be about early."

"Yes; I reckon it's the best time for sport at the end of June."

"'Tis so, sir. Shall I fetch a net and come along?"

"No, thank you, I'll manage the ladle myself. But which do you call the best water?"

"They be both middling good. There aint much odds atwixt 'em. But I sees most fish movin' o' mornins in the deep water down below."

"I don't know; the night was too hot," said Tom, who had examined the water the day before, and made up his mind where he was going. "I'm for deep water on cold days; I shall begin with the stickles up above. There's good head of water on, I suppose?"

"Plenty down the last week, sir."

"Come along, then; we'll walk together, if you're going that way." So Tom stepped off, brushing through the steaming long grass, gemmed with wild flowers, followed by the keeper; and, as the grasshoppers bounded chirrupping out of his way, and the insect life hummed and murmured, and the lark rose and sang above his head, he felt happier than he had done for many a long month. So his heart opened towards his companion who kept a little behind him.

"What size do you take 'em out, keeper?"

"Any thing over nine inches, sir. But there's a smartish few fish of three pounds, for them as can catch 'em."

"Well, that's good; but they aint easy caught, eh?"

"I don't rightly know, sir; but there's gents comes as stands close by the water, and flogs down stream with the sun in their backs, and uses all manner o' vlies, wi' long names; and then they gwoes away, and says, 'taint no use flying here, 'cos there's so much cadis bait and that like."

"Ah, very likely," said Tom, with a chuckle.

"The chaps as catches the big fishes, sir," went on the keeper, getting confidential, "is thay cussed night-line poachers. There's one o' thay as has come here this last spring-tide — the artfullest chap as ever I come across, and down to every move on the board. He don't use no shove nets nor such like tackle, not he; I s'pose he don't call that sport. Besides, I got master to stake the whole water, and set old knives and razors about in the holes, so that don't answer; and this joker allus goes alone — which, in course, he couldn't do with nets. Now, I knows within five or six yards where that chap sets his lines, and I finds 'em, now and again, set the artfullest you ever see. But 'twould take a man's life to look arter him, and I knows he gets maybe a dozen big fish a week, do all as I knows."

"How is it you can't catch him, keeper?" said Tom, much amused.

"Why, you see, sir, he don't come at any hours. Drat un!" said the keeper, getting hot; "blessed if I don't think he sometimes comes down among the haymakers and folk at noon, and up lines and off, while thay chaps does nothing but snigger at un — all I knows is, as I've watched till midnight, and then on again at dawn for'n, and no good come on it but once."

"How was that?"

"Well, one mornin', sir, about last Lady-day, I comes quite quiet up stream about dawn. When I gets to Farmer Giles' piece (that little rough bit, sir, as you sees t'other side the stream, two fields from our outside bounds), I sees un a stooping down and hauling in's line. 'Now's your time, Billy,' says I, and up the hedge I cuts hotfoot, to get betwixt he and our bounds. Wether he seen me or not, I can't mind; least ways, when I up's head t'other side the hedge, vorrights where I seen him last, there was he a-trotting up stream quite-cool, a-pocketing a two-pounder. Then he seen me, and away we goes side by side for the bounds — he this side the hedge and I t'other; he takin' the fences like our old greyhound-bitch, Clara. We takes the last fence on to that fuzzy field as you sees there, sir (parson's glebe, and out of our liberty), neck and neck, and I turns short to the left, 'cos there warn't no fence now betwixt he and I. Well, I thought he'd a dodged on about the fuz. Not he; he slouches his hat over's eyes, and stands quite cool by fust fuz bush — I minded then as we was out o' our beat. Hows'ever, my blood was up; so I at's him then and there, no words lost, and fetches a crack at's head wi' my stick. He fends wi' his'n; and then, as I rushes in to collar'n, dashed if 'e didn't meet I full, and catch I by the thigh and collar, and send I slap over's head into a fuz bush. Then he chuckles fit to bust hisself, and cuts his stick, while I creeps out full o' prickles, and wi' my breeches tore shameful. Dang un!" cried the keeper, while Tom roared, "he's a lissum wosbird, that I 'ool say, but I'll be upsides wi' he next time I sees un. Whorson fool as I was not to stop and look at 'n and speak to un! Then I should ha' know'd 'n again; and now he med be our parish clerk for all as I knows."

"And you've never met him since?"

"Never sot eye on un, sir, arly or late — wishes I had."

"Well, keeper, here's half a crown to go towards mending the hole in your breeches, and better luck at the return match. I shall begin fishing here."

"Thank'ee, sir; you keep your cast pretty nigh that there off bank, and you med have a rare good un ther'.

I seen a fish suck there just now as warn't spawned this year nor last nether."

And away went the keeper.

"Stanch fellow, the keeper," said Tom to himself, as he reeled out yard after yard of his tapered line, and with a gentle sweep dropped his collar of flies lightly on the water, each cast covering another five feet of the dimpling surface. "Good fellow, the keeper — don't mind telling a story against himself — can stand being laughed at — more than his master can. Ah, there's the fish he saw sucking, I'll be bound. Now, you beauties, over his nose, and fall light — don't disgrace your bringing up!" and away went the flies quivering through the air and lighting close to the opposite bank, under a bunch of rushes. A slight round eddy followed below the rushes, as the cast came gently back across the current.

"Ah, you see them, do you, old boy?" thought Tom. "Say your prayers, then, and get shrived!" and away went the flies again, this time a little below. No movement. The third throw, a great lunge and splash, and the next moment the lithe rod bent double, and the gut collar spun along, cutting through the water like mad. Up goes the great fish twice into the air, Tom giving him the point, then up stream again, Tom giving him the butt and beginning to reel up gently. Down goes the great fish into the swaying weeds, working with his tail like a twelve-horse screw. "If I can only get my nose to ground," thinks he. So thinks Tom, and trusts to his tackle, keeping a steady strain on trouty, and creeping gently down stream. "No go," says the fish, as he feels his nose steadily hauled round, and turns with a swirl down stream. Away goes Tom, reeling in, and away goes the fish in hopes of a slack — away, for twenty or thirty yards — the fish coming to the top lazily, now and again, and holding on to get his second wind. Now a cart track crossed the stream, no weeds, and shallow water at the side. " Here we must have it out," thinks Tom, and turns fish's nose up stream again. The big fish gets sulky, twice drifts towards the shallow, and twice plunges away at the sight of his enemy into the deep water. The third time he comes swaying in, his yellow side gleaming and his mouth open; and the next moment Tom scoops him out on to the grass, with a " whoop" that might have been heard at the house.

" Two-pounder, if he's an ounce," says Tom, as he gives him the *coup de grace,* and lays him out lovingly on the fresh green sward.

Who amongst you, dear readers, can appreciate the intense delight of grassing your first big fish after a nine months' fast? All first sensations have their special pleasure, but none can be named, in a small way, to beat this of the first fish of the season. The first clean leg-hit for four in your first match at Lords — the grating of the bows of your racing boat against the stern of the boat ahead in your first race — the first half-mile of a burst from the cover side in November when the hounds in the field ahead may be covered with a tablecloth, and no one but the huntsman and a top sawyer or two lies between you and them — the first brief after your call to the bar, if it comes within the year — the sensations produced by these are the same in kind; but cricket, boating, getting briefs, even hunting, lose their edge as time goes on. As to lady readers, it is impossible, probably, to give them an idea of the sensation in question. Perhaps some may have experienced something of the kind at their first balls, when they heard whispers, and saw all eyes turning their way, and knew that their dresses and gloves fitted perfectly. But this joy can be felt but once in a life, and the first fish comes back as fresh as ever, or ought to come, if all men had their rights, once in a season. So, good luck to the gentle craft, and its professors, and may the Fates send us much into their company! The trout-fisher, like the landscape painter, haunts the loveliest places of the earth, and haunts them alone. Solitude, nature, and his own thoughts — he must be on the best terms with all of these; and he who can take kindly the largest allowance of these, is likely to be the kindliest and truest with his fellow-men.

Tom had splendid sport that summer morning. As the great sun rose higher, the light morning breeze which had curled the water, died away; the light mist drew up into light cloud, and the light cloud vanished into cloudland, for any thing I know; and still the fish rose, strange to say, though Tom felt it was an affair of minutes, and acted accordingly. At eight o'clock he was about a quarter of a mile from the house, at a point in the stream of rare charms both for the angler and the lover of gentle river beauty. The main stream was crossed by a lock, formed of a solid brick bridge with no parapets, under which the water rushed through four small arches, each of which could be closed in an instant by letting down a heavy wooden lock gate, fitted in grooves on the upper side of the bridge. Such locks are frequent in the west-country streams, even at long distances from mills and millers, for whose behoof they were made in old days, that the supply of water to the mill might be easily regulated. All pious anglers should bless the memories of the old builders of them, for they are the very paradises of the great trout, who frequent the old brickwork and timber foundations. The water, in its rush through the arches, had of course worked for itself a deep hole, and then, some twenty yards below, spread itself out in wanton joyous ripples and eddies over a broad surface some fifty yards across, and dashed away towards a little island some two hundred yards below, or rolled itself slowly back towards the bridge again, up the backwater by the side of the bank, as if longing for another merry rush through one of those narrow arches. The island below was crowned with splendid alders, willows forty feet high, which wept into the water, and two or three poplars; a rich mile of water meadow, with an occasional willow or alder lay gleaming beyond; and the view was bounded by a glorious wood, which crowned the gentle slope, at the foot of which the river ran. Another considerable body of water, which had been carried off above from the main stream to flush the water meadows, rejoined its parent at this point; it came slowly down a broad artificial ditch, running parallel with the main stream; and the narrow strip of land which divided the two streams ended abruptly just below the lock, forming a splendid point for bather or angler. Tom had fixed on this pool as his *bonne bouche*, as a child keeps its plums till the last, and stole over the bridge, stooping low, to gain the point above indicated. Having gained it, he glanced round to be aware of the dwarf ash-trees and willows which were scattered along the strip and might catch heedless collars and spoil sport, when, lying lazily almost on the surface where the backwater met the stream from the meadows, he beheld the great-grandfather of all trout, a fellow two feet long and a foot in girth at the shoulders, just moving fin enough to keep him from turning over on to his back. He threw himself flat on the ground and crept away to the other side of the strip; the king-fish had not seen him; and the next moment my uncle saw him suck in a bee laden with his morning's load of honey, who touched the water unwarily close to his nose. With a trembling hand Tom took off his tail fly, and, on his knees, substituted a governor; then, shortening his line after wetting his mimic bee in the pool behind him, tossed him gently into the monster's very jaws. For a moment the fish seemed scared, but the next, conscious in his strength, lifted his nose slowly to the surface and sucked in the bait. My uncle struck gently, and then sprang to his feet. But the Heavens had other work for the king-fish, who dived swiftly under the bank; a slight jar followed, and Tom's rod was straight over his head, the line and scarce a yard of his trusty gut collar dangling about his face. He seized this remnant with horror and unsatisfied longing, and examined it with care. Could he have overlooked any fraying which the gut might have got in the morning's work? No; he had gone over every inch of it not five minutes before, as he neared the pool. Besides, it was cut clean through, not a trace of bruise or fray about it. How could it have happened? He went to the spot and looked into the water; it was slightly discolored, and he could not see the bottom. He threw his fishing coat off, rolled up the sleeve of his flannel shirt, and, lying on his side, felt about the bank and tried to reach the bottom, but couldn't. So, hearing the half-hour bell ring, he deferred further inquiry, and stripped in silent disgust for a plunge in the pool. Three times he hurled himself into the delicious rush of the cold chalk stream, with that utter abandon in which man, whose bones are brittle, can only indulge when there are six or seven feet of water between him and mother earth; and, letting the stream bear him away at its own sweet will to the shallows below, struck up again through the rush and the roar to his plunging place. Then slowly and luxuriously dressing, he lit his short pipe, — companion of meditation, — and began to ruminate on the escape of his king-fish. What could have cut his collar? The more he thought, the less he could make it out. When suddenly he was aware of the keeper on his way back to the house for orders and breakfast.

"What sport, sir?"

"Pretty fair," said Tom, carelessly; lugging five plump speckled fellows, weighing some seven and a half pounds, out of his creel, and laying them out for the keeper's inspection.

"Well, they be in prime order, sir, surely," says the keeper, handling them; "they allus gets mortal thick across the shoulders while the May fly be on. Lose any, sir?"

"I put in some little ones up above, and lost one screamer just up the back ditch there. He must have been a four pounder, and went off, and be hanged to him, with two yards of my collar and a couple of firstrate flies. How on earth he got off I can't tell!" and he went on to unfold the particulars of the short struggle.

The keeper could hardly keep down a grin. "Ah, sir," said he, "I thinks I knows what spwiled your sport. You owes it all to that chap as I was a-telling you of, or my name's not Willum Goddard;" and then, fishing the lock-pole with a hook at the end of it out of the rushes, he began groping under the bank, and presently hauled up a sort of infernal machine, consisting of a heavy lump of wood, a yard or so long, in which were carefully inserted the blades of four or five old knives and razors, while a crop of rusty, jagged nails filled up the spare space.

Tom looked at it in wonder. "What devil's work have you got hold of there?" he said at last.

"Bless you, sir," said the keeper, "'tis only our shove-net traps as I wur a-telling you of. I keeps hard upon a dozen on 'em, and shifts 'em about in the likeliest holes;

and I takes care to let the men as is about the water meadows see me a-sharpening on 'em up a bit, wi' a file, now and again. And, since master gev me orders to put 'em in, I don't think they tries that game on not once a month."

"Well, but where do you and your master expect to go to if you set such things as those about?" said Tom, looking serious. "Why, you'll be cutting some fellow's hand or foot half off one of these days. Suppose I'd waded up the bank to see what had become of my cast?"

"Lor, sir, I never thought o' that," said the keeper, looking sheepish, and lifting the back of his short hat off his head to make room for a scratch; "but," added he, turning the subject, "if you wants to keep thay artful wosbirds off the water, you must frighten 'em wi' summat out o' the way. Drattle 'em, I knows they puts me to my wits' end; but you'd never 'a' had five such fish as them afore breakfast, sir, if we didn't stake the waters unmussiful."

"Well, and I don't want 'em, if I can't get 'em without. I'll tell you what it is, keeper, this razor business is going a bit too far; men aint to be maimed for liking a bit of sport. You set spring-guns in the woods, and you know what that came to. Why don't you, or one of your watchers, stop out here at night, and catch the fellows, like men?"

"Why, you see, sir, master don't allow me but one watcher, and he's mortal feared o' the water he be, specially o' nights. He'd sooner by half stop up in the woods. Daddy Collins (that's an old woman as lives on the heath, sir, and a bad sort she be, too), well, she told he once, when he wouldn't gee her some baccchy as he'd got, and she'd a mind to, as he'd fall twice into the water for once as he'd get out; and th' poor chap ever since can't think but what he'll be drownded. And there's queer sights and sounds by the river o' nights, too, I ool say, sir, let alone the white mist, as makes every thing look unket, and gives a chap the rheumatics."

"Well, but *you* aint afraid of ghosts and rheumatism?"

"No; I don't know as I be, sir. But then, there's the pheasants a breedin', and there's four brood of flappers in the withey bed, and a sight o' young hares in the spinneys. I be hard put to to mind it all."

"I dare say you are," said Tom, putting on his coat, and shouldering his rod; "I've a good mind to take a turn at it myself, to help you, if you'll only drop those razors."

"I wishes you would, sir," said the keeper, from behind; "if gen'l'men'd sometimes take a watch at nights, they'd find out as keepers hadn't all fair-weather work, I'll warrant, if they're to keep a good head o' game about a place; 'taint all popping off guns, and lunching under hayricks, I can tell 'em — no, nor half on it."

"Where do you think, now, this fellow we were talking of sells his fish?" said Tom, after a minute's thought.

"Mostly at Reading Market, I hears tell, sir. There's the guard of the mail, as goes by the cross-roads three days a week, he wur a rare poaching chap hisself down in the west afore he got his place along of his bugle-playing. They do say as he's open to any game, he is, from a buck to a snipe, and drives a trade all down the road with the country chaps."

"What day is Reading Market?"

"Tuesdays and Saturdays, sir."

"And what time does the mail go by?"

"Six o'clock in the morning, sir, at the cross-roads."

"And they're three miles off, across the fields?"

"Thereabouts, sir; I reckons it about a forty minutes' stretch, and no time lost."

"There'll be no more big fish caught on the fly to-day," said Tom, after a minute's silence, as they neared the house.

The wind had fallen dead, and not a spot of cloud in the sky.

"Not afore nightfall, I think, sir;" and the keeper disappeared towards the offices.

## CHAPTER XIV.

### THE NIGHT-WATCH.

"You may do as you please, but I'm going to see it out."

"No; but I say, do come along; that's a good fellow."

"Not I; why, we've only just come out. Didn't you hear? Wurley dared me to do a night's watching and I said I meant to do it."

"Yes; so did I. But we can change our minds. What's the good of having a mind if you can't change it! αἱ δεύτεραι πως φροντίδες σοφώτεραι; isn't that good Greek and good sense?"

"I don't see it. They'll only laugh and sneer if we go back now."

"They'll laugh at us twice as much if we don't. Fancy! they're just beginning pool now on that stunning table. Come along, Brown; don't miss your chance. We shall be sure to divide the pools, as we've missed the claret. Cool hands and cool heads, you know! Green on brown, pink your player in hand! That's a good deal pleasanter than squatting here all night on the damp grass."

"Very likely."

"But you wont? Now, do be reasonable. Will you come if I stop with you another half-hour?"

"No."

"An hour then? Say till ten o'clock?"

"If I went at all, I would go at once."

"Then you wont come?"

"No."

"I'll bet you a sovereign you never see a poacher, and then how sold you will be in the morning! It will be much worse coming in to breakfast with empty hands and a cold in the head, than going in now. They will chaff then, I grant you."

"Well, then, they may chaff and be hanged, for I sha'n't go in now."

Tom's interlocutor put his hands in the pockets of his heather mixture shooting-coat, and took a turn or two of some dozen yards, backwards and forwards above the place where our hero was sitting. He didn't like going in and facing the pool-players by himself; so he stopped once more and re-opened the conversation.

"What do you want to do by watching all night, Brown?"

"To show the keeper, and those fellows in-doors, that I mean what I say. I said I'd do it, and I will."

"You don't want to catch a poacher, then?"

"I don't much care: I'll catch one if he comes in my way — or try it on, at any rate."

"I say, Brown, I like that; as if you don't poach yourself. Why, I remember when the Whitcham keeper spent the best part of a week outside the college gates, on the look-out for you and Drysdale, and some other fellows."

"What has that to do with it?"

"Why, you ought to have more fellow-feeling. I suppose you go on the principle of set a thief to catch a thief."

Tom made no answer, and his companion went on,—

"Come along now, like a good fellow. If you'll come

in now, we can come out again all fresh, when the rest go to bed."

"Not we. I sha'n't go in. But you can come out again, if you like; you'll find me hereabouts."

The man in the heather mixture had now shot his last bolt, and took himself off to the house, leaving Tom by the river side. How they got there may be told in a few words. After his morning's fishing, and conversation with the keeper, he had gone in full of his subject, and propounded it at the breakfast-table. His strictures on the knife and razor business produced a rather warm discussion, which merged in the question whether a keeper's life was a hard one, till something was said implying that Wurley's men were overworked. The master took this in high dudgeon, and words ran high. In the discussion, Tom remarked (*apropos* of night-work) that he would never ask another man to do what he would not do himself; which sentiment was endorsed by, amongst others, the man in the heather mixture. The host had retorted, that they had better in that case try it themselves; which remark had the effect of making Tom resolve to cut short his visit, and in the mean time had brought him and his ally to the river side on the night in question.

The first hour, as we have seen, had been enough for the ally, and so Tom was left in company with a plaid, a stick, and a pipe, to spend the night by himself.

It was by no means the first night he had spent in the open air, and promised to be a pleasant one for camping out. It was almost the longest day in the year, and the weather was magnificent. There was yet an hour of daylight, and the place he had chosen was just the right one for enjoying the evening.

He was sitting under one of a clump of huge old alders, growing on the thin strip of land already noticed,

which divided the main stream from the deep artificial
ditch which fed the water-meadows. On his left the
emerald-green meadows stretched away till they met the
enclosed corn land. On his right ran the main stream,
some fifty feet in breadth at this point; on the opposite
side of which was a rough piece of ground, half withey
bed, half copse, with a rank growth of rushes at the
water's edge. These were the chosen haunts of moor-hen
and water-rat, whose tracks could be seen by dozens, like
small open doorways, looking out on to the river, through
which ran mysterious little paths into the rush-wilderness
beyond.

The sun was now going down behind the copse, through
which his beams came aslant, chequered and mellow.
The stream ran dimpling down by him, sleepily swaying
the masses of weed, under the surface and on the surface;
and the trout rose under the banks, as some moth or gnat
or gleaming beetle fell into the stream; here and there
one more frolicsome than his brethren would throw himself joyously into the air. The swifts rushed close by
him, in companies of five or six, and wheeled, and
screamed, and dashed away again, skimming along the
water, baffling his eye as he tried to follow their flight.
Two kingfishers shot suddenly up on to their supper
station, on a stunted willow stump, some twenty yards
below him, and sat there in the glory of their blue backs
and cloudy red waistcoats, watching with long, sagacious
beaks pointed to the water beneath, and every now and
then dropping like flashes of light into the stream, and
rising again with what seemed one motion, to their
perches. A heron or two were fishing about the meadows; and he watched them stalking about in their sober
quaker coats, or rising on slow heavy wing, and lumbering away home with a weird cry. He heard the strong

pinions of the wood pigeon in the air, and then from the trees above his head came the soft call, "Take-two-cow-Taffy, take-two-cow-Taffy," with which that fair and false bird is said to have beguiled the hapless Welchman to the gallows. Presently, as he lay motionless, the timid and graceful little water-hens peered out from their doors in the rushes opposite, and, seeing no cause for fear, stepped daintily into the water, and were suddenly surrounded by little bundles of black soft down, which went paddling about in and out of the weeds, encouraged by the occasional sharp, clear, parental "keck — keck," and merry little dabchicks popped up in mid-stream, and looked round, and nodded at him, pert and voiceless, and dived again; even old cunning water-rats sat up on the bank with round black noses and gleaming eyes, or took solemn swims out, and turned up their tails and disappeared for his amusement. A comfortable low came at intervals from the cattle, revelling in the abundant herbage. All living things seemed to be disporting themselves, and enjoying, after their kind, the last gleams of the sunset, which were making the whole vault of heaven glow and shimmer; and, as he watched them, Tom blessed his stars as he contrasted the river side with the glare of lamps and the click of balls in the noisy pool-room.

Before it got dark he bethought him of making sure of his position once more; matters might have changed since he chose it before dinner. With all that he could extract from the keeper, and his own experience in such matters, it had taken him several hours hunting up and down the river that afternoon before he had hit on a night-line. But he had persevered, knowing that this was the only safe evidence to start from, and at last had found several, so cunningly set that it was clear that it was a firstrate artist in the poaching line against whom he had pitted himself. These lines must have been laid almost under his nose on that very day, as the freshness of the baits proved. The one which he had selected to watch by was under the bank, within a few yards of the clump of alders where he was now sitting. There was no satisfactory cover near the others; so he had chosen this one, where he would be perfectly concealed behind the nearest trunk from any person who might come in due time to take up the line. With this view, then, he got up, and, stepping carefully on the thickest grass where his foot would leave no mark, went to the bank, and felt with the hook of his stick after the line. It was all right, and he returned to his old seat.

And then the summer twilight came on, and the birds disappeared, and the hush of night settled down on river and copse and meadow — cool and gentle summer twilight after the hot, bright day. He welcomed it too, as it folded up the landscape, and the trees lost their outline, and settled into soft black masses rising here and there out of the white mist, which seemed to have crept up to within a few yards all around him unawares. There was no sound now but the gentle murmur of the water, and an occasional rustle of reeds, or of the leaves over his head, as a stray wandering puff of air passed through them on its way home to bed. Nothing to listen to, and nothing to look at; for the moon had not risen, and the light mist hid every thing except a star or two right up above him. So, the outside world having left him for the present, he was turned inwards on himself.

This was all very well at first; and he wrapped the plaid round his shoulders and leant against his tree, and indulged in a little self-gratulation. There was something of strangeness and adventure in his solitary night-watch, which had its charm for a youngster of twenty-one; and the consciousness of not running word, of doing what he had said he would do, while others shirked and broke down, was decidedly pleasant.

But this satisfaction did not last very long, and the night began to get a little wearisome, and too cool to be quite comfortable. By degrees doubts as to the wisdom of his self-imposed task crept into his head. He dismissed them for a time by turning his thoughts to other matters. The neighborhood of Englebourn, some two miles up above him, reminded him of the previous summer; and he wondered how he should get on with his cousin when they met. He should probably see her the next day, for he would lose no time in calling. Would she receive him well? Would she have much to tell him about Mary?

He had been more hopeful on this subject of late, but the loneliness, the utter solitude and silence of his position, as he sat there in the misty night, away from all human habitations, was not favorable somehow to hopefulness. He found himself getting dreary and sombre in heart, more and more so as the minutes rolled on, and the silence and loneliness pressed on him more and more heavily. He was surprised at his own down-heartedness, and tried to remember how he had spent former nights so pleasantly out of doors. Ah, he had always had a companion within call, and something to do — cray fishing, bat fowling, or something of the kind? Sitting there, doing nothing, he fancied, must make it so heavy to-night. By a strong effort of will he shook off the oppression. He moved, and hummed a tune to break the silence; he got up and walked up and down, lest it should again master him. If wind, storm, pouring rain, any thing to make sound or movement, would but come!

But neither of them came, and there was little help in sound or movement made by himself. Besides, it occurred to him that much walking up and down might defeat the object of his watch. No one would come near while he was on the move; and he was probably making marks already which might catch the eye of the setter of the night-lines at some distance, if that cunning party waited for the morning light, and might keep him away from the place altogether.

So he sat down again on his old seat, and leant hard against the alder trunk, as though to steady himself, and keep all troublesome thoughts well in front of him. In this attitude of defence, he reasoned with himself on the absurdity of allowing himself to be depressed by the mere accidents of place and darkness and silence; but all the reasoning at his command didn't alter the fact. He felt the enemy advancing again, and, casting about for help, fell back on the thought that he was going through a task, holding to his word, doing what he had said he would do; and this brought him some relief for the moment. He fixed his mind steadily on this task of his; but alas, here again, in his very last stronghold the enemy began to turn his flank, and the position every minute became more and more untenable.

He had of late fallen into a pestilent habit of cross-questioning himself on any thing which he was about—setting up himself like a cock at Shrove-tide, and pelting himself with inexorable "whys?" and "wherefores?" A pestilent habit truly he had found it, and one which left a man no peace of his life—a relentless, sleepless habit, always ready to take advantage of him, but never so viciously alert, that he remembered, as on this night.

And so this questioning self, which would never be denied for long, began to examine him as to his proposed night's work. This precious task, which he was so proud of going through with, on the score of which he had been in his heart crowing over others, because they had not taken it on them, or had let it drop, what then was the meaning of it?

"What was he out there for? What had he come out to do?" They were awkward questions. He tried several answers, and was driven from one to another till he was bound to admit that he was out there that night, partly out of pique, and partly out of pride: and that his object (next to earning the pleasure of thinking himself a better man than his neighbors) was, if so be, to catch a poacher. "To catch a poacher? What business had he to be catching poachers? If all poachers were to be caught, he would have to be caught himself." He had just had an unpleasant reminder of this fact from him of the heather mixtures—a Parthian remark which he had thrown over his shoulder as he went off, and which had stuck. "But then," Tom argued, "it was a very different thing, his poaching—going out for a day's lark after game, which he didn't care a straw for, but only for the sport—and that of men making a trade of it, like the man the keeper spoke of. Why? How different? If there were any difference, was it one in his favor?" Avoiding this suggestion, he took up new ground. "Poachers were always the greatest blackguards in their neighborhoods, pests of society, and ought to be put down. Possibly—at any rate he had been one of the fraternity in his time, and was scarcely the man to be casting stones at them. But his poaching had always been done thoughtlessly. How did he know that others had worse motives?"

And so he went on, tossing the matter backwards and forwards in his mind, and getting more and more uncomfortable, and unable to answer to his own satisfaction the simple question, "What right have you to be out here on this errand?"

He got up a second time and walked up and down, but with no better success than before. The change of position and exercise did not help him out of his difficulties. And now he got a step further. If he had no right to be there, hadn't he better go up to the house and say so, and go to bed like the rest? No, his pride couldn't stand that. But if he couldn't go in, he might turn into a barn or outhouse; nobody would be any the wiser then, and after all he was not pledged to stop on one spot all night? It was a tempting suggestion, and he was very near yielding to it at once. While he wavered, a new set of thoughts came up to back it. How, if he stayed there, and a gang of night poachers came? He knew that many of them were desperate men. He had no arms; what could he do against them? Nothing; but he might be maimed for life in a night row which he had no business to be in— murdered, perhaps. He stood still and listened, long and painfully.

Every moment, as he listened, the silence mastered him more and more, and his reason became more and more powerless. It was such a silence—a great, illimitable, vague silence! The silence of a deserted house, where he could at least have felt that he was bounded somewhere, by wall and floor and roof—where men must have lived and worked once, though they might be there no longer—would have been nothing; but this silence of the huge, wide, out-of-doors world, where there was nothing but air and space around and above him and the ground beneath, it was getting irksome, intolerable, awful! The great silence seemed to be saying to him, "You are alone, alone, alone!" and he had never known before what horror lurked in that thought.

Every moment that he stood, still the spell grew on him, and yet he dared not move; and a strange, wild feeling of fear—unmistakable physical fear, which made his heart beat and his limbs tremble—seized on him. He was ready to cry out, to fall down, to run, and yet there he stood listening, still and motionless.

The critical moment in all panics must come at last. A wild and grewsome hissing and snoring, which seemed to come from the air just over his head, made him start and spring forward, and gave him the use of his limbs again, at any rate, though they would not have been worth much to him had the ghost or hobgoblin appeared whom he half expected to see the next moment. Then came a screech, which seemed to flit along the rough meadow opposite, and come towards him. He drew a long breath, for he knew that sound well enough; it was nothing after all but the owls.

The mere realized consciousness of the presence of some living creatures, were they only owls, brought him to his senses. And now the moon was well up, and the wayward mist had cleared away, and he could catch glimpses of the solemn birds every now and then, beating over the rough meadow backwards and forwards and over the shallow water, as regularly as trained pointers.

He threw himself down again under his tree, and now bethought himself of his pipe. Here was a companion which, wonderful to say, he had not thought of before since the night set in. He pulled it out, but paused before lighting. Nothing was so likely to betray his whereabouts as tobacco. True, but any thing was better than such another fright as he had had, "so here goes," he thought; "if I keep off all the poachers in Berkshire;" and he accordingly lighted up, and, with the help of his pipe, once more debated with himself the question of beating a retreat.

After a sharp inward struggle, he concluded to stay and see it out. He should despise himself, more than he cared to face, if he gave in now. If he left that spot before morning, the motive would be sheer cowardice. There might be fifty other good reasons for going; but if he went, *his* reason would be fear and nothing else. It might have been wrong and foolish to come out; it must be to go in now. "Fear never made a man do a right action," he summed up to himself; "so here I stop, come what may of it. I think I've seen the worst of it now. I was in a real blue funk, and no mistake. Let's see, wasn't I laughing this morning at the watcher who didn't like passing a night by the river? Well, he has got the laugh of me now, if he only knew it. I've learnt one lesson tonight at any rate; I don't think I shall ever be very hard on cowards again."

By the time he had finished his pipe, he was a man again, and, moreover, notwithstanding the damp, began to feel sleepy, now that his mind was thoroughly made up, and his nerves were quiet. So he made the best of his plaid, and picked a softish place, and went off soon into a sort of dog sleep, which lasted at intervals through the rest of the short summer night. A poor thin sort of sleep it was, in which he never altogether lost his consciousness, and broken by short intervals of actual wakefulness, but a blessed release from the self-questionings and panics of the early night.

He woke at last with a shiver. It was colder than he had yet felt it, and it seemed lighter. He stretched his half-torpid limbs, and sat up. Yes, it was certainly getting light, for he could just make out the figures on the face of his watch which he pulled out. The dawn was almost upon him, and his night-watch was over. Nothing had come of it as yet, except his fright, at which he could now laugh comfortably enough; probably nothing more might come of it after all, but he had done the task he had set himself without flinching, and that was a satisfaction. He wound up his watch, which he had forgotten to do the night before, and then stood up, and threw his damp plaid aside, and swung his arms across his chest to restore circulation. The crescent moon was high up in the sky, faint and white, and he could scarcely now make out the stars, which were fading out as the glow in the north-east got stronger and broader.

Forgetting for a moment the purpose of his vigil, he was thinking of a long morning's fishing, and had turned to pick up his plaid and go off to the house for his fishing-rod, when he thought he heard the sound of dry wood snapping. He listened intently; and the next moment it came again, some way off, but plainly to be heard in the intense stillness of the morning. Some living thing was moving down the stream. Another moment's listening, and he was convinced that the sound came from a hedge some hundred yards below.

He had noticed the hedge before; the keeper had stopped up a gap in it the day before, at the place where it came down to the water, with some old hurdles and dry thorns. He drew himself up behind his alder, looking out from behind it cautiously towards the point from which the sound came. He could just make out the hedge through the mist, but saw nothing.

But now the crackling began again, and he was sure that a man was forcing his way over the keeper's barricade. A moment afterwards he saw a figure drop from the hedge into the slip in which he stood. He drew back his head hastily, and his heart beat like a hammer as he waited the approach of the stranger. In a few seconds the suspense was too much for him, for again there was perfect silence. He peered out a second time cautiously round the tree, and now he could make out the figure of a man stooping by the water-side just above the hedge, and drawing in a line. This was enough, and he drew back again, and made himself small behind the tree; now he was sure that the keeper's enemy, the man he had come out to take, was here. His next halt would be at the line which was set within a few yards of the place where he stood. So the struggle which he had courted was come! All his doubts of the night wrestled in his mind for a minute; but, forcing them down, he strung himself up for the encounter, his whole frame trembling with the excitement, and his blood tingling through his veins as though it would burst them. The next minute was as severe a trial of nerve as he had ever been put to, and the sound of a stealthy tread on the grass just below came to him as a relief. It stopped, and he heard the man stoop, then came a stir in the water, and the flapping as of a fish being landed.

Now was his time! He sprang from behind the tree, and, the next moment, was over the stooping figure of the poacher. Before he could seize him, the man sprang up, and grappled with him. They had come to a tight lock at once, for the poacher had risen so close under him that he could not catch his collar and hold him off. Too close to strike, it was a desperate trial of strength and bottom.

Tom knew in a moment that he had his work cut out for him. He felt the nervous power of the frame he had got hold of as he drove his chin into the poacher's shoulder, and arched his back, and strained every muscle in his body to force him backwards, but in vain. It was all he could do to hold his own; but he felt that he might hold it yet, as they staggered on the brink of the back ditch, stamping the grass and marsh marigolds into the ground, and drawing deep breath through their set teeth. A slip, a false foothold, a failing muscle, and it would be over; down they must go — who would be uppermost?

The poacher trod on a soft place, and Tom felt it, and, throwing himself forward, was reckoning on victory, but reckoning without his host; for, recovering himself with a twist of the body which brought them still closer together, the poacher locked his leg behind Tom's in a crook which brought the wrestlings of his boyhood into his head with a flash, as they tottered for another moment, and then losing balance, went headlong over with a heavy plunge and splash into the deep back ditch, locked tight in each other's arms.

The cold water closed over them, and for a moment Tom held as tight as ever. Under or above the surface, it was all the same, he couldn't give in first. But a gulp of water, and the singing in his ears, and a feeling of choking, brought him to his senses, helped too by the thought of his mother and Mary, and love of the pleasant world up above. The folly and uselessness of being drowned in a ditch on a point of honor stood out before him as clearly as if he had been thinking of nothing else all his life; and he let go his hold — much relieved to find that his companion of the bath seemed equally willing to be quit of him — and struggled to the surface, and seized the bank, gasping and exhausted.

His first thought was to turn round and look for his adversary. The poacher was by the bank too, a few feet from him. His cap had fallen off in the struggle, and, all chance of concealment being over, he too had turned to face the matter out, and their eyes met.

"Good God! Harry! is it you?"

Harry Winburn answered nothing; and the two dragged their feet out of the soft, muddy bottom, and scrambled on to the bank, and then with a sort of common instinct sat down, dripping and foolish, each on the place he had reached, and looked at one another. Probably two more thoroughly bewildered lieges of her majesty were not at that moment facing one another in any corner of the United Kingdom.

# CHAPTER XV.

### MARY IN MAYFAIR.

On the night which our hero spent by the side of the river, with the results detailed in the last chapter, there was a great ball in Brook Street, Mayfair. It was the height of the season; and, of course, balls, concerts, and parties of all kinds were going on in all parts of the Great Babylon, but the entertainment in question was *the* event of that evening. Persons behind the scenes would have told you at once, had you happened to meet them, and inquire on the subject during the previous ten days, that Brook Street was the place in which everybody who went anywhere ought to spend some hours between eleven and three on this particular evening. If you did not happen to be going there, you had better stay quietly at your club, or elsewhere, and not speak of your engagements for that night.

A great awning had sprung up in the course of the day over the pavement in front of the door, and as the evening closed in, tired lawyers and merchants, on their return from the city, and the riders and drivers on their way home from the park, might have seen Holland's men laying red drugget over the pavement, and Gunter's carts coming and going, and the police "moving on" the street boys and servant-maids, and other curious members of the masses, who paused to stare at the preparations.

Then came the lighting up of the rooms, and the blaze

of pure white light from the uncurtained ball-room windows spread into the street, and the musicians passed in with their instruments. Then, after a short pause, the carriages of a few intimate friends, who came early at the hostess' express desire, began to drive up, and the Hansom cabs of the contemporaries of the eldest son, from which issued guardsmen and foreign-office men, and other dancing-youth of the most approved description. Then the crowd collected again round the door — a sadder crowd now to the eye of any one who has time to look at it; with sallow, haggard-looking men here and there on the skirts of it, and tawdry women joking and pushing to the front, through the powdered footmen, and linkmen in red waistcoats, already clamorous and redolent of gin and beer, and scarcely kept back by the half-dozen constables of the A division, told off for the special duty of attending and keeping order on so important an occasion.

Then comes a rush of carriages, and by eleven o'clock the line stretches away half round Grosvenor Square, and moves at a foot's-pace towards the lights and the music and the shouting street. In the middle of the line is the comfortable chariot of our friend, Mr. Porter — the corners occupied by himself and his wife, while Miss Mary sits well forward between them, her white muslin dress, looped up with sprigs of heather, spread delicately on either side over their knees, and herself in a pleasant tremor of impatience and excitement.

"How very slow Robert is to-day, mamma! we shall never get to the house."

"He cannot get on faster, my dear. The carriages in front of us must set down, you know."

"But I wish they would be quicker. I wonder whether we shall know many people? Do you think I shall get partners?"

Not waiting for her mother's reply, she went on to name some of her acquaintance, whom she knew would be there, and bewailing the hard fate which was keeping her out of the first dances. Mary's excitement and impatience were natural enough. The ball was not like most balls. It was a great battle in the midst of the skirmishes of the season, and she felt the greatness of the occasion.

Mr. and Mrs. Porter had for years past dropped into a quiet sort of dinner-giving life, in which they saw few but their own friends and contemporaries. They generally left London before the season was at its height, and had altogether fallen out of the ball-giving and party-going world. Mary's coming out had changed their way of life. For her sake they had spent the winter at Rome, and, now that they were at home again, were picking up the threads of old acquaintance, and encountering the disagreeables of a return into habits long disused and almost forgotten. The giver of the ball was a stirring man in political life, rich, clever, well connected, and much sought after. He was an old schoolfellow of Mr. Porter, and their intimacy had never been wholly laid aside, notwithstanding the severance of their paths in life. Now that Mary must be taken out, the Brook Street house was one of the first to which the Porters turned, and the invitation to this ball was one of the first consequences.

If the truth must be told, neither her father nor mother were in sympathy with Mary as they gradually neared the place of setting down, and would far rather have been going to a much less imposing place, where they could have driven up at once to the door, and would not have been made uncomfortable by the shoutings of their names from servant to servant. However, after the first plunge, when they had made their bows to their kind and smiling hostess, and had passed on into the already well-filled rooms, their shyness began to wear off, and they could in some sort enjoy the beauty of the sight from a quiet corner. They were not long troubled with Miss Mary. She had not been in the ball-room two minutes before the eldest son of the house had found her out and engaged her for the next waltz. They had met several times already, and were on the best terms; and the freshness and brightness of her look and manner, and the evident enjoyment of her partner, as they laughed and talked together in the intervals of the dance, soon attracted the attention of other young men, who began to ask one another " Who is Norman dancing with?" and to ejaculate with various strength, according to their several temperaments, as to her face and figure and dress.

As they were returning towards Mrs. Porter, Norman was pulled by the sleeve more than once, and begged to be allowed to introduce first one and then another of his friends.

Mary gave herself up to the fascination of the scene. She had never been in rooms so perfectly lighted, with such a floor, such exquisite music, and so many pretty and well-bred looking people, and she gave herself up to enjoy it with all her heart and soul, and danced and laughed and talked herself into the good graces of partner after partner, till she began to attract the notice of some of the ill-natured people who are to be found in every room, and who cannot pardon the pure and buoyant and unsuspecting mirth which carries away all but themselves in its bright stream. So Mary passed on from one partner to another, with whom we have no concern, until at last a young lieutenant in the guards, who had just finished his second dance with her, led up a friend whom he begged to introduce. "Miss Porter—

Mr. St. Cloud;" and then, after the usual preliminaries, Mary left her mother's side again and stood up by the side of her new partner.

"It is your first season, I believe, Miss Porter?"

"Yes; my first in London."

"I thought so; and you have only just come to town?"

"We came back from Rome six weeks ago, and have been in town ever since."

"But I am sure I have not seen you anywhere this season until to-night. You have not been out much yet?"

"Yes, indeed; papa and mamma are very good-natured, and go wherever we are asked to a ball, as I am fond of dancing."

"How very odd! and yet I am quite sure I should have remembered it if we had met before in town this year."

"Is it so very odd?" asked Mary, laughing. "London is a very large place. It seems very natural that two people should be able to live in it for a long time without meeting."

"Indeed, you are quite mistaken. You will find out very soon how small London is — at least, how small society is; and you will get to know every face quite well — I mean the face of every one in society."

"You must have a wonderful memory?"

"Yes; I have a good memory for faces, and, by the way, I am sure I have seen you before; but not in town, and I cannot remember where. But it is not at all necessary to have a memory to know everybody in society by sight; you meet every night almost; and altogether there are only two or three hundred faces to remember. And then there is something in the look of people, and the way they come into a room or stand about, which tells you at once whether they are amongst those whom you need trouble yourself about."

"Well, I cannot understand it. I seem to be in a whirl of faces, and can hardly ever remember any of them."

"You will soon get used to it. By the end of the season you will see that I am right. And you ought to make a study of it, or you will never feel at home in London."

"I must make good use of my time then. I suppose I ought to know everybody here, for instance?"

"Almost everybody."

"And I really do not know the names of a dozen people."

"Will you let me give you a lesson?"

"Oh, yes; I shall be much obliged."

"Then let us stand here, and we will take them as they pass to the supper-room."

So they stood near the door-way of the ball-room, and he ran on, exchanging constant nods and remarks with the passers-by, as the stream flowed to and from the ices and cup, and then rattling on to his partner with the names and short sketches of the characters and peculiarities of his large acquaintance. Mary was very much amused, and had no time to notice the ill-nature of most of his remarks; and he had the wit to keep within what he considered the most innocent bounds.

"There, you know him, of course," he said, as an elderly soldier-like looking man with a star, passed them.

"Yes; at least, I mean I know him by sight. I saw him at the Commemoration at Oxford last year. They gave him an honorary degree on his return from India."

"At Oxford! Were you at the Grand Commemoration then?"

"Yes. The Commemoration Ball was the first public ball I was ever at."

"Ah! that explains it all. I must have seen you there. I told you we had met before. I was perfectly sure of it."

"What! were you there, then!"

"Yes. I had the honor of being present at your first ball, you see."

"But how curious that you should remember me!"

"Do you really think so? Surely, there are some faces which, once seen, one can never forget."

"I am so glad that you know dear Oxford."

"I know it too well, perhaps, to share your enthusiasm."

"How do you mean?"

"I spent nearly three years there."

"What, were you at Oxford last year?"

"Yes; I left before Commemoration: but I went up for the gayeties, and I am glad of it, as I shall have one pleasant memory of the place now."

"Oh, I wonder you don't love it! But what college were you of?"

"Why, you talk like a graduate. I was of St. Ambrose."

"St. Ambrose! That is my college!"

"Indeed! I wish we had been in residence at the same time."

"I mean that we almost lived there at the Commemoration."

"Have you any relation there, then?"

"No, not a relation, only a distant connection."

"May I ask his name?"

"Brown. Did you know him?"

"Yes. We were not in the same set. He was a boating man, I think?"

She felt that he was watching her narrowly now, and had great difficulty in keeping herself reasonably composed. As it was she could not help showing a little that she felt embarrassed, and looked down; and changed color slightly, busying herself with her bouquet. She longed to continue the conversation, but somehow the manner of her partner kept her from doing so. She resolved to recur to the subject carelessly, if they met again, when she knew him better. The fact of his having been at St. Ambrose made her wish to know him better, and gave him a good start in her favor. But for the moment she felt that she must change the subject; so, looking up, she fixed on the first people who happened to be passing, and asked who they were.

"Oh, nobody. Constituents, probably, or something of that sort."

"I don't understand."

"Why, you see, we are in a political house to-night. So you may set down the people whom nobody knows, as troublesome ten-pounders, or that kind of thing, who would be disagreeable at the next election, if they were not asked."

"Then you do not include them in society?"

"By no manner of means."

"And I need not take the trouble to remember their faces?"

"Of course not. There is a sediment of rubbish at almost every house. At the parties here it is political rubbish. To-morrow night, at Lady Aubrey's—you will be there, I hope?"

"No, I think not."

"I am sorry for that. Well, there we shall have the scientific rubbish; and at other houses you see queer artists, and writing people. In fact, it is the rarest thing in the world to get a party where there is nothing of the kind, and, after all, it is rather amusing to watch the habits of the different species."

"Well, to me the rubbish, as you call it, seems much like the rest. I am sure those people were ladies and gentlemen."

"Very likely," he said, lifting his eyebrows; "but you may see at a glance that they have not the air of society. Here again, look yourself. You can see that these are constituents."

To the horror of St. Cloud, the advancing constituents made straight for his partner.

"Mary, my dear!" exclaimed the lady, "where have you been? We have lost you ever since the last dance."

"I have been standing here, mamma," she said; and then, slipping from her late partner's arm, she made a demure little bow, and passed into the ball-room with her father and mother.

St. Cloud bit his lip, and swore at himself, under his breath, as he looked after them. "What an infernal idiot I must have been not to know that her people would be sure to turn out something of that sort!" thought he. "By Jove, I'll go after them, and set myself right, before the little minx has time to think it over!" He took a step or two towards the ball-room, but then thought better of it, or his courage failed him. At any rate, he turned round again, and sought the refreshment-room, where he joined a knot of young gentlemen indulging in delicate little raised pies and salads, and liberal potations of iced claret or champagne cup. Amongst them was the guardsman, who had introduced him to Mary, and who received him, as he came up, with,—

"Well, St. Cloud, I hope you're alive to your obligations to me."

"For shunting your late partner on to me? Yes, quite."

"You be hanged!" replied the guardsman; "you may pretend what you please now, but you wouldn't let me alone till I had introduced you."

"Are you talking about the girl in white muslin with fern leaves in her hair?" asked another.

"Yes; what do you think of her?"

"Devilish taking, I think. I say, can't you introduce me? They say she has tin."

"I can't say I think much of her looks," said St. Cloud, acting up to his principle of telling a lie sooner than let his real thoughts be seen.

"Don't you?" said the guardsman. "Well, I like her form better than any thing out this year. Such a clean stepper! You should just dance with her."

And so they went on, criticising Mary and others of their partners, exactly as they would have a stud of racers, till they found themselves sufficiently refreshed to encounter new labors, and broke up, returning in twos and threes towards the ball-room.

St. Cloud attached himself to the guardsman, and returned to the charge.

"You seem hit by that girl," he began. "Have you known her long?"

"About a week — I met her once before to-night."

"Do you know her people? Who is her father?"

"A plain-headed old party — you wouldn't think it to look at her — but I hear he is very solvent."

"Any sons?"

"Don't know. I like your talking of my being hit, St. Cloud. There she is; I shall go and try for another waltz."

The guardsman was successful, and carried off Mary from her father and mother, who were standing together watching the dancing. St. Cloud, after looking them well over, sought out the hostess, and begged to be introduced to Mr. and Mrs. Porter, gleaning, at the same time, some particulars of who they were. The introduction was affected in a minute, the lady of the house being glad to get any one to talk to the Porters, who were almost strangers amongst her other guests. She managed, before leaving them, to whisper to Mrs. Porter that he was a young man of excellent connections.

St. Cloud made the most of his time. He exerted himself to the utmost to please, and, being fluent of speech, and thoroughly satisfied with himself, had no shyness or awkwardness to get over, and jumped at once into the good graces of Mary's parents. When she returned after the waltz, she found him, to her no small astonishment, deep in conversation with her mother, who was listening with a pleased expression to his small talk. He pretended not to see her at first, and then begged Mrs. Porter to introduce him formally to her daughter, though he had already had the honor of dancing with her.

Mary put on her shortest and coldest manner, and thought she had never heard of such impertinence. That he should be there talking so familiarly to her mother after the slip he had made to her was almost too much even for her temper. But she went off for another dance, and again returned and found him still there; this time entertaining Mr. Porter with political gossip. The unfavorable impression began to wear off, and she soon resolved not to make up her mind about him without some further knowledge.

In due course he asked her to dance again, and they stood up in a quadrille. She stood by him looking straight before her, and perfectly silent, wondering how he would open the conversation. He did not leave her long in suspense.

"What charming people your father and mother are, Miss Porter!" he said; "I am so glad to have been introduced to them."

"Indeed! You are very kind. We ought to be flattered by your study of us, and I am sure I hope you will find it amusing."

St. Cloud was a little embarrassed by the rejoinder, and was not sorry at the moment to find himself called upon to perform the second figure. By the time he was at her side again he had recovered himself.

"You can't understand what a pleasure it is to meet some one with a little freshness"—he paused to think how he should end his sentence.

"Who has not the air of society," she suggested. "Yes, I quite understand."

"Indeed, you quite mistake me. Surely, you have not taken seriously the nonsense I was talking just now?"

"I am a constituent, you know—I don't understand how to take the talk of society."

"Oh, I see, then, that you are angry at my joke, and will not believe that I knew your father perfectly by sight. You really cannot seriously fancy that I was alluding to any one connected with you;" and then he proceeded to retail the particulars he had picked up from the lady of the house, as if they had been familiar to him for years, and to launch out again into praises of her father and mother. Mary looked straight up in his face, and, though he did not meet her eye, his manner was so composed, that she began to doubt her own senses, and then he suddenly changed the subject to Oxford and the Commemoration, and by the end of the set could flatter himself that he had quite dispelled the cloud which had looked so threatening.

Mary had a great success that evening. She danced every dance, and might have had two or three partners at once, if they would have been of any use to her. When, at last, Mr. Porter insisted that he would keep his horses no longer, St. Cloud and the guardsman accompanied her to the door, and were assiduous in the cloak-room. Young men are pretty much like a drove of sheep; any one who takes a decided line on certain matters, is sure to lead all the rest. The guardsman left the ball in the firm belief, as he himself expressed it, that Mary "had done his business for life;" and, being quite above concealment, persisted in singing her praises over his cigar at the club, to which many of the dancers adjourned; and from that night she became the fashion with the set in which St. Cloud lived. The more enterprising of them he amongst the foremost, were soon intimate in Mr. Porter's house, and spoke well of his dinners. Mr. Porter changed his hour of riding in the park at their suggestion, and now he and his daughter were always sure of companions. Invitations multiplied, for Mary's success was so decided, that she floated her astonished parents into a whirl of balls and breakfasts. Mr. Porter and his wife were flattered themselves, and pleased to see their daughter admired and enjoying herself; and in the next six weeks Mary had the opportunity of getting all the good and the bad which a girl of eighteen can extract from a London season.

The test was a severe one. Two months of constant

excitement, of pleasure-seeking pure and simple, will not leave people just as they found them; and Mary's habits, and thoughts, and ways of looking at and judging of people and things, were much changed by the time that the gay world melted away from Mayfair and Belgravia, and it was time for all respectable people to pull down the blinds and shut the shutters of their town houses.

# CHAPTER XVI.

### WHAT CAME OF THE NIGHT-WATCH.

The last knot of the dancers came out of the club, and were strolling up St. James' Street, and stopping to chaff the itinerant coffee vendor, who was preparing his stand at the corner of Piccadilly for his early customers, just about the time that Tom was beginning to rouse himself under the alder tree, and stretch his stiffened limbs, and sniff the morning air. By the time the guardsman had let himself into his lodgings in Mount Street, our hero had undergone his unlooked-for bath, and was sitting in a state of utter bewilderment as to what was next to be said or done, dripping and disconcerted, opposite to the equally dripping, and, to all appearance, equally disconcerted, poacher.

At first he did not look higher than his antagonist's boots and gaiters, and spent a few seconds by the way in considering whether the arrangement of nails on the bottom of Harry's boots was better than his own. He settled that it must be better for wading on slippery stones, and that he would adopt it, and then passed on to wonder whether Harry's boots were as full of water as his own, and whether corduroys, wet through, must not be very uncomfortable so early in the morning, and congratulated himself on being in flannels.

And so he hung back for second after second, playing with any absurd little thought that would come into his head and give him ever so brief a respite from the effort of facing the situation, and hoping that Harry might do or say something to open the ball. This did not happen. He felt that the longer he waited the harder it would be. He must begin himself. So he raised his head gently, and took a sidelong look at Harry's face, to see whether he could not get some hint for starting, from it. But scarcely had he brought his eyes to bear, when they met Harry's, peering dolefully up from under his eyebrows, on which the water was standing unwiped, while a piece of green weed, which he did not seem to have presence of mind enough to remove, trailed over his dripping locks. There was something in the sight which tickled Tom's sense of humor. He had been prepared for sullen black looks and fierce words; instead of which he was irresistibly reminded of schoolboys caught by their master using a crib, or in other like flagrant delict.

Harry lowered his eyes at once, but lifted them the next moment with a look of surprise, as he heard Tom burst into a hearty fit of laughter. After a short struggle to keep serious, he joined in it himself.

"By Jove, though, Harry, it's no laughing matter," Tom said at last, getting on to his legs, and giving himself a shake.

Harry only replied by looking most doleful again, and picking the weed out of his hair, as he, too, got up.

"What in the world's to be done?"

"I'm sure I don't know, Master Tom."

"I'm very much surprised to find you at this work, Harry."

"I'm sure, so be I, to find you, Master Tom."

Tom was not prepared for this line of rejoinder. It seemed to be made with perfect innocence, and yet it put him in a corner at once. He did not care to inquire into the reason of Harry's surprise, or to what work he alluded; so he went off on another tack.

"Let us walk up and down a bit to dry ourselves. Now, Harry, you'll speak to me openly, man to man, as an old friend should — wont you?"

"Ay, Master Tom, and glad to do it."

"How long have you taken to poaching?"

"Since last Michaelmas, when they turned me out o' our cottage, and tuk away my bit o' land, and did all as they could to break me down."

"Who do you mean?"

"Why, Squire Wurley as was then — not this one, but the last — and his lawyer, and Farmer Tester."

"Then it was through spite to them that you took to it?"

"Nay, 'twarn't altogether spite, tho' I wont say but what I might ha' thought o' bein' upsides wi' them."

"What was it then besides spite?"

"Want o' work. I haven't had no more 'n a matter o' six weeks' reg'lar work ever since last fall."

"How's that? Have you tried for it?"

"Well, Master Tom, I wont tell a lie about it. I don't see as I wur bound to go round wi' my cap in my hand a beggin' for a day's work to the likes o' them. They knowed well enough as I wur there, ready and willing to work, and they knowed as I wur able to do as good a day's work as e'er a man in the parish; and ther's been plenty o' work goin', but they thought as I should starve, and have to come and beg for't from one or t'other on 'em. They would ha' liked to ha' seen me clean broke down, that's wut they would, and in the house," and he paused as if his thoughts were getting a little unmanageable.

"But you might have gone to look for work elsewhere."

"I can't see as I had any call to leave the place where I wur bred up, Master Tom. That wur just wut they wanted. Why should I let 'em drive m'out?"

"Well, Harry, I'm not going to blame you. I only want to know more about what has been happening to you, that I may be able to advise and help you. Did you ever try for work, or go and tell your story, at the Rectory?"

"Try for work there! No, I never went arter work there."

Tom went on without noticing the change in Harry's tone and manner,—

"Then I think you ought to have gone. I know my cousin, Miss Winter, is so anxious to help any man out of work, and particularly you; for —" The whole story of Patty flashed into his mind, and made him stop short, and stammer, and look anywhere except at Harry. How he could have forgotten it for a moment in that company was the wonder. All his questioning and patronizing powers went out of him, and he felt that their positions were changed, and that he was the culprit. It was clear that Harry knew nothing yet of his own relations with Patty. Did he even suspect them? It must all come out now at any rate, for both their sakes, however it might end. So he turned again, and met Harry's eye, which was now cold and keen, and suspicious.

"You knows all about it, then?"

"Yes; I know that you have been attached to Simon's daughter for a long time, and that he is against it. I wish I could help you with all my heart. In fact, I did feel my way towards speaking to him about it last year, when I was in hopes of getting you the gardener's place there. But I could see that I should do no good."

"I've heard say as you was acquainted with her when she was away?"

"Yes, I was, when she was with her aunt in Oxford. What then?"

"'Twas there as she larnt her bad ways."

"Bad ways! What do you mean?"

"I means as she larnt to dress fine, and to gee herself airs to them as she'd known from a child, and as'd ha' gone through fire to please her."

"I never saw any thing of the kind in her. She was a pleasant, lively girl, and dressed neatly, but never above her station. And I'm sure she has too good a heart to hurt an old friend."

"Wut made her keep shut up in the house when she cum back? ah, for weeks and weeks;—and arter that, wut made her so flighty and fickle? carryin' of herself as proud as a lady, a mincin' and a trapesin' along, wi' all the young farmers a follerin' her, like a fine gentleman's miss?"

"Come, Harry, I wont listen to that. You don't believe what you're saying, you know her better."

"You knows her well enough by all seemin'."

"I know her too well to believe any harm of her."

"What call have you and the likes o' you wi' her? 'Tis no good comes o' such company keepin'."

"I tell you again, no harm has come of it to her."

"Whose hair does she carry about then in that gold thing as she hangs round her neck?"

Tom blushed scarlet, and lowered his eyes without answering.

"Dost know? 'Tis thine, by —." The words came hissing out between his set teeth. Tom put his hands behind him, expecting to be struck, as he lifted his eyes, and said, —

"Yes, it is mine; and I tell you again, no harm has come of it."

"'Tis a lie. I knowed how 'twas, and 'tis thou hast done it."

Tom's blood tingled in his veins and wild words rushed to his tongue, as he stood opposite the man who had just given him the lie, and who waited his reply with clenched hands and laboring breast and fierce eye. But the discipline of the last year stood him in good stead. He stood for a moment or two crushing his hands together behind his back, drew a long breath, and answered, —

"Will you believe my oath, then? I stood by your side at your mother's grave. A man who did that wont lie to you, Harry. I swear to you there's no wrong between me and her. There never was fault on her side. I sought her. She never cared for me; she doesn't care for me. As for that locket, I forced it on her. I own I have wronged her, and wronged you. I have repented it bitterly. I ask your forgiveness, Harry; for the sake of old times, for the sake of your mother!" He spoke from the heart, and saw that his words went home. "Come, Harry," he went on, "you wont turn from an old playfellow, who owns the wrong he has done, and will do all he can to make up for it. You'll shake hands, and say you forgive me."

Tom paused, and held out his hand.

The poacher's face worked violently for a moment or two, and he seemed to struggle once or twice to get his hand out in vain. At last he struck it suddenly into Tom's, turning his head away at the same time. "'Tis what mother would ha' done," he said, "thou cassn't say more. There 'tis then, though I never thought to do't."

The curious and unexpected explanation brought thus to a happy issue, put Tom into high spirits, and at once roused the castle-building power within him, which was always ready enough to wake up.

His first care was to persuade Harry that he had better give up poaching, and in this he had much less difficulty than he expected. Harry owned himself sick of the life he was leading already. He admitted that some of the men with whom he had been associating more or less for the last year were the greatest blackguards in the neighborhood. He asked nothing better than to get out of it. But how?

This was all Tom wanted. He could see to that; nothing could be easier.

"I shall go with you back to Englebourn this morning. I'll just leave a note for Wurley to say that I'll be back some time in the day to explain matters to him, and then we will be off at once. We shall be at the Rectory by breakfast-time. Ah, I forgot; — well, you can stop at David's while I go and speak to my uncle and to Miss Winter."

Harry didn't seem to see what would be the good of this; and David, he said, was not so friendly to him as he had been.

"Then you must wait at the Red Lion. Don't see the good of it! Why, of course, the good of it is that you must be set right with the Englebourn people — that's the first thing to do. I shall explain how the case stands to my uncle, and I know I can get him to let you have your land again if you stay in the parish, even if he can't give you work himself. But what he must do is, to take you up, to show people that he is your friend, Harry. Well then, if you can get good work — mind it must be real, good, regular work — at Farmer Grove's, or one of the best farmers, stop here by all means, and I will take myself the first cottage which falls vacant and let you have it, and meantime you must lodge with old David. Oh, I'll go and talk him round, never fear. But if you can't get regular work here, why you go off with flying colors; no sneaking off under a cloud and leaving no address. You'll go off with me, as my servant, if you like. But just as you please about that. At any rate, you'll go with me, and I'll take care that it shall be known that I consider you as an old friend. My father has always got plenty of work and will take you on. And then, Harry, after a bit you may be sure all will go right, and I shall be your best man, and dance at your wedding before a year's out."

There is something in this kind of thing which is contagious and irresistible. Tom thoroughly believed all that he was saying; and faith, even of such a poor kind as believing in one's own castles, has its reward. Common sense in vain suggested to Harry that all the clouds which had been gathering round him for a year were not likely to melt away in a morning. Prudence suggested that the sooner he got away the better; which suggestion, indeed, he handed on for what it was worth. But Tom treated prudence with sublime contempt. They would go together, he said, as soon as any one was up at the house, just to let him in to change his things and write a note. Harry needn't fear any unpleasant consequences. Wurley wasn't an ill-natured fellow at bottom, and wouldn't mind a few fish. Talking of fish, where was the one he had heard kicking just now as Harry hauled in the line? They went to the place, and, looking in the long grass, soon found the dead trout, still on the night line, of which the other end remained in the water. Tom seized hold of it, and pulling it carefully in, landed another fine trout, while Harry stood by, looking rather sheepish. Tom inspected the method of the lines, which was simple but awfully destructive. The line was long enough to reach across the stream. At one end was a heavy stone, at the other a short stake cut sharp, and driven into the bank well under the water. At intervals of four feet along the line short pieces of fine gimp were fastened, ending in hooks baited alternately with lobworms and gudgeon. Tom complimented his companion on the killing nature of his cross-line.

"Where are your other lines, Harry?" he asked; "we may as well go and take them up."

"A bit higher up stream, Master Tom;" and so they walked up stream and took up the other lines.

"They'll have the finest dish of fish they've seen this long time at the house to-day," said Tom, as each line came out with two or three fine thick-shouldered fish on it; "I'll tell you what, Harry, they're deuced well set, these lines of yours, and do you credit. They do; I'm not complimenting you."

"I should rather like to be off, Master Tom, if you don't object. The mornin's gettin' on, and the men'll be about. 'Twould be unked for I to be caught."

"Well, Harry, if you're so set on it off with you, but—"

"'Tis too late now; here's keper."

Tom turned sharp round, and, sure enough, there was the keeper coming down the bank towards them, and not a couple of hundred yards off.

"So it is," said Tom; "well, only hold your tongue, and do just what I tell you."

The keeper came up quickly, and touching his hat to

Tom, looked inquiringly at him, and then at Harry. Tom nodded to him, as if every thing were just as it should be. He was taking a two-pound fish off the last line; having finished which feat, he threw it on the ground by the rest. "There, keeper," he said, "there's a fine dish of fish. Now pick 'em up and come along."

Never was keeper more puzzled. He looked from one to the other, lifting the little short hat from the back of his head, and scratching that somewhat thick skull of his, as his habit was when engaged in what he called thinking, conscious that somebody ought to be tackled, and that he, the keeper, was being mystified, but quite at sea as to how he was to set himself straight.

"Wet, bain't 'ee, sir?" he said at last, nodding at Tom's clothes.

"Dampish, keeper," answered Tom; "I may as well go and change, the servants will be up at the house by this time. Pick up the fish and come along. You do up the lines, Harry."

The keeper and Harry performed their tasks, looking at one another out of the corners of their eyes, like the terriers of rival butchers when the carts happen to stop suddenly in the street close to one another. Tom watched them, mischievously delighted with the fun, and then led the way up to the house. When they came to the stable-yard he turned to Harry, and said, "Stop here; I sha'n't be ten minutes;" adding in an undertone, "Hold your tongue now;" and then vanished through the back-door, and, hurrying up to his room, changed as quickly as he could.

He was within the ten minutes, but as he descended the back stairs in his dry things, became aware that his stay had been too long. Noise and laughter came up from the stable-yard, and shouts of "Go it keper,"

"Keper's down," "No he bain't," greeted his astonished ears. He sprang down the last steps and rushed into the stable-yard, where he found Harry at his second wrestling match for the day, while two or three stablemen, and a footman, and the gardener, looked on and cheered the combatants with the remarks he had heard on his way down.

Tom made straight to them, and tapping Harry on the shoulder, said, —

"Now then, come along; I'm ready."

Whereupon the keeper and Harry disengaged, and the latter picked up his cap.

"You bain't goin', sir?" said the keeper.

"Yes, keeper."

"Not along wi' he?"

"Yes, keeper."

"What, bain't I to take un?"

"Take him! No, what for?"

"For night poachin', look at all them fish," said the keeper indignantly, pointing to the shining heap.

"No, no, keeper; you've nothing to do with it. You may give him the lines though, Harry. I've left a note for your master on my dressing-table," Tom said, turning to the footman, "let him have it at breakfast. I'm responsible for him," nodding at Harry. "I shall be back in a few hours, and now come along."

And, to the keeper's astonishment, Tom left the stable-yard, accompanied by Harry.

They were scarcely out of hearing before the stable-yard broke out into uproarious laughter at the keeper's expense, and much rude banter was inflicted on him for letting the poacher go. But the keeper's mind for the moment was full of other things. Disregarding their remarks, he went on scratching his head, and burst out at last with, —

"Dang un; I knows I should ha' drowed un."

"Drow your grandmother," politely remarked one of the stablemen, an acquaintance of Harry Winburn, who knew his repute as a wrestler.

"I should, I tell 'ee," said the keeper, as he stooped to gather up the fish; "and to think as he should ha' gone off. Master'll be like any wild beast when he hears on't. Hows'mever, 'tis Mr. Brown's doin's. 'Tis a queer start for a gen'l'man like he to be goin' off wi' a poacher chap, and callin' of un Harry. 'Tis past me altogether. But I s'pose he baint right in's 'ead;" and, so soliloquizing, he carried off the fish to the kitchen.

Meantime, on their walk to Englebourn, Harry, in answer to Tom's inquiries, explained that in his absence the stableman, his acquaintance, had come up and begun to talk. The keeper had joined in and accused him point-blank of being the man who had thrown him into the furze bush. The story of the keeper's discomfiture on that occasion being well known, a laugh had been raised in which Harry had joined. This brought on a challenge to try a fall then and there, which Harry had accepted, notwithstanding his long morning's work and the ducking he had had. They laughed over the story, though Harry could not help expressing his fears as to how it might all end. They reached Englebourn in time for breakfast. Tom appeared at the Rectory, and soon he and Katie were on their old terms. She was delighted to find that he had had an explanation with Harry Winburn, and that there was some chance of bringing that sturdy offender once more back into decent ways;—more delighted perhaps to hear the way in which he spoke of

Patty, to whom after breakfast she paid a visit, and returned in due time with the unfortunate locket.

Tom felt as if another coil of the chain he had tied about himself had fallen off. He went out into the village, consulted again with Harry, and returned to the Rectory to consider what steps were to be taken to get him work. Katie entered into the matter heartily, though foreseeing the difficulties of the case. At luncheon the rector was to be sounded on the subject of the allotments. But in the middle of their plans they were startled by the news that a magistrate's warrant had arrived in the village for the arrest of Harry as a night poacher.

Tom returned to the Grange furious, and before night had had a worse quarrel with young Wurley than with his uncle before him. Had duelling been in fashion still in England they would probably have fought in a quiet corner of the park before night. As it was they only said bitter things, and parted, agreeing not to know one another in future.

Three days afterwards, at petty sessions, where Tom brought upon himself the severe censure of the bench for his conduct on the trial, Harry Winburn was committed to Reading gaol for three months.

Readers who will take the trouble to remember the picture of our hero's mental growth during the past year, attempted to be given in a late chapter, and the state of restless dissatisfaction into which his experiences and thoughts and readings had thrown him by the time long vacation had come round again, will perhaps be prepared for the catastrophe which ensued on the conviction and sentence of Harry Winburn at petty sessions.

Hitherto, notwithstanding the strength of the new and revolutionary forces which were mustering round it, there had always been a citadel holding out in his mind, garrisoned by all that was best in the Toryism in which he had been brought up — by loyalty, reverence for established order and established institutions; by family traditions, and the pride of an inherited good name. But now the walls of that citadel went down with a crash, the garrison being put to the sword, or making a way to hide in out-of-the-way corners, and wait for a reaction.

It was much easier for a youngster, whose attention was once turned to such subjects as had been occupying Tom, to get hold of wild and violent beliefs and notions in those days than now. The state of Europe generally was far more dead and hopeless. There were no wars, certainly, and no expectations of wars. But there was a dull, beaten-down, pent-up feeling abroad, as if the lid were screwed down on the nations, and the thing which had been, however cruel and heavy and mean, was that which was to remain to the end. England was better off than her neighbors, but yet in bad case. In the south and west particularly, several causes had combined to spread a very bitter feeling abroad amongst the agricultural poor. First amongst these stood the new poor law, the provisions of which were rigorously carried out in most districts. The poor had as yet felt the harshness only of the new system. Then the land was in many places in the hands of men on their last legs, the old sporting farmers, who had begun business as young men while the great war was going on, had made money hand over hand for a few years out of the war prices, and had tried to go on living with greyhounds and yeomanry uniforms — horse to ride and weapon to wear — through the hard years which had followed. These were bad masters in every way, unthrifty, profligate, needy, and narrow-minded. The younger men who were supplanting them were introducing machinery, threshing-machines, and winnowing-machines, to take the little bread which a poor man was still able to earn out of the mouths of his wife and children — so at least the poor thought and muttered to one another; and the mutterings broke out every now and then in the long nights of the winter months in blazing ricks and broken machines. Game preserving was on the increase. Australia and America had not yet become familiar words in every English village, and the labor market was everywhere overstocked; and last, but not least, the corn laws were still in force, and the bitter and exasperating strife in which they went out was at its height. And while Swing and his myrmidons were abroad in the counties, and could scarcely be kept down by yeomanry and poor law guardians, the great towns were in almost worst case. Here, too, emigration had not yet set in to thin the labor market; wages were falling, and prices rising; the corn-law struggle was better understood and far keener than in the country; and Chartism was gaining force every day, and rising into a huge threatening giant, waiting to put forth his strength, and eager for the occasion which seemed at hand.

You generation of young Englishmen, who were too young then to be troubled with such matters, and have grown into manhood since, you little know — may you never know! — what it is to be living the citizens of a divided and distracted nation. For the time that danger is past. In a happy hour, and so far as man can judge, in time, and only just in time, came the repeal of the corn laws, and the great cause of strife, and the sense of injustice passed away out of men's minds. The nation was roused by the Irish famine, and the fearful distress in other parts of the country, to begin looking steadily and seriously at some of the sores which were festering in its body, and undermining health and life. And so the tide had turned, and England had already passed the critical point, when 1848 came upon Christendom, and the whole of Europe leapt up into a wild blaze of revolution.

Is any one still inclined to make light of the danger that threatened England in that year, to sneer at the 10th of April, and the monster petition, and the monster meetings on Kennington and other commons? Well, if there be such persons amongst my readers, I can only say that they can have known nothing of what was going on around them and below them, at that time, and I earnestly hope that their vision has become clearer since then, and that they are not looking with the same eyes that see nothing, at the signs of to-day. For that there are questions still to be solved by us in England, in this current half-century, quite as likely to tear the nation in pieces as the corn laws, no man with half an eye in his head can doubt. They may seem little clouds like a man's hand on the horizon just now, but they will darken the whole heaven before long unless we can find wisdom enough amongst us to take the little clouds in hand in time, and make them descend in soft rain.

But such matters need not be spoken of here. All I want to do is to put my young readers in a position to understand how it was that our hero fell away into beliefs and notions, at which Mrs. Grundy and all decent people could only lift up eyes and hands in pious and respectable horror, and became, soon after the incarceration of his friend for night poaching, little better than a physical force Chartist at the age of twenty-one. In which unhappy condition we shall now have to take a look or two at him in future numbers.

## CHAPTER XVII.

#### HUE AND CRY.

At the end of a gusty, wild October afternoon a man leading two horses was marching up and down the little plot of short turf at the top of the Hawk's Lynch. Every now and then he would stop on the brow of the hill to look over the village, and seemed to be waiting for somebody from that quarter. After being well blown he would turn to his promenade again, or go in under the clump of firs, through which the rising south-west wind, rushing up from the vale below, was beginning to make a moan; and, hitching the horses to some stump or bush, and patting and coaxing them to induce them, if so might be, to stand quiet for awhile, would try to settle himself to leeward of one of the larger trees.

But the fates were against all attempts at repose. He had scarcely time to produce a cheroot from his case and light it under many difficulties, when the horses would begin fidgeting, and pulling at their bridles, and shifting round to get their tails to the wind. They clearly did not understand the necessity of the position, and were inclined to be moving stablewards. So he had to get up again, sling the bridles over his arm, and take to his march up and down the plot of turf; now stopping for a moment or two to try to get his cheroot to burn straight, and pishing and pshawing over its perverseness; now going again and again to the brow, and looking along the road which led to the village, holding his hat on tight with one hand — for by this time it was blowing half a gale of wind.

Though it was not yet quite the hour for his setting, the sun had disappeared behind a heavy bank of wicked slate-colored cloud, which looked as though it were rising straight up into the western heavens, while the wind whirled along and twisted into quaint shapes a ragged rift of light vapor, which went hurrying by, almost touching the tops of the moaning firs. Altogether an uncanny evening to be keeping tryst at the top of a wild knoll; and so thought our friend with the horses, and showed it, too, clearly enough, had any one been there to put a construction on his impatient movements.

There was no one nearer than the village, half a mile and more away; so, by way of passing the time, we must exercise our privilege of putting into words what he is half thinking, half muttering to himself, —

"A pleasant night I call this, to be out on a wild goose chase. If ever I saw a screaming storm brewing, there it comes. I'll be hanged if I stop up here to be caught in it for all the crack-brained friends I ever had in the world; and I seem to have a faculty for picking up none but cracked-brained ones. I wonder what the plague can keep him so long: he must have been gone an hour. There steady, steady, old horse. Confound this weed! What rascals tobacconists are! You never can get a cheroot now worth smoking. Every one of them goes spluttering up the side, or charring up the middle, and tasting like tow soaked in saltpetre and tobacco juice. Well, I suppose I shall get the real thing in India.

"India! In a month from to-day we shall be off. To hear our senior major talk, one might as well be going to the bottomless pit at once. Well, he'll sell out, that's a comfort. Gives us a step, and gets rid of an old ruffian.

I don't seem to care much what the place is like if we only get some work; and there will be some work there before long, by all accounts. No more garrison town life, at any rate. And if I have any luck — a man may get a chance there.

"What the deuce can he be about? This all comes of sentiment, now. Why couldn't I go quietly off to India without bothering up to Oxford to see him? Not but what it's a pleasant place enough. I've enjoyed my three days there uncommonly. Food and drink all that can be wished, and plenty of good fellows and good fun. The look of the place, too, makes one feel respectable. But, by George, if their divinity is at all like their politics, they must turn out a queer set of parsons — at least, if Brown picked up his precious notions at Oxford. He always was a headstrong beggar. What was it he was holding forth about last night? Let's see. 'The sacred right of insurrection.' Yes, that was it, and he talked as if he believed it all too; and, if there should be a row, which don't seem unlikely, by Jove I think he'd act on it in the sort of temper he's in. How about the sacred right of getting hung or transported? I shouldn't wonder to hear of that some day. Gad! suppose he should be in for an instalment of his sacred right to-night. He's capable of it, and of lugging me in with him. What did he say we were come here for? To get some fellow out of a scrape, he said — some sort of poaching radical foster-brother of his, who had been in gaol, and deserved it, too, I'll be bound. And we couldn't go down quietly into the village and put up at the public, where I might have sat in the tap, and not run the chance of having my skin blown over my ears, and my teeth down my throat, on this cursed look-out place, because he's *too well known* there. What does that mean? Upon my soul it looks bad. They may be lynching a J. P. down there, or making a spread eagle of the parish-constable at this minute, for any thing I know, and as sure as fate if they are I shall get my foot in it.

"It will read sweetly in the *Army News:* 'A court-martial was held this day at Chatham, president, Colonel Smith, of Her Majesty's 101st Regiment, to try Henry East, a lieutenant in the same distinguished corps, who has been under arrest since the 10th ult., for aiding and abetting the escape of a convict, and taking part in a riot in the village of Englebourn, in the county of Berks. The defence of the accused was that he had a sentimental friendship for a certain Thomas Brown, an undergraduate of St. Ambrose College, Oxford, etc., etc.; and the sentence of the court—'

"Hang it! It's no laughing matter. Many a fellow has been broken for not making half such a fool of himself as I have done, coming out here on this errand. I'll tell T. B. a bit of my mind as sure as—

"Hullo! didn't I hear a shout? Only the wind, I believe. How it does blow! One of these firs will be down, I expect, just now. The storm will burst in a quarter of an hour. Here goes! I shall ride down into the village, let what will come of it. Steady now, steady. Stand still, you old fool; can't you?

"There, now I'm all right. Solomon said something about a beggar on horseback. Was it Solomon, though? Never mind. He couldn't ride. Never had a horse till he was grown up. But he said some uncommon wise things about having nothing to do with such friends as T. B. So, Harry East, if you please, no more tomfoolery after to-day. You've got a whole skin, and a lieutenant's commission to make your way in the world with, and are troubled with no particular crotchets yourself that need ever get you into trouble. So just you keep clear of other people's. And if your friends must be mending the world, and poor man's plastering, and running their heads against stone walls, why, just you let go of their coat tails."

So muttering and meditating, Harry East paused a moment after mounting, to turn up the collar of the rough shooting coat which he was wearing, and button it up to the chin, before riding down the hill, when, in the hurly-burly of the wind, a shout came spinning past his ears, plain enough this time; he heard the gate at the end of Englebourn Lane down below him shut with a clang, and saw two men running at full speed towards him, straight up the hill.

"Oh! here you are at last," he said, as he watched them. "Well, you don't lose your time now. Somebody must be after them. What's he shouting and waving his hand for? I'm to bring the cavalry supports down the slope, I suppose. Well, here goes: he has brought off his pal the convict, I see —

"'Says he, you've 'scaped from transportation
    All upon the briny main,
So never give way to no temptation,
    And don't get drunk nor prig again!'

There goes the gate again. By Jove, what's that? Dragoons, as I'm a sinner! There's going to be the d———st bear-fight."

Saying which, Harry East dug his heels into his horse's sides, holding him up sharply with the curb at the same time, and in another moment was at the bottom of the solitary mound on which he had been perched for the last hour, and on the brow of the line of hill out of which it rose so abruptly, just at the point for which the two runners were making. He had only time to glance at the pursuers, and saw that one or two rode straight on the track of the fugitives, while the rest skirted away along a parish road which led up the hill-side by an easier ascent, when Tom and his companion were by his side. Tom seized the bridle of the led horse, and was in the saddle with one spring.

"Jump up behind," he shouted; "now then come along."

"Who are they?" roared East—in that wind nothing but a shout could be heard—pointing over his shoulder with his thumb as they turned to the heath.

"Yeomanry?"

"After you?"

Tom nodded, as they broke into a gallop, making straight across the heath towards the Oxford road. They were some quarter of a mile in advance before any of their pursuers showed over the brow of the hill behind them. It was already getting dusk, and the great bank of cloud was by this time all but upon them, making the atmosphere denser and darker every second. Then, first one of the men appeared who had ridden straight up the hill under the Hawk's Lynch, and, pulling up for a moment, caught sight of them and gave chase. Half a minute later, and several of those who had kept to the road were also in sight, some distance away on the left, but still near enough to be unpleasant; and they, too, after a moment's pause, were in full pursuit. At first the fugitives held their own, and the distance between them and their pursuers was not lessened, but it was clear that this could not last. Any thing that horseflesh is capable of, a real good Oxford hack, such as they rode, will do; but to carry two full-grown men at the end of a pretty long day, away from fresh horses and moderate weights, is too much to expect even of Oxford horse-flesh; and the gallant beast which Tom rode was beginning to show signs of distress when they struck into the road. There was a slight dip in the ground at this place, and a little further on the heath rose suddenly again, and the road ran between high banks for a short distance.

As they reached this point they disappeared for the moment from the yeomanry, and the force of the wind was broken by the banks, so that they could breath more easily, and hear one another's voices.

Tom looked anxiously round at the lieutenant, who shrugged his shoulders in answer to the look, as he bent forward to ease his own horse, and said,—

" Can't last another mile."

" What's to be done ? "

East again shrugged his shoulders, but said nothing.

" I know, Master Tom," said Harry Winburn.

" What ? "

" Pull up a bit, sir."

Tom pulled up, and his horse fell into a walk willingly enough, while East passed on a few strides ahead. Harry Winburn sprang off.

" You ride on, now, Master Tom," he said, " I knows the heath well; you let me bide."

" No, no, Harry, not I. I wont leave you now; so let them come, and be hanged."

East had pulled up, and listened to their talk.

" Look here, now," he said to Harry; " put your arm over the hind part of his saddle, and run by the side; you'll find you can go as fast as the horse. Now, you two push on, and strike across the heath. I'll keep the road, and take off this joker behind, who is the only dangerous customer."

" That's like you, old boy," said Tom, " then we'll meet at the first public beyond the heath ? " and they passed ahead in their turn, and turned on to the heath, Harry running by the side, as the lieutenant had advised.

East looked after them, and then put his horse into a steady trot, muttering, —

"Like me! yes, devilish like me: I know that well enough. Didn't I always play cat's-paw to his monkey at school? but that convict don't seem such a bad lot, after all."

Meantime Tom and Harry struck away over the heath, as the darkness closed in, and the storm drove down. They stumbled on over the charred furze roots, and splashed through the sloppy peat cuttings, casting anxious, hasty looks over their shoulders as they fled, straining every nerve to get on, and longing for night and the storm.

"Hark, wasn't that a pistol-shot?" said Tom, as they floundered on. The sound came from the road they had left.

"Look! here's some on 'em, then," said Harry; and Tom was aware of two horsemen coming over the brow of the hill on their left, some three hundred yards to the rear. At the same instant his horse stumbled, and came down on his nose and knees. Tom went off over his shoulder, tumbling against Harry, and sending him headlong to the ground, but keeping hold of the bridle; they were up again in a moment.

"Are you hurt?"

"No."

"Come along, then," and Tom was in the saddle again, when the pursuers raised a shout. They had caught sight of them now, and spurred down the slope towards them. Tom was turning his horse's head straight away, but Harry shouted, —

"Keep to the left, Master Tom, to the left, right on."

It seemed like running into the lion's jaws, but he yielded, and they pushed on down the slope on which they were. Another shout of triumph rose on the howling wind; Tom's heart sank within him. The enemy was closing on them every moment; another hundred yards, and they must meet at the bottom of the slope. What could Harry be dreaming of? The thought had scarcely time to cross his brain, when down went the two yeomen, horse and man, floundering in a bog above their horses' girths. At the same moment the storm burst on them, with driving mist and pelting rain. The chase was over. They could not have seen a regiment of men at fifty yards' distance.

"You let me lead the horse, Master Tom," shouted Harry Winburn; "I knowed where they was going; 'twill take they the best part o' the night to get out o' that, I knows."

"All right, let's get back to the road, then, as soon as we can," said Tom, surrendering his horse's head to Harry, and turning up his collar to meet the pitiless deluge which was driving on their flanks. They were drenched to the skin in two minutes; Tom jumped off, and plodded along on the opposite side of his horse to Harry. They did not speak; there was very little to be said under the circumstances, and a great deal to be thought about.

Harry Winburn probably knew the heath as well as any man living, but even he had much difficulty in finding his way back to the road through that storm. However, after some half-hour spent in beating about, they reached it, and turned their faces northwards towards Oxford. By this time night had come on; but the fury of the storm had passed over them, and the moon began to show every now and then through the driving clouds. At last Tom roused himself out of the brown study in which he had been hitherto plodding along, and turned down his coat collar, and shook himself, and looked up at the sky, and across at his companion, who was still leading the horse along mechanically. It was too dark to see his face, but his walk and general look was listless and dogged; at last Tom broke silence.

"You promised not to do any thing, after you came out, without speaking to me." Harry made no reply; so presently he went on, —

"I didn't think you'd have gone in for such a business as that to-night. I shouldn't have minded so much if it had only been machine-breaking; but robbing the cellar and staving in ale casks and maiming cattle — "

"I'd no hand in that," interrupted Harry.

"I'm glad to hear it. You were certainly leaning against the gate when I came up, and taking no part in it; but you were one of the leaders of the riot."

"He brought it on hisself," said Harry, doggedly.

"Tester is a bad man, I know that; and the people have much to complain of: but nothing can justify what was done to-night." Harry made no answer.

"You're known, and they'll be after you the first thing in the morning. I don't know what's to be done."

"'Tis very little odds what happens to me."

"You've no right to say that, Harry. Your friends — "

"I hain't got no friends."

"Well, Harry, I don't think you ought to say that after what has happened to-night. I don't mean to say that my friendship has done you much good yet; but I've done what I could, and — "

"So you hev', Master Tom, so you hev'."

"And I'll stick by you through thick and thin, Harry. But you must take heart and stick by yourself, or we shall never pull you through." Harry groaned, and then, turning at once to what was always uppermost in his mind, said,—

" 'Tis no good, now I've been in gaol. Her father wur allus agin me. And now, how be I ever to hold up my head at whoam? I seen her once arter I came out."

" Well, and what happened?" said Tom, after waiting a moment or two.

" She just turned red and pale, and was all flustered like, and made as though she'd have held out her hand: and then tuk and hurried off like a frighted hare, as though she heerd somebody a comin'. Ah! 'tis no good! 'tis no good!"

" I don't see any thing very hopeless in that," said Tom.

" I've knowed her since she wur that high," went on Harry, holding out his hand about as high as the bottom of his waistcoat, without noticing the interruption, " when her and I went a-gleanin' together. 'Tis what I've thought on, and lived for, and 'tis four year since she and I broke a sixpence auver't. And at times it sim'd as tho' 'twould all cum right, when my poor mother wur livin',— tho' her never tuk to it kindly, mother didn't. But 'tis all gone now! and I be that mad wi' myself, and mammered, and down, I be ready to hang myself, Master Tom; and if they just teks and transpworts me —"

" Oh, nonsense, Harry! You must keep out of that. We shall think of some way to get you out of that before morning. And you must get clear away, and go to work on the railways or somewhere. There's nothing to be down-hearted about so far as Patty is concerned."

" Ah! 'tis they as wears it as knows where the shoe pinches. You'd say different if 'twas you, Master Tom."

" Should I?" said Tom; and, after pausing a moment

or two, he went on. "What I'm going to say is in confidence. I've never told it to any man yet, and only one has found it out. Now, Harry, I'm much worse off than you at this minute. Don't I know where the shoe pinches? Why, I haven't seen — I've scarcely heard of — of — well, of my sweetheart — there, you'll understand that — for this year and more. I don't know when I may see her again. I don't know that she hasn't clean forgotten me. I don't know that she ever cared a straw for me. Now, you know quite well that you're better off than that."

"I bean't so sure o' that, Master Tom. But I be terrible vexed to hear about you."

"Never mind about me. You say you're not sure, Harry. Come, now, you said, not two minutes ago, that you two had broken a sixpence over it. What does that mean, now?"

"Ah! but 'tis four years gone. Her's bin a leadin' o' me up and down, and a dancin' o' me round and round, purty nigh ever since, let alone the time as she wur at Oxford, when —"

"Well, we wont talk of that, Harry. Come, will yesterday do for you? If you thought she was all right yesterday, would that satisfy you?"

"Ees; and summat to spare."

"You don't believe it, I see. Well, why do you think I came after you to-night? How did I know what was going on?"

"That's just what I've been a axin' o' myself as we cum along."

"Well, then, I'll tell you. I came because I got a note from her yesterday at Oxford." Tom paused, for he heard a muttered growl from the other side of the horse's head, and could see, even in the fitful moonlight, the

angry toss of the head with which his news was received.
"I didn't expect this, Harry," he went on presently,
"after what I told you just now about myself. It was a
hard matter to tell it at all; but, after telling you, I didn't
think you'd suspect me any more. However, perhaps
I've deserved it. So, to go on with what I was saying,
two years ago, when I came to my senses about her, and
before I cared for any one else, I told her to write if ever
I could do her a service. Any thing that a man could do
for his sister I was bound to do for her, and I told her so.
She never answered till yesterday, when I got this note,"
and he dived into the inner breast pocket of his shooting-
coat. "If it isn't soaked to pulp, it's in my pocket now.
Yes, here it is," and he produced a dirty piece of paper,
and handed it across to his companion. "When there's
light enough to read it, you'll see plain enough what she
means, though your name is not mentioned."

Having finished his statement, Tom retired into himself, and walked along watching the hurrying clouds.
After they had gone some hundred yards, Harry cleared
his throat once or twice, and at last brought out, —

"Master Tom."

"Well."

"You bean't offended wi' me, sir, I hopes?"

"No, why should I be offended?"

"'Cause I knows I be so all-fired jealous, I can't abear
to hear o' her talkin', let alone writin' to —"

"Out with it. To me, you were going to say."

"Nay, 'tis mwore nor that."

"All right, Harry, if you only lump me with the rest
of mankind, I don't care. But you needn't be jealous of
me, and you musn't be jealous of me, or I sha'n't be able
to help you as I want to do. I'll give you hand and
word on it, as man to man, there's no thought in my heart

24*

towards her that you mightn't see this minute. Do you believe me?"

"Ees, and you'll forgie—"

"There's nothing to forgive, Harry. But now you'll allow your case isn't such a bad one. She must keep a good look-out after you to know what you were likely to be about to-day. And if she didn't care for you she wouldn't have written to me. That's good sense, I think."

Harry assented, and then Tom went into a consideration of what was to be done, and, as usual, fair castles began to rise in the air. Harry was to start down the line at once, and take work on the railway. In a few weeks he would be captain of a gang, and then what was to hinder his becoming a contractor, and making his fortune, and buying a farm of his own at Englebourn? To all which Harry listened with open ears till they got off the heath, and came upon a small hamlet of some half-dozen cottages scattered along the road.

"There's a public here, I suppose," said Tom, returning to the damp realities of life. Harry indicated the humble place of entertainment for man and horse.

"That's all right. I hope we shall find my friend here;" and they went towards the light which was shining temptingly through the latticed window of the road-side inn.

## CHAPTER XVIII.

#### THE LIEUTENANT'S SENTIMENTS AND PROBLEMS.

"STOP! It looks so bright that there must be something going on. Surely, they can never have come on here already?"

Tom laid his hand on the bridle, and they halted on the road opposite the public-house, which lay a little back, with an open space of ground before it. The sign-post, and a long water-trough for the horses of guests to drink at, were pushed forward to the side of the road to intimate the whereabouts of the house, and the hack which Harry led was already drinking eagerly.

"Stay here for a minute, and I'll go to the window, and see what's up inside. It's very unlucky, but it will never do for us to go in if there are any people there."

Tom stole softly up to the window out of which the light came. A little scrap of a curtain was drawn across a portion of it, but he could see easily into the room on either side of the curtain. The first glance comforted him, for he saw at once that there was only one person in the kitchen; but who and what he might be was a puzzle. The only thing which was clear at a first glance was, that he was making himself at home.

The room was a moderate-sized kitchen, with a sanded floor, and a large fireplace; a high wooden screen, with a narrow seat in front of it, ran along the side on which the door from the entrance-passage opened. In the middle there was a long, rough, walnut table, on which stood a large loaf, some cold bacon and cheese, and a yellow jug; a few heavy rush-bottomed chairs and a settle composed the rest of the furniture. On the walls were a few samplers, a warming pan, and shelves with some common delf plates, and cups and saucers. But though the furniture was meagre enough, the kitchen had a look of wondrous comfort for a drenched mortal outside. Tom felt this keenly, and, after a glance round, fixed his attention on the happy occupant, with the view of ascertaining whether he would be a safe person to intrude on under the circumstances. He was seated on a low, three-cornered oak seat, with his back to the window, steadying a furze faggot on the fire with the poker. The faggot blazed and crackled, and roared up the chimney, sending out the bright, flickering light which had attracted them, and forming a glorious top to the glowing clear fire of wood embers beneath, into which was inserted a long, funnel-shaped tin, out of which the figure helped himself to some warm compound, when he had settled the faggot to his satisfaction. He was enveloped as to his shoulders in a heavy, dirty-white coat, with huge cape and high collar, which hid the back of his head, such as was then in use by country carriers; but the garment was much too short for him, and his bare arms came out a foot beyond the end of the sleeves. The rest of his costume was even more eccentric, being nothing more or less than a coarse flannel petticoat; and his bare feet rested on a mat in front of the fire.

Tom felt a sudden doubt as to his sanity, which doubt was apparently shared by the widow woman, who kept the house, and her maid-of-all-work, one or other of whom might be seen constantly keeping an eye on their guest from behind the end of the wooden screen. However, it was no time to be over particular; they must rest before going further, and, after all, it was only one man. So Tom thought, and was just on the point of calling Harry to come on, when the figure turned round towards the window, and the face of the lieutenant disclosed itself between the highpeaked gills of the carrier's coat. Tom burst into a loud laugh, and called out, —

"It's all right, come along."

"I'll just look to the hosses, Master Tom."

"Very well, and then come into the kitchen;" saying which, he hurried into the house, and after tumbling against the maid-of-all-work in the passage, emerged from behind the screen.

"Well, here we are at last, old fellow," he said, slapping East on the shoulder.

"Oh, it's you, is it? I thought you were in the lock-up by this time."

East's costume, as he sat looking up, with a hand on each knee, was even more ridiculous on a close inspection, and Tom roared with laughter again.

"I don't see the joke," said East, without moving a muscle.

"You would, though, if you could see yourself. You wonderful old Guy, where did you pick up that toggery?"

"The late lamented husband of the Widow Higgs, our landlady, was the owner of the coat. He also bequeathed to her several pairs of breeches, which I have vainly endeavored to get into. The late lamented Higgs was an abominably small man. He must have been very much her worse half. So, in default of other clothing, the widow has kindly obliged me by the loan of one of her own garments."

"Where are your own clothes?"

"There," said East, pointing to a clothes' horse, which

Tom had not hitherto remarked, which stood well into the chimney corner; "and they are dry, too," he went on, feeling them; "at least the flannel shirt and trousers are, so I'll get into them again."

"I say, ma'am," he called out, addressing the screen, "I'm going to change my things. So you had better not look in just now. In fact, we can call now if we want any thing."

At this strong hint the Widow Higgs was heard bustling away behind the screen, and after her departure East got into some of his own clothes again, offering the cast-off garments of the Higgs family to Tom, who, however declined, contenting himself with taking off his coat and waistcoat, and hanging them up on the horse. He had been blown comparatively dry in the last half-hour of his walk.

While East was making his toilet, Tom turned to the table, and made an assault on the bread and bacon, and then poured himself out a glass of beer and began to drink it, but was pulled up half way, and put it down with a face all drawn up into puckers by its sharpness.

"I thought you wouldn't appreciate the widow's tap," said East, watching him, with a grin. "Regular whistle-belly vengeance, and no mistake! Here, I don't mind giving you some of my compound, though you don't deserve it."

So Tom drew his chair to the fire, and smacked his lips over the long-necked glass, which East handed to him.

"Ah! that's not bad tipple after such a ducking as we've had. Dog's nose, isn't it?"

East nodded.

"Well, old fellow, I will say you're the best hand I know at making the most of your opportunities. I don't know any one else who could have made such a good brew out of that stuff and a drop of gin."

East was not to be mollified by any such compliment.

"Have you got any more such jobs as to-day's on hand? I should think they must interfere with reading."

"No. But I call to-day's a real good job."

"Do you? I don't agree. Of course it's a matter of taste. I have the honor of holding her majesty's commission; so I may be prejudiced perhaps."

"What difference does it make whose commission you hold? You wouldn't hold any commission, I know, which would bind you to be a tyrant and oppress the weak and the poor."

"Humbug about your oppressing! Who's the tyrant, I should like to know, the farmer, or the mob that destroys his property? I don't call Swing's mob the weak and the poor."

"That's all very well; but I should like to know how you'd feel if you had no work and a starving family. You don't know what the people have to suffer. The only wonder is that all the country isn't in a blaze; and it will be, if things last as they are much longer. It must be a bad time which makes such men as Harry Winburn into rioters."

"I don't know any thing about Harry Winburn. But I know there's a good deal to be said on the yeomanry side of the question."

"Well, now, East, just consider this—"

"No, I'm not in the humor for considering. I don't want to argue with you."

"Yes, that's always the way. You wont hear what a fellow's got to say, and then set him down for a mischievous fool, because he wont give up beliefs founded on the evidence of his own eyes and ears and reason."

"I don't quarrel with any of your beliefs. You've got 'em — I haven't — that's just the difference between us. You've got some sort of faith to fall back upon, in equality and brotherhood and a lot of cursed nonsense of that kind. So, I dare say, you could drop down into a navigator, or a shoe black, or something in that way to-morrow, and think it pleasant. You might rather enjoy a trip across the water at the expense of your country, like your friend the convict here."

"Don't talk such rot, man. In the first place, he isn't a convict — you know that, well enough."

"He is just out of prison, at any rate. However, this sort of thing isn't my line of country at all. So the next time you want to do a bit of gaol-delivery on your own hook, don't ask me to help you."

"Well, if I had known all that was going to happen, I wouldn't have asked you to come, old fellow. Come, give us another glass of your dog's-nose, and no more of your sermon, which isn't edifying."

The lieutenant filled the long-necked glass which Tom held out with the creaming mixture, which he was nursing in the funnel-shaped tin. But he was not prepared to waive his right to lecture, and so continued, while Tom sipped his liquor with much relish, and looked comically across at his old schoolfellow.

"Some fellows have a call to set the world right — I haven't. My gracious sovereign pays me seven and sixpence a day; for which sum I undertake to be shot at on certain occasions and by proper persons, and I hope when the time comes I shall take it as well as another. But that doesn't include turning out to be potted at like a woodcock on your confounded Berkshire wilds by a turnip-headed yeoman. It isn't to be done at the figure."

"What in the world do you mean?"

"I mean just what I say."

"That one of those blessed yeomanry has been shooting at you?"

"Just so."

"No, you don't really mean it? Wh-e-e-w! Then that shot we heard was fired at you. 'Pon my honor, I'm very sorry."

"Much good your sorrow would have done me if your precious countryman had held straight."

"Well, what can I say more, East? If there's any thing I can do to show you that I really am very sorry, and ashamed at having brought you into such a scrape, only tell me what it is."

"I don't suppose your word would go for much at the Horse Guards, or I'd ask you to give me a character for coolness under fire."

"Come, I see you're joking now, old fellow. Do tell us how it happened."

"Well, when you turned off across the common I pulled up for half a minute, and then held on at a steady, slow trot. If I had pushed on ahead, my friends behind would have been just as likely to turn after you as after me. Presently I heard Number One coming tearing along behind; and as soon as he got from between the banks, he saw me, and came straight after me down the road. You were well away to the left, so now I just clapped on a bit, to lead him further away from the right scent, and on he came whooping and hallooing to me to pull up. I didn't see why I hadn't just as good a right to ride along the road at my own pace as he; so the more he shouted, the more I didn't stop. But the beggar had the legs of me. He was mounted on something deuced like a thoroughbred, and gained on me hand over hand. At last when I judged he must be about twenty yards behind, I thought

I might as well have a look at him — so I just turned for a moment, and, by Jove, there was my lord, lugging a pistol out of his right holster. He shouted again to me to stop. I turned, ducked my head, and the next moment he pulled trigger and missed me."

"And what happened then?" said Tom, drawing a long breath.

"Why, I flatter myself I showed considerable generalship. If I had given him time to get at his other pistol, or his toasting-fork, it was all up. I dived into my pocket, where by good luck there was some loose powder, and copper caps, and a snuff-box; upset the snuff, grabbed a handful of the mixture, and pulled hard at my horse. Next moment he was by my side, lifting his pistol to knock me over. So I gave him the mixture right in his face, and let him go by. Up went both his hands, and away went he and his horse, somewhere over the common out of sight. I just turned round, and walked quietly back. I didn't see the fun of accepting any more attacks in rear. Then up rides Number Two, a broad-faced young farmer on a big gray horse, blowing like a grampus. He pulled up short when we met, and stared, and I walked past him. You never saw a fellow look more puzzled, I had regularly stale-mated him. However, he took heart, and shouted, had I met the captain? I said, a gentleman had ridden by on a bright bay. 'That was he: which way had he gone?' So I pointed generally over the common, and Number Two departed; and then down came the storm, and I turned again and came on here."

"The captain! It must have been Wurley, then, who fired at you."

"I don't know who it was. I only hope he wont be blinded."

"It's a strange business altogether," said Tom, looking into the fire, " I scarcely know what to think of it. We should never have pulled through but for you, that's certain."

"I know what to think of it well enough," said East. "But now let's hear what happened to you. They didn't catch you, of course?"

"No, but it was touch and go. I thought it was all up at one time, for Harry would turn right across their line. But he knew what he was about; there was a bog between us, and they came on right into it, and we left them floundering."

"The convict seems to have his head about him, then. Where is he, by the way? I'm curious to have a look at him."

"Looking after the horses. I'll call him in. He ought to have something to drink."

Tom went to the door, and called Harry, who came out from the rough shed which served as a stable in his shirt, with a whisp of hay in his hand. He had stripped off coat and waistcoat, and braces, and had been warming himself by giving the horses a good dressing.

"Why, Harry, you haven't had any thing," said Tom; "come across, and have a glass of something hot."

Harry followed into the kitchen, and stood by the end of the screen, looking rather uncomfortable, while Tom poured him out a glass of the hot mixture, and the lieutenant looked him over with keen eyes.

"There, take that off. How are the horses?"

"Pretty fresh, Master Tom. But they'd be the better of a bran mash or somethin' cumfable. I've spoken to the missus about it, and 'tis ready to put on the fire."

"That's right, then; let them have it as quick as you can."

"Then I med fetch it and warm it up here, sir?" said Harry.

"To be sure; the sooner the better."

Harry took off his glass, making a shy sort of duck with his head, accompanied by "Your health, sir," to each of his entertainers, and then disappeared into the back kitchen, returned with the mash, which he put on the fire, and went off to the stable again.

"What do you think of him?" said Tom.

"I like to see a fellow let his braces down when he goes to work," said East.

"It's not every fellow who would be strapping away at those horses, instead of making himself at home in the back kitchen."

"No, it isn't," said East.

"Don't you like his looks now?"

"He's not a bad sort, your convict."

"I say, I wish you wouldn't call him names."

"Very good; your unfortunate friend, then. What are you going to do with him?"

"That's just what I've been puzzling about all the way here: what do you think?" and then they drew to the fire again, and began to talk over Harry's prospects. In some ten minutes he returned to the kitchen for the mash, and this time drew a complimentary remark from the lieutenant.

Harry was passionately fond of animals, and especially of horses, and they found it out quickly enough, as they always do. The two hacks were by this time almost fresh again, with dry coats, and feet well washed and cleansed; and, while working at them, Harry had been thinking over all he had heard that evening, and found himself getting more hopeful every minute. No one who had seen his face an hour before on the heath would have believed it was the same man who was now patting and fondling the two hacks as they slowly ate up the mash he had prepared for them.  When they had finished he leant back against the manger, rubbing the ears of Tom's hack — the one which had carried double so well in their first flight — gently with his two hands, while the delighted beast bent down its head, and pressed it against him, and stretched its neck, expressing in all manner of silent ways its equine astonishment and satisfaction.  By the light of the single dip Harry's face grew shorter and shorter, until the old merry look began to creep back into it.

As we have already taken the liberty of putting the thoughts of his betters into words, we must now do so for him; and, if he had expressed his thoughts as he rubbed the hack's ears in the stable, his speech would have been much as follows: —

"How cums it as I be all changed like, as tho' sum un had tuk and rubbed all the down-heartedness out o' me? Here I be, two days out o' gaol, wi' nothin' in the world but the things I stands in — for in course I med just give up the bits o' things as is left at Daddy Collins' — and they all draggled wi' the wet — and I med be tuk in the mornin' and sent across the water — and yet I feels sumhow as peert as a yukkel. So fur as I can see, 'tis jest nothin' but talkin' wi' our Master Tom. What a fine thing 'tis to be schollard, and yet seemin'ly 'tis nothin' but talk arter all's said and done. But 'tis allus the same; whenever I gets talkin' wi' he, it all cums out as smooth as crame. Fust time as ever I seen him since we wur bwys he talked just as a do now; and then my poor mother died. Then he cum in arter the tuneral, and talked me up again, till I thought as I wur to hev our cottage and all the land as I could do good by; but our cottage wur tuk away, and my 'lotment besides. Then cum last summer, and 'twur jest the same agen arter his talk, but I got dree months auver that job. And now here I be wi' un agen, a runnin' from the constable, and like to be tuk up and transpworted, and 'tis just the same — and I s'pose 'twill be just the same if ever I gets back, and sees un, and talks wi' un, if I be gwine to be hung. 'Tis a wunnerful thing to be a schollard, to be able to make things look all straight when they be ever so akkered and unked."

And then Harry left off rubbing the horse's ears; and, pulling the damp piece of paper which Tom had given him out of his breeches pocket, proceeded to flatten it out tenderly on the palm of his hand, and read it by the light of the dip, when the landlady came to inform him that the gentlefolk wanted him in the kitchen. So he folded his treasure up again, and went off to the kitchen. He found Tom standing with his back to the fire, while the lieutenant was sitting at the table writing on a scrap of paper, which the landlady had produced after much hunting over of drawers. Tom began, with some little hesitation: —

"O Harry, I've been talking your matters over with my friend here, and I've changed my mind. It wont do after all for you to stay about at railway work, or any thing of that sort. You see you wouldn't be safe. They'd be sure to trace you, and you'd get into trouble about this day's work. And then, after all, it's a very poor opening for a young fellow like you. Now, why shouldn't you enlist into Mr. East's regiment? You'll be in his company, and it's a splendid profession. What do you say now?"

East looked up at poor Harry, who was quite taken aback at this change in his prospects, and could only mutter he had never turned his mind to "sodgerin."

"It's just the thing for you," Tom went on. "You can write and keep accounts, and you'll get on famously.

Ask Mr. East if you wont. And don't you fear about matters at home. You'll see that'll all come right. I'll pledge you my word it will, and I'll take care that you shall hear every thing that goes on there, and depend upon it, it's your best chance. You'll be back at Englebourn as a sergeant in no time, and be able to snap your fingers at them all. You'll come with us to Steventon station, and take the night train to London, and then in the morning go to Whitehall, and find Mr. East's sergeant. He'll give you a note to him, and they'll send you on to Chatham, where the regiment is. You think it's the best thing for him, don't you?" said Tom, turning to East.

"Yes; I think you'll do very well if you only keep steady. Here's a note to the sergeant, and I shall be back at Chatham in a day or two myself."

Harry took the note mechanically; he was quite unable yet to make any resistance.

"And now get something to eat as quick as you can, for we ought to be off. The horses are all right, I suppose?"

"Yes, Master Tom," said Harry, with an appealing look.

"Where are your coat and waistcoat, Harry?"

"They be in the stable, sir."

"In the stable! Why, they're all wet then still?"

"Oh, 'tis no odds about that, Master Tom."

"No odds! Get them in directly, and put them to dry here."

So Harry Winburn went off to the stable to fetch his clothes.

"He's a fine fellow," said East, getting up and coming to the fire; "I've taken a fancy to him, but he doesn't fancy enlisting."

"Poor fellow! he has to leave his sweetheart. It's a sad business, but it's the best thing for him, and you'll see he'll go."

Tom was right. Poor Harry came in and dried his clothes, and got his supper, and while he was eating it, and all along the road afterwards, till they reached the station at about eleven o'clock, pleaded in his plain way with Tom against leaving his own country side. And East listened silently, and liked him better and better.

Tom argued with him gently, and turned the matter round on all sides, putting the most hopeful face upon it; and, in the end, talked first himself, and then Harry, into the belief that it was the very best thing that could have happened to him, and more likely than any other course of action to bring every thing right between him and all folk at Englebourn.

So Harry got into the train at Steventon in pretty good heart, with his fare paid, and half a sovereign in his pocket, more and more impressed in his mind with what a wonderful thing it was to be a "schollard."

The two friends rode back to Oxford at a good pace. They had both of them quite enough to think about, and were not in the humor for talk, had place and time served, so that scarce a word passed between them, till they had left their horses at the livery stables, and were walking through the silent streets a few minutes before midnight. Then East broke silence.

"I can't make out how you do it. I'd give half a year's pay to get the way of it."

"The way of what? What are you talking about?"

"Why, your way of shutting your eyes, and going in blind."

"Well, that's a queer wish for a fighting man," said Tom, laughing. "We always thought a rusher no good at school, and that the thing to learn was to go in with your own eyes open, and shut up other people's."

"Ah, but we hadn't cut our eyeteeth then. I look at these things from a professional point of view. My business is to get fellows to shut their eyes tight, and I begin to think, you can't do it as it should be done, without shutting your own first."

"I don't take."

"Why, look at the way you talked your convict — I beg your pardon — your unfortunate friend — into enlisting to-night. You talked as if you believed every word you were saying to him."

"So I did."

"Well, I should like to have you for a recruiting sergeant, if you could only drop that radical bosh. If I had had to do it, instead of enlisting, he would have gone straight off and hung himself in the stable."

"I'm glad you didn't try your hand at it, then."

"Look again at me. Do you think any one but such a — well, I don't want to say any thing uncivil — a headlong dog like you could have got me into such a business as to-day's? Now I want to be able to get other fellows to make just such fools of themselves as I've made of myself to-day. How do you do it?"

"I don't know, unless it is that I can't help always looking at the best side of things myself, and so —"

"Most things haven't got a best side."

"Well a better, then."

"Nor a better."

"If they haven't got a better, of course, it don't matter."

"No, I don't believe it does — much. Still, I should like to be able to make a fool of myself, too, when I want — with the view of getting others to do ditto, of course."

"I wish I could help you, old fellow; but I don't see my way to it."

"I shall talk to our regimental doctor about it, and get put through a course of fool's-diet before we start for India."

"Flap-doodle, they call it, what fools are fed on. But it's odd that you should have broken out in this place, when all the way home I've been doing nothing but envying your special talent."

"What's that?"

"Just the opposite one — the art of falling on your feet. I should like to exchange with you."

"You'd make a precious bad bargain of it, then."

"There's twelve striking. I must knock in. Goodnight. You'll be round to breakfast at nine?"

"All right. I believe in your breakfasts, rather," said East, as they shook hands at the gate of St. Ambrose, into which Tom disappeared, while the lieutenant strolled back to the Mitre.

# CHAPTER XIX.

### THIRD YEAR.

East returned to his regiment in a few days, and at the end of the month the gallant 101st embarked for India. Tom wrote several letters to the lieutenant, inclosing notes to Harry with gleanings of news from Englebourn, where his escape on the night of the riot had been a nine-days' wonder, and, now that he was fairly "listed" and out of the way, public opinion was beginning to turn in his favor. In due course a letter arrived from the lieutenant, dated Cape Town, giving a prosperous account of the voyage so far. East did not say much about "your convict," as he still insisted on calling Harry; but the little he did say was very satisfactory, and Tom sent off this part of the letter to Katie, to whom he had confided the whole story, entreating her to make the best use of it in the interests of the young soldier. And, after this out-of-the-way beginning, he settled down into the usual routine of his Oxford life.

The change in his opinions and objects of interest brought him now into more intimate relations with a set of whom he had as yet seen little. For want of a better name, we may call them "the party of progress." At their parties, instead of practical jokes and boisterous mirth and talk of boats and bats and guns and horses, the highest and deepest questions of morals and politics and metaphysics were discussed, and discussed with a freshness and enthusiasm which is apt to wear off when doing has to take the place of talking, but has a strange charm of its own while it lasts, and is looked back to with loving regret by those for whom it is no longer a possibility.

With this set Tom soon fraternized, and drank in many new ideas, and took to himself also many new crotchets besides those with which he was already weighted. Almost all his new acquaintance were Liberal in politics, but a few only were ready to go all lengths with him. They were all Union men, and Tom, of course, followed the fashion, and soon propounded theories in that institution which gained him the name of Chartist Brown.

There was a strong mixture of self-conceit in it all. He had a kind of idea that he had discovered something which it was creditable to have discovered, and that it was a very fine thing to have all these feelings for, and sympathies with, the masses, and to believe in democracy and glorious humanity and a good time coming, and I know not what other big matters. And, although it startled and pained him at first to hear himself called ugly names, which he had hated and despised from his youth up, and to know that many of his old acquaintance looked upon him, not simply as a madman, but as a madman with snobbish proclivities; yet, when the first plunge was over, there was a good deal on the other hand which tickled his vanity, and was far from being unpleasant.

To do him justice, however, the disagreeables were such that, had there not been some genuine belief at the bottom, he would certainly have been headed back very speedily into the fold of political and social orthodoxy. As it was, amidst the cloud of sophisms and platitudes and big one-sided ideas half mastered, which filled his thoughts and overflowed in his talk, there was growing in him and taking firmer hold on him daily a true and broad sympathy for men as men, and especially for poor men as poor men, and a righteous and burning hatred against all laws, customs, or notions, which, according to his light, either were or seemed to be setting aside, or putting any thing else in the place of, or above the man. It was with him the natural outgrowth of the child's and boy's training (though his father would have been much astonished to be told so), and the instincts of those early days were now getting rapidly set into habits and faiths, and becoming a part of himself.

In this stage of his life, as in so many former ones, Tom got great help from his intercourse with Hardy, now the rising tutor of the college. Hardy was travelling much the same road himself as our hero, but was somewhat further on, and had come into it from a different country, and through quite other obstacles. Their early lives had been so different; and, both by nature and from long and severe self-restraint and discipline, Hardy was much the less impetuous and demonstrative of the two. He did not rush out, therefore (as Tom was too much inclined to do), the moment he had seized hold of the end of a new idea which he felt to be good for *him* and what *he* wanted, and brandish it in the face of all comers, and think himself a traitor to the truth if he wasn't trying to make everybody he met with eat it. Hardy, on the contrary, would test his new idea, and turn it over, and prove it as far as he could, and try to get hold of the whole of it, and ruthlessly strip off any tinsel or rose-pink sentiment with which it might happen to be connected.

Often and often did Tom suffer under this severe method, and rebel against it, and accuse his friend, both to his face and in his own secret thoughts, of coldness and want of faith, and all manner of other sins of omission and commission. In the end, however, he generally came round, with more or less of rebellion, according to the severity of the treatment, and acknowledged that, when Hardy brought him down from riding the high horse, it was not without good reason, and that the dust in which he was rolled was always most wholesome dust.

For instance, there was no phrase more frequently in the mouths of the party of progress than "the good cause." It was a fine, big-sounding phrase, which could be used with great effect in perorations of speeches at the Union, and was sufficiently indefinite to be easily defended from ordinary attacks, while it saved him who used it the trouble of ascertaining accurately for himself or settling for his hearers what it really did mean. But, however satisfactory it might be before promiscuous audiences, and so long as vehement assertion or declaration was all that was required to uphold it, this same "good cause" was liable to come to much grief when it had to get itself defined. Hardy was particularly given to persecution on this subject, when he could get Tom, and, perhaps, one or two others, in a quiet room by themselves. While professing the utmost sympathy for "the good cause," and a hope as strong as theirs that all its enemies might find themselves suspended to lamp-posts as soon as possible, he would pursue it into corners from which escape was most difficult, asking it and its supporters what it exactly was, and driving them from one cloud-land to another, and from "the good cause" to the "people's cause," "the cause of labor," and other like troublesome definitions, until the great idea seemed to have no shape or existence any longer even in their own brains.

But Hardy's persecution, provoking as it was for the time, never went to the undermining of any real conviction in the minds of his juniors, or the shaking of any thing which did not need shaking, but only helped them to clear their ideas and brains as to what they were talking and thinking about, and gave them glimpses — soon clouded over again, but most useful, nevertheless — of the truth, that there were a good many knotty questions to be solved before a man could be quite sure that he had found out the way to set the world thoroughly to rights, and heal all the ills that flesh is heir to.

Hardy treated another of his friend's most favorite notions even with less respect than this one of "the good cause." Democracy, that "universal democracy," which their favorite author had recently declared to be "an inevitable fact of the days in which we live," was, perhaps, on the whole the pet idea of the small section of liberal young Oxford, with whom Tom was now hand and glove. They lost no opportunity of worshipping it, and doing battle for it; and, indeed, did most of them very truly believe that that state of the world which this universal democracy was to bring about, and which was coming no man could say how soon, was to be in fact that age of peace and good-will which men had dreamed of in all times, when the lion should lie down with the kid, and nation should not vex nation any more.

After hearing something to this effect from Tom on several occasions, Hardy cunningly lured him to his rooms on the pretence of talking over the prospects of the boat club, and then, having seated him by the fire, which he himself proceeded to assault gently with the poker, propounded suddenly to him the question,—

"Brown, I should like to know what you mean by 'democracy'?"

Tom at once saw the trap into which he had fallen, and made several efforts to break away, but unsuccessfully;

and, being seated to a cup of tea, and allowed to smoke, was then and there grievously oppressed and mangled and sat upon, by his oldest and best friend. He took his ground carefully, and propounded only what he felt sure that Hardy himself would at once accept, — what no man of any worth could possibly take exception to. He meant much more, he said, than this, but for the present purpose it would be enough for him to say that, whatever else it might mean, democracy in his mouth always meant that every man should have a share in the government of his country.

Hardy, seeming to acquiesce, and making a sudden change in the subject of their talk, decoyed his innocent guest away from the thought of democracy for a few minutes, by holding up to him the flag of hero-worship, in which worship Tom was, of course, a sedulous believer. Then, having involved him in most difficult country, his persecutor opened fire upon him from masked batteries of the most deadly kind, the guns being all from the armory of his own prophets.

"You long for the rule of the ablest man, everywhere, at all times? To find your ablest man, and then give him power, and obey him — that you hold to be about the highest act of wisdom which a nation can be capable of?"

"Yes; and you know you believe that too, Hardy, just as firmly as I do."

"I hope so. But then, how about our universal democracy, and every man having a share in the government of his country?"

Tom felt that his flank was turned; in fact, the contrast of his two beliefs had never struck him vividly before, and he was consequently much confused. But Hardy went on tapping a big coal gently with the poker, and gave him time to recover himself and collect his thoughts.

"I don't mean, of course, that every man is to have an actual share in the government," he said, at last.

"But every man is somehow to have a share; and, if not an actual one, I can't see what the proposition comes to."

"I call it having a share in the government when a man has a share in saying who shall govern him."

"Well, you'll own that's a very different thing. But, let's see; will that find our wisest governor for us — letting all the foolishest men in the nation have a say as to who he is to be?"

"Come now, Hardy; I've heard you say that you are for manhood suffrage."

"That's another question; you let in another idea there; at present we are considering whether the *vox populi* is the best test for finding your best man. I'm afraid all history is against you."

"That's a good joke. Now, there I defy you, Hardy."

"Begin at the beginning, then, and let us see."

"I suppose you'll say, then, that the Egyptian and Babylonian empires were better than the little Jewish republic."

"Republic! well, let that pass. But I never heard that the Jews elected Moses, or any of the judges."

"Well, never mind the Jews; they're an exceptional case: you can't argue from them."

"I don't admit that. I believe just the contrary. But go on."

"Well, then, what do you say to the glorious Greek republics, with Athens at the head of them?"

"I say that no nation ever treated their best men so badly. I see I must put on a lecture in Aristophanes for your special benefit. Vain, irritable, shallow, suspicious old Demus, with his two oboli in his cheek, and doubting only between Cleon and the sausage-seller, which he shall choose for his wisest man — not to govern, but to serve his whims and caprices. You must call another witness, I think."

"But that's a caricature."

"Take the picture, then, out of Thucydides, Plato, Xenophon, how you will, and where you will — you wont mend the matter much. You shouldn't go so fast, Brown; you wont mind my saying so, I know. You don't get clear in your own mind before you pitch into every one who comes across you, and so do your own side (which I admit is often the right one) more harm than good."

Tom couldn't stand being put down so summarily, and fought over the ground from one country to another, from Rome to the United States, with all the arguments he could master, but with little success. That unfortunate first admission of his, he felt it throughout like a millstone round his neck, and could not help admitting to himself, when he left, that there was a good deal in Hardy's concluding remark, "You'll find it rather a tough business to get your 'universal democracy,' and 'government by the wisest,' to pull together in one coach."

Notwithstanding all such occasional reverses and cold baths, however, Tom went on strengthening himself in his new opinions, and maintaining them with all the zeal of a convert. The shelves of his bookcase, and the walls of his rooms, soon began to show signs of the change which was taking place in his ways of looking at men and things. Hitherto a framed engraving of George III. had hung over his mantelpiece; but early in this, his third year, the frame had disappeared for a few days, and when it re-appeared, the solemn face of John Milton looked out from it, while the honest monarch had retired into a portfolio. A fac-simile of Magna Charta soon displaced a large colored print of "A Day with the Pychelcy;" and soon afterwards the death-warrant of Charles I. with its grim and resolute rows of signatures and seals, appeared on the wall in a place of honor, in the neighborhood of Milton.

Squire Brown was passing through Oxford, and paid his son a visit soon after this last arrangement had been completed. He dined in hall, at the high table, being still a member of the college, and afterwards came with Hardy to Tom's rooms to have a quiet glass of wine, and spend the evening with his son and a few of his friends, who had been asked to meet "the governor."

Tom had a struggle with himself whether he should not remove the death-warrant into his bedroom for the evening, and had actually taken it down with this view; but in the end he could not stomach such a backsliding, and so restored it to its place. "I have never concealed my opinions from my father," he thought, "though I don't think he quite knows what they are. But if he doesn't, he ought, and the sooner the better. I should be a sneak to try to hide them. I know he wont like it, but he is always just and fair, and will make allowances. At any rate, up it goes again."

And so he rehung the death-warrant, but with the devout secret hope that his father might not see it.

The wine-party went off admirably. The men were nice, gentlemanly, intelligent fellows; and the squire, who had been carefully planted by Tom with his back to the death-warrant, enjoyed himself very much. At last they all went, except Hardy; and now the nervous time approached. For a short time longer the three sat at the wine-table, while the squire enlarged upon the great improvement in young men, and the habits of the university, especially in the matter of drinking. Tom had only opened three bottles of port. In his time the men would have drunk certainly not less than a bottle a man; and other like remarks he made, as he sipped his coffee, and then, pushing back his chair, said, "Well, Tom, hadn't your servant better clear away? and then we can draw round the fire, and have a talk."

"Wouldn't you like to take a turn while he is clearing? There's the Martyr's Memorial you haven't seen."

"No, thank you. I know the place well enough. I don't come to walk about in the dark. We sha'n't be in your man's way."

And so Tom's scout came in to clear away, took out the extra leaves of his table, put on the cloth, and laid tea. During these operations Mr. Brown was standing with his back to the fire, looking about him as he talked: when there was more space to move in, he began to walk up and down, and very soon took to remarking the furniture and arrangements of the room. One after another the pictures came under his notice, — most of them escaped without comment, the squire simply pausing a moment, and then taking up his walk again. Magna Charta drew forth his hearty approval. It was a capital notion to hang such things on your walls, instead of bad prints of steeple-chases, or trash of that sort. "Ah, here's something else of the same kind. Why, Tom, what's this?" said the squire, as he paused before the death-warrant. There was a moment or two of dead silence, while the squire's eye ran down the names, from Jo. Bradshaw to Miles Corbet; and then he turned, and came and sat down opposite to his son. Tom expected his father to be vexed, but was not the least prepared for the tone of pain and sorrow and anger, in which he first inquired, and then remonstrated.

For some time past the squire and his son had not felt

so comfortable together as of old. Mr. Brown had been annoyed by much that Tom had done in the case of Harry Winburn, though he did not know all. There had sprung up a barrier somehow or other between them, neither of them knew how. They had often felt embarrassed at being left alone together during the last year, and found that there were certain topics which they could not talk upon, which they avoided by mutual consent. Every now and then the constraint and embarrassment fell off for a short time, for at bottom they loved and appreciated one another heartily; but the divergences in their thoughts and habits had become very serious, and seemed likely to increase rather than not. They felt keenly the chasm between the two generations; as they looked at one another from the opposite banks, each in his secret heart blamed the other in great measure for that which was the fault of neither. Mixed with the longings which each felt for a better understanding was enough of reserve and indignation to prevent them from coming to it. The discovery of their differences was too recent, and they were too much alike in character and temper for either to make large enough allowances for, or to be really tolerant of, the other.

This was the first occasion on which they had come to outspoken and serious difference, and, though the collision had been exceedingly painful to both, yet, when they parted for the night, it was with a feeling of relief that the ice had been thoroughly broken. Before his father left the room, Tom had torn the fac-simile of the death-warrant out of its frame, and put it in the fire, protesting, however, at the same time, that, though "he did this out of deference to his father, and was deeply grieved at having given him pain, he could not and would not give up his honest convictions, or pretend that they were changed, or even shaken."

The squire walked back to his hotel deeply moved.

Who can wonder? He was a man full of living and vehement convictions. One of his early recollections had been the arrival in England of the news of the beheading of Louis XVI., and the doings of the reign of terror. He had been bred in the times when it was held impossible for a gentleman or a Christian to hold such views as his son had been maintaining, and, like many of the noblest Englishmen of his time, had gone with and accepted the creed of the day.

Tom remained behind, dejected and melancholy; now accusing his father of injustice and bigotry, now longing to go after him, and give up every thing. What were all his opinions and convictions compared with his father's confidence and love? At breakfast the next morning, however, after each of them had had time for thinking over what had passed, they met with a cordiality which was as pleasant to each as it was unlooked for; and from this visit of his father to him at Oxford Tom dated a new and more satisfactory epoch in their intercourse.

The fact had begun to dawn on the squire that the world had changed a good deal since his time. He saw that young men were much improved in some ways, and acknowledged the fact heartily; on the other hand, they had taken up with a lot of new notions which he could not understand, and thought mischievous and bad. Perhaps Tom might get over them as he got to be older and wiser, and in the mean time he must take the evil with the good. At any rate, he was too fair a man to try to dragoon his son out of any thing which he really believed. Tom on his part gratefully accepted the change in his father's manner, and took all means of showing his gratitude by consulting and talking freely to him on such subjects as they could agree upon, which were numerous, keeping in the background the questions which had provoked painful discussions between them. By degrees these even could be tenderly approached; and, now, that they were approached in a different spirit, the honest beliefs of the father and son no longer looked so monstrous to one another, the hard and sharp outlines began to wear off, and the views of each of them to be modified. Thus, bit by bit, by a slow but sure process, a better understanding than ever was re-established between them.

This beginning of a better state of things in his relations with his father consoled Tom for many other matters that seemed to go wrong with him, and was a constant bit of bright sky to turn to when the rest of his horizon looked dark and dreary, as it did often enough.

For it proved a very trying year to him, this his third and last year at the university; a year full of large dreams and small performances, of unfulfilled hopes, and struggles to set himself right, ending ever more surely in failure and disappointment. The common pursuits of the place had lost their freshness, and with it much of their charm. He was beginning to feel himself in a cage, and to beat against the bars of it.

Often, in spite of all his natural hopefulness, his heart seemed to sicken and turn cold, without any apparent reason; his old pursuits palled on him, and he scarcely cared to turn to new ones. What was it that made life so blank to him at these times? How was it that he could not keep the spirit within him alive and warm?

It was easier to ask such questions than to get an answer. Was it not this place he was living in, and the ways of it? No, for the place and its ways were the same as ever, and his own way of life in it better than ever before. Was it the want of sight or tidings of Mary? Sometimes he thought so, and then cast the thought away as treason. His love for her was ever sinking deeper into him, and raising and purifying him. Light and strength and life came from that source; craven weariness and coldness of heart, come from whence they might, were not from that quarter. But, precious as his love was to him, and deeply as it affected his whole life, he felt that there must be something beyond it — that its full satisfaction would not be enough for him. The bed was too narrow for a man to stretch himself on. What he was in search of must underlie and embrace his human love, and support it. Beyond and above all private and personal desires and hopes and longings he was conscious of a restless craving and feeling about after something which he could not grasp, and yet which was not avoiding him, which seemed to be mysteriously laying hold of him and surrounding him.

The routine of chapels and lectures and reading for degree, boating, cricketing, Union debating — all well enough in their way — left this vacuum unfilled. There was a great outer visible world, the problems and puzzles of which were rising before him and haunting him more and more; and a great inner and invisible world opening round him in awful depth. He seemed to be standing on the brink of each — now, shivering and helpless, feeling like an atom, about to be whirled into the great flood and carried he knew not where — now, ready to plunge in and take his part, full of hope and belief that he was meant to buffet in the strength of a man with the seen and the unseen, and to be subdued by neither.

In such a year as this a bit of steady, bright, blue sky was a boon beyond all price, and so he felt it to be. And it was not only with his father that Tom regained lost ground in this year. He was in a state of mind in which he could not bear to neglect or lose any particle of human sympathy, and so he turned to old friendships, and revived the correspondence with several of his old schoolfellows, and particularly with Arthur, to the great delight of the latter, who had mourned bitterly over the few half-yearly lines, all he had got from Tom of late, in answer to his own letters, which had themselves, under the weight of neglect, gradually dwindled down to mere formal matters. A specimen of the later correspondence may fitly close the chapter,—

"*St. Ambrose.*

" Dear Geordie,—I can hardly pardon you for having gone to Cambridge, though you have got a Trinity scholarship—which I suppose is, on the whole, quite as good a thing as any thing of the sort you could have got up here. I had so looked forward to having you here though, and now I feel that we shall probably scarcely ever meet. You will go your way and I mine; and one alters so quickly, and gets into such strange new grooves, that, unless one sees a man about once a week at least, you may be just like strangers when you are thrown together again. If you had come up here it would have been all right, and we should have gone on all through life as we were when I left school, and as I know we should be again in no time if you had come here. But now who can tell?

" What makes me think so much of this is a visit of a few days that East paid me just before his regiment went to India. I feel that if he hadn't done it, and we had not met till he came back,—years hence perhaps,—we should never have been to one another what we shall be now. The break would have been too great. Now it's all right. You would have so liked to see the old fellow grown into a man, but not a bit altered—just the quiet, old way, pooh poohing you, and pretending to care for nothing, but ready to cut the nose off his face, or go through fire and water for you at a pinch if you'll only let him go his own way about it, and have his grumble, and say that he does it all from the worst possible motives.

"But we must try not to lose hold of one another, Geordie. It would be a bitter day to me if I thought any thing of the kind could ever happen again. We must write more to one another. I've been awfully lazy, I know, about it for this last year and more; but then I always thought you would be coming up here, and so that it didn't matter much. But now I will turn over a new leaf, and write to you about 'my secret thoughts, my works, and ways;' and you must do it too. If we can only tide over the next year or two we shall get into plain sailing, and I suppose it will all go right then. At least, I can't believe that one is likely to have many such up-and-down years in one's life as the last two. If one is, goodness knows where I shall end. You know the outline of what has happened to me from my letters, and the talks we have had in my flying visits to the old school; but you haven't a notion of the troubles of mind I've been in, and the changes I've gone through. I can hardly believe it myself when I look back. However, I'm quite sure I have *got on;* that's my great comfort. It is a strange blind sort of world, that's a fact, with lots of blind alleys, down which you go blundering in the fog after some seedy gaslight, which you take for the sun till you run against the wall at the end, and find out that the light is a gaslight, and that there's no thoroughfare. But for all that one does get on. You get to know the sun's light better and better, and to keep out of the blind alleys; and I am surer and surer every day, that there's always sunlight enough for every honest fellow,— though I didn't think so a few months back,—and a good sound road under his feet, if he will only step out on it.

"Talking of blind alleys puts me in mind of your last. Aren't you going down a blind alley, or something worse? There's no wall to bring you up, that I can see, down the turn you've taken; and then, what's the practical use of it all? What good would you do to yourself, or any one else, if you could get to the end of it? I can't for the life of me fancy, I confess, what you think will come of speculating about necessity and free will. I only know that I can hold out my hand before me, and can move it to the right or left, despite of all powers in heaven or earth. As I sit here writing to you I can let into my heart, and give the reins to, all sorts of devils' passions, or to the spirit of God. Well, that's enough for me. I *know* it of myself, and I believe you know it of yourself, and everybody knows it of themselves or himself; and why you can't be satisfied with that, passes my comprehension. As if one hasn't got puzzles enough, and bothers enough, under one's nose, without going a-field after a lot of metaphysical quibbles. No, I'm wrong,—not going a-field,—any thing one has to go a-field for is all right. What a fellow meets outside himself he isn't responsible for, and must do the best he can with. But to go on forever looking inside of one's self, and groping about amongst one's own sensations and ideas and whimsies of one kind and another, I can't conceive a poorer line of business than that. Don't you get into it now, that's a dear boy.

"Very likely you'll tell me you can't help it; that every one has his own difficulties, and must fight them out, and that mine are one sort, and yours another. Well, perhaps you may be right. I hope I'm getting to know that my plummet isn't to measure all the world. But it does seem a pity that men shouldn't be thinking about how to cure some of the wrongs which poor dear old England is pretty near dying of, instead of taking the edge off their brains, and spending all their steam in speculating about all kinds of things, which wouldn't make any poor man in the world — or rich one either, for that matter — a bit better off, if they were all found out, and settled to-morrow. But here I am at the end of my paper. Don't be angry at my jobation; but write me a long answer of your own free will, and believe me ever affectionately yours, T. B."

## CHAPTER XX.

### AFTERNOON VISITORS.

Miss Mary Porter was sitting alone in the front drawing-room of her father's house, in Belgravia, on the afternoon of a summer's day in this same year. Two years and more have passed over her head since we first met her, and she may be a thought more sedate and better dressed, but there is no other change to be noticed in her. The room was for the most part much like other rooms in that quarter of the world. There were few luxuries in the way of furniture which fallen man can desire which were not to be found there; but, over and above this, there was an elegance in the arrangement of all the knick-knacks and ornaments, and an appropriateness and good taste in the placing of every piece of furniture and vase of flowers, which showed that a higher order of mind than the upholsterer's or housemaid's was constantly overlooking and working there. Every thing seemed to be in its exact place, in the best place which could have been thought of for it, and to be the best thing which could have been thought of for the place; and yet this perfection did not strike you particularly at first, or surprise you in any way, but sank into you gradually, so that, until you forced yourself to consider the matter, you could not in the least say why the room had such a very pleasant effect on you.

The young lady to whom this charm was chiefly owing was sitting by a buhl work-table, on which lay her embroidery and a book. She was reading a letter, which seemed deeply to interest her; for she did not hear the voice of the butler, who had just opened the door and disturbed her solitude, until he had repeated for the second time, "Mr. Smith." Then Mary jumped up, and, hastily folding her letter, put it into her pocket. She was rather provoked at having allowed herself to be caught there alone by afternoon visitors, and with the servants for having let any one in; nevertheless, she welcomed Mr. Smith with a cordiality of manner which perhaps rather more than represented her real feelings, and, with a "let mamma know," to the butler, set to work to entertain her visitor. She would have had no difficulty in doing this under ordinary circumstances, as all that Mr. Smith wanted was a good listener. He was a somewhat heavy and garrulous old gentleman, with many imaginary, and a few real, troubles, the constant contemplation of which served to occupy the whole of his own time, and as much of his friends' as he could get them to give him. But scarcely had he settled himself comfortably in an easy-chair opposite to his victim, when the butler entered again, and announced "Mr. St. Cloud."

Mary was now no longer at her ease. Her manner of receiving her new visitor was constrained; and yet it was clear that he was on easy terms in the house. She asked the butler where his mistress was, and heard with vexation that she had gone out, but was expected home almost immediately. Charging him to let her mother know the moment she returned, Mary turned to her unwelcome task, and sat herself down again with such resignation as she was capable of at the moment. The conduct of her visitors was by no means calculated to restore her composure, or make her comfortable between them. She was sure that they knew one another; but neither of them would speak to the other. There the two sat on, each resolutely bent on tiring the other out; the elder crooning on to her in an undertone, and ignoring the younger, who in his turn put on an air of serene unconsciousness of the presence of his senior, and gazed about the room, and watched Mary, making occasional remarks to her as if no one else were present. On and on they sat, her only comfort being the hope that neither of them would have the conscience to stay on after the departure of the other.

Between them Mary was driven to her wits' end, and looked for her mother or for some new visitor to come to her help, as Wellington looked for the Prussians on the afternoon of June 18th. At last youth and insolence prevailed, and Mr. Smith rose to go. Mary got up too, and after his departure remained standing, in hopes that her other visitor would take the hint and follow the good example. But St. Cloud had not the least intention of moving.

"Really, your good-nature is quite astonishing, Miss Porter," he said, leaning forwards with his elbows on his knees, and following the pattern of one of the flowers on the carpet with his cane, which gave him the opportunity of showing his delicately gloved hand to advantage.

"Indeed, why do you think so?" she asked; taking up her embroidery, and pretending to begin working.

"Have I not got good reason, after sitting this half-hour and seeing you enduring old Smith — the greatest bore in London? I don't believe there are three houses where the servants dare let him in. It would be as much as their places were worth. No porter could hope for a character who let him in twice in the season."

"Poor Mr. Smith," said Mary, smiling. "But you know we have no porter, and," she suddenly checked herself, and added, gravely, "he is an old friend, and papa and mamma like him."

"But the wearisomeness of his grievances! those three sons in the Plungers, and their eternal scrapes! How you could manage to keep a civil face! It was a masterpiece of polite patience."

"Indeed, I am very sorry for his troubles. I wonder where mamma can be? We are going to drive. Shall you be in the Park? I think it must be time for me to dress."

"I hope not. It is so seldom that I see you, except in crowded rooms. Can you wonder that I should value such a chance as this?"

"Were you at the new opera last night?" asked Mary, carefully avoiding his eye, and sticking to her work, but scarcely able to conceal her nervousness and discomfort.

"Yes, I was there; but —"

"Oh, do tell me about it, then; I hear it was a great success."

"Another time. We can talk of the opera anywhere. Let me speak now of something else. You must have seen, Miss Porter —"

"How can you think I will talk of any thing till you have told me about the opera?" interrupted Mary, rapidly and nervously. "Was Grisi very fine? The chief part was composed for her, was it not? and dear old Lablache —"

"I will tell you all about it presently if you will let me, in five minutes' time — I only ask for five minutes —"

"Five minutes! Oh, no, not five seconds. I must hear about the new opera before I will listen to a word of any thing else."

"Indeed, Miss Porter, you must pardon me for disobeying. But I may not have such a chance as this again for months."

With which prelude he drew his chair towards hers, and Mary was just trying to make up her mind to jump up and run right out of the room, when the door opened, and the butler walked in with a card on a waiter. Mary had never felt so relieved in her life, and could have hugged the solemn old domestic when he said, presenting the card to her, —

"The gentleman asked if Mrs. or you were in, Miss, and told me to bring it up, and find whether you would see him on business. A clergyman, I think, Miss. He's waiting in the hall."

"Oh, yes, I know. Of course. Yes, say I will see him directly. I mean, ask him to come up now."

"Shall I show him into the library, Miss?"

"No, no; in here; do you understand?"

"Yes, Miss," replied the butler, with a deprecatory look at St. Cloud, as much as to say, "You see I can't help it," in answer to his impatient telegraphic signals. St. Cloud had been very liberal to the Porters' servants.

Mary's confidence had all come back. Relief was at hand. She could trust herself to hold St. Cloud at bay now, as it could not be for more than a few minutes. When she turned to him the nervousness had quite gone out of her manner, and she spoke in her old tone again, as she laid her embroidery aside.

"How lucky that you should be here. Look; I think you must be acquainted," she said, holding out the card which the butler had given her to St. Cloud.

He took it mechanically, and looked at it, and then crushed it in his hand, and was going to speak. She prevented him.

"I was right, I'm sure. You do know him?"

"I didn't see the name," he said, almost fiercely.

"The name on the card which I gave you just now?— Mr. Grey. He is curate in one of the poor Westminster districts. You must remember him, for he was of your college. He was at Oxford with you. I made his acquaintance at the Commemoration. He will be so glad to meet an old friend."

St. Cloud was too much provoked to answer; and the next moment the door opened, and the butler announced Mr. Grey.

Grey came into the room timidly, carrying his head a little down as usual, and glancing uncomfortably about in the manner which used to make Drysdale say that he always looked as though he had just been robbing a hen-roost. Mary went forward to meet him, holding out her hand cordially.

"I am so glad to see you," she said. "How kind of you to call when you are so busy! Mamma will be here directly. I think you must remember Mr. St. Cloud, Mr. Grey?"

St. Cloud's patience was now quite gone. He drew himself up, making the slightest possible inclination towards Grey, and then, without taking any further notice of him, turned to Mary, with a look which he meant to be full of pitying admiration for her, and contempt of her visitor; but, as she would not look at him, it was thrown away. So he made his bow and stalked out of the room, angrily debating with himself, as he went down the stairs, whether she could have understood him. He was so fully convinced of the sacrifice which a man in his position was making in paying serious attentions to a girl with little fortune and no connection, that he soon consoled himself in the belief that her embarrassment only arose from shyness, and that the moment he could explain himself she would be his obedient and grateful servant. Meantime, Mary sat down opposite to the curate, and listened to him as he unfolded his errand awkwardly enough. An execution was threatened in the house of a poor struggling widow, whom Mrs. Porter had employed to do needlework occasionally, and who was behind with her rent through sickness. He was afraid that her things would be taken and sold in the morning, unless she should borrow two sovereigns. He had so many claims on him that he could not lend her the money himself, and so had come out to see what he could do amongst those who knew her.

By the time Grey had arrived at the end of his story, Mary had made up her mind — not without a little struggle — to sacrifice the greater part of what was left of her quarter's allowance. After all, it would only be wearing cleaned gloves instead of new ones, and giving up her new riding-hat till next quarter. So she jumped up, and said gayly, "Is that all, Mr. Grey? I have the money, and I will lend it her with pleasure. I will fetch it directly." She tripped off to her room, and soon came back with the money; and just then the butler came in with tea, and Mary asked Mr. Grey to take some. He looked tired, she said, and if he would wait a little time, he would see her mother, who would be sure to do something more for the poor woman.

Grey had got up to leave, and was standing, hat in hand, ready to go. He was in the habit of reckoning with himself strictly for every minute of his day, and was never quite satisfied with himself unless he was doing the most disagreeable thing which circumstances for the time being allowed him to do. But greater and stronger men than Grey, from Adam downwards, have yielded to the temptation before which he now succumbed. He looked out of the corners of his eyes; and there was something so fresh and bright in the picture of the dainty little tea-service and the young lady behind it, the tea which she was beginning to pour out smelt so refreshing, and her hand and figure looked so pretty in the operation, that, with a sigh to departing resolution, he gave in, put his hat on the floor, and sat down opposite to the tempter.

Grey took a cup of tea, and then another. He thought he had never tasted any thing so good. The delicious rich cream, and the tempting plate of bread and butter, were too much for him. He fairly gave way, and resigned himself to physical enjoyment, and sipped his tea, and looked over his cup at Mary, sitting there bright and kind, and ready to go on pouring out for him to any extent. It seemed to him as if an atmosphere of light and joy surrounded her, within the circle of which he was sitting and absorbing. Tea was the only stimulant that Grey ever took, and he had more need of it than usual, for he had given away the chop, which was his ordinary dinner, to a starving woman. He was faint with fasting and the bad air of the hovels in which he had been spending his morning. The elegance of the room, the smell of the flowers, the charm of companionship with a young woman of his own rank, and the contrast of the whole to his common way of life, carried him away, and hopes and thoughts began to creep into his head to which he had long been a stranger. Mary did her very best to make his visit pleasant to him. She had a great respect for the self-denying life which she knew he was leading; and the nervousness and shyness of his manners were of a kind, which, instead of infecting her, gave her confidence, and made her feel quite at her ease with him. She was so grateful to him for having delivered her out of her recent embarrassment, that she was more than usually kind in her manner.

She saw how he was enjoying himself, and thought

what good it must do him to forget his usual occupations for a short time. So she talked positive gossip to him, asked his opinion on riding-habits, and very soon was telling him the plot of a new novel which she had just been reading, with an animation and playfulness which would have warmed the heart of an anchorite. For a short quarter of an hour Grey resigned himself; but at the end of that time he became suddenly and painfully conscious of what he was doing, and stopped himself short in the middle of an altogether worldly compliment, which he detected himself in the act of paying to his too fascinating young hostess. He felt that retreat was his only chance, and so grasped his hat again, and rose with a deep sigh, and a sudden change of manner which alarmed Mary.

"My dear Mr. Grey," she said, anxiously, "I hope you are not ill?"

"No, not the least, thank you. But — but — in short, I must go to my work. I ought to apologize, indeed, for having stayed so long."

"Oh, you have not been here more than twenty minutes. Pray stay, and see mamma; she must be in directly."

"Thank you; you are very kind. I should like it very much, but indeed, I cannot."

Mary felt that it would be no kindness to press it further, and so rose herself, and held out her hand. Grey took it, and it is not quite certain to this day whether he did not press it in that farewell shake more than was absolutely necessary. If he did, we may be quite sure that he administered exemplary punishment to himself afterwards for so doing. He would gladly have left now, but his over-sensitive conscience forbade it. He had forgotten his office, he thought, hitherto, but there was time yet not to be altogether false to it. So he looked grave and shy again, and said,—

"You will not be offended with me, Miss Porter, if I speak to you as a clergyman?"

Mary was a little disconcerted, but answered almost immediately,—

"Oh, no. Pray say any thing which you think you ought to say."

"I am afraid there must be a great temptation in living always in beautiful rooms like this, with no one but prosperous people. Do you not think so?"

"But one cannot help it. Surely, Mr. Grey, you do not think it can be wrong?"

"No, not wrong. But it must be very trying. It must be very necessary to do something to lessen the temptation of such a life."

"I do not understand you. What could one do?"

"Might you not take up some work which would not be pleasant, such as visiting the poor?"

"I should be very glad; but we do not know any poor people in London."

"There are very miserable districts near here."

"Yes, and papa and mamma are very kind, I know, in helping whenever they can hear of a proper case. But it is so different from the country. There it is so easy and pleasant to go into the cottages where every one knows you, and most of the people work for papa, and one is sure of being welcomed, and that nobody will be rude. But here I should be afraid. It would seem so impertinent to go to people's houses of whom one knows nothing. I should never know what to say."

"It is not easy or pleasant duty which is the best for us. Great cities could never be evangelized, Miss Porter, if all ladies thought as you do."

"I think, Mr. Grey," said Mary, rather nettled, "that every one has not the gift of lecturing the poor, and setting them right; and, if they have not, they had better not try to do it. And as for all the rest, there is plenty of the same kind of work to be done, I believe, amongst the people of one's own class."

"You are joking, Miss Porter."

"No, I am not joking at all. I believe that rich people are quite as unhappy as poor. Their troubles are not the same, of course, and are generally of their own making. But troubles of the mind are worse, surely, than troubles of the body?"

"Certainly; and it is the highest work of the ministry to deal with spiritual trials. But, you will pardon me for saying that I cannot think this is the proper work for — for —"

"For me, you would say. We must be speaking of quite different things, I am sure. I only mean that I can listen to the troubles and grievances of any one who likes to talk of them to me, and try to comfort them a little, and to make things look brighter, and to keep cheerful. It is not easy always even to do this."

"It is not, indeed. But would it not be easier if you could do as I suggest? Going out of one's own class, and trying to care for and to help the poor, braces the mind more than any thing else."

"You ought to know my Cousin Katie," said Mary, glad to make a diversion; "that is just what she would say. Indeed, I think you must have seen her at Oxford; did you not?"

"I believe I had the honor of meeting her at the rooms of a friend. I think he said she was also a cousin of his."

"Mr. Brown, you mean? Yes; did you know him?"

"Oh, yes. You will think it strange, as we are so

very unlike; but I knew him better than I knew almost any one."

"Poor Katie is very anxious about him. I hope you thought well of him. You do not think he is likely to go very wrong?"

"No, indeed. I could wish he were sounder on Church questions, but that may come. Do you know that he is in London?"

"I had heard so."

"He has been several times to my schools. He used to help me at Oxford, and has a capital way with the boys."

At this moment the clock on the mantelpiece struck a quarter. The sound touched some chord in Grey which made him grasp his hat again, and prepare for another attempt to get away.

"I hope you will pardon —" He pulled himself up short, in the fear lest he were going again to be false (as he deemed it) to his calling, and stood the picture of nervous discomfort.

Mary came to his relief. "I am sorry you must go, Mr. Grey," she said; "I should so like to have talked to you more about Oxford. You will call again soon, I hope?"

At which last speech Grey, casting an imploring glance at her, muttered something which she could not catch, and fled from the room.

Mary stood looking dreamily out of the window for a few minutes, till the entrance of her mother roused her, and she turned to pour out a cup of tea for her.

"It is cold, mamma dear; do let me make some fresh."

"No, thank you, dear; this will do very well," said Mrs. Porter; and she took off her bonnet and sipped the cold tea. Mary watched her silently for a minute, and then, taking the letter she had been reading, out of her pocket, said, —

"I have a letter from Katie, mamma."

Mrs. Porter took the letter and read it; and, as Mary still watched, she saw a puzzled look coming over her mother's face. Mrs. Porter finished the letter, and then looked stealthily at Mary, who on her side was now busily engaged in putting up the tea-things.

"It is very embarrassing," said Mrs. Porter.

"What, mamma?"

"Oh, of course, my dear, I mean of Katie's telling us of her cousin's being in London, and sending us his address —" and then she paused.

"Why, mamma?"

"Your papa will have to make up his mind whether he will ask him to the house. Katie would surely never have told him that she has written."

"Mr. and Mrs. Brown were so very kind. It would seem so strange, so ungrateful, not even to ask him."

"I am afraid he is not the sort of young man — in short, I must speak to your papa."

Mrs. Porter looked hard at her daughter, who was still busied with the tea-things. She had risen, bonnet in hand, to leave the room; but now changed her mind, and, crossing to her daughter, put her arm round her neck. Mary looked up steadily into her eyes, then blushed slightly, and said, quietly, —

"No, mamma; indeed it is not as you think."

Her mother stooped and kissed her, and left the room, telling her to get dressed, as the carriage would be round in a few minutes.

Her trials for the day were not over. She could see by their manner at dinner that her father and mother had been talking about her. Her father took her to a ball in the evening, where they met St. Cloud, who fastened himself to them. She was dancing a quadrille, and her father stood near her, talking confidentially to St. Cloud. In the intervals of the dance scraps of their conversation reached her.

"You knew him, then, at Oxford?"

"Yes, very slightly."

"I should like to ask you now, as a friend —" Here Mary's partner reminded her that she ought to be dancing. When she had returned to her place again she heard —

"You think, then, that it was a bad business?"

"It was notorious in the college. We never had any doubt on the subject."

"My niece has told Mrs. Porter that there really was nothing wrong in it."

"Indeed? I am happy to hear it."

"I should like to think well of him, as he is a connection of my wife. In other respects now —" Here again she was carried away by the dance, and, when she returned, caught the end of a sentence of St. Cloud's, "You will consider what I have said in confidence."

"Certainly," answered Mr. Porter; "and I am exceedingly obliged to you;" and then the dance was over, and Mary returned to her father's side. She had never enjoyed a ball less than this, and persuaded her father to leave early, which he was delighted to do.

When she reached her own room Mary took off her wreath and ornaments, and then sat down and fell into a brown study, which lasted for some time. At last she roused herself with a sigh, and thought she had never had so tiring a day, though she could hardly tell why, and felt half inclined to have a good cry, if she could only have made up her mind what about. However, being a sensible young woman, she resisted the temptation, and, hardly taking the trouble to roll up her hair, went to bed and slept soundly.

Mr. Porter found his wife sitting up for him; they were evidently both full of the same subject.

"Well, dear?" she said, as he entered the room.

Mr. Porter put down his candle, and shook his head.

"You don't think Katie can be right, then? She must have capital opportunities of judging, you know, dear."

"But she is no judge. What can a girl like Katie know about such things?"

"Well, dear, do you know I really cannot think there was any thing very wrong, though I did think so at first, I own."

"But I find that his character was bad — decidedly bad — always. Young St. Cloud didn't like to say much to me; which was natural, of course. Young men never like to betray one another; but I could see what he thought. He is a right-minded young man, and very agreeable."

"I do not take to him very much."

"His connections and prospects, too, are capital. I sometimes think he has a fancy for Mary. Haven't you remarked it?"

"Yes, dear. But as to the other matter? Shall you ask him here?"

"Well, dear, I do not think there is any need. He is only in town, I suppose, for a short time, and it is not at all likely that we should know where he is, you see."

"But if he should call?"

"Of course then we must be civil. We can consider then what is to be done."

## CHAPTER XXI.

### THE INTERCEPTED LETTER-BAG.

"DEAR KATIE,— At home, you see, without having answered your last kind letter of counsel and sympathy. But I couldn't write in town, I was in such a queer state all the time. I enjoyed nothing, not even the match at Lords, or the race; only walking at night in the square, and watching her window, and seeing her at a distance in Rotten Row.

"I followed your advice at last, though it went against the grain uncommonly. It did seem so unlike what I had a right to expect from them — after all the kindness my father and mother had shown them when they came into our neighborhood, and after I had been so intimate there, running in and out just like a son of their own — that they shouldn't take the slightest notice of me all the time I was in London. I shouldn't have wondered if you hadn't explained; but after that, and after you had told them my direction, and when they knew that I was within five minutes' walk of their house constantly (for they knew all about Grey's schools, and that I was there three or four times a week), I do think it was too bad. However, as I was going to tell you, I went at last, for I couldn't leave town without trying to see her; and I believe I have finished it all off. I don't know. I'm very low about it, at any rate, and want to tell you all that passed, and to hear what you think. I have no one to consult but you, Katie. What should I do without you? But you were born to help and comfort all the world. I sha'n't rest till I know what you think about this last crisis in my history.

"I put off going till my last day in town, and then called twice. The first time, 'not at home.' But I was determined now to see somebody, and make out something; so I left my card, and a message that, as I was leaving town next day, I would call again. When I called again at about six o'clock, I was shown into the library, and presently your uncle came in. I felt very uncomfortable, and I think he did too; but he shook hands cordially enough, asked why I had not called before, and said he was sorry to hear I was going out of town so soon. Do you believe he meant it? I didn't. But it put me out, because it made it look as if it had been my fault that I hadn't been there before. I said I didn't know that he would have liked me to call, but I felt that he had got the best of the start.

"Then he asked after all at home, and talked of his boys, and how they were getting on at school. By this time I had got my head again; so I went back to my calling, and said that I had felt I could never come to their house as a common acquaintance, and, as I did not know whether they would ever let me come in any other capacity, I had kept away till now.

"Your uncle didn't like it, I know; for he got up and walked about, and then said he didn't understand me. Well, I had got quite reckless by this time. It was my last chance I felt; so I looked hard into my hat, and said that I had been over head and ears in love with Mary for two years. Of course there was no getting out of the business after that. I kept on staring into my hat; so I don't know how he took it; but the first thing he said was that he had had some suspicions of this, and now my coufession gave him a right to ask me several questions. In the first place, Had I ever spoken to her? No; never directly. What did I mean by directly? I meant that I had never either spoken or written to her on the subject, — in fact, I hadn't seen her, except at a distance, for the last two years, — but I could not say that she might not have found it out from my manner. Had I ever told any one else? No; and this was quite true, Katie, for both you and Hardy found it out.

"He took a good many more turns before speaking again. Then he said I had acted as a gentleman hitherto, and he should be very plain with me. Of course, I must see that, looking at my prospects and his daughter's, it could not be an engagement which he could look on with much favor from a worldly point of view. Nevertheless, he had the highest respect and regard for my family, so that, if in some years' time I was in a position to marry, he should not object on this score; but there were other matters which were in his eyes of more importance. He had heard (who could have told him?) that I had taken up very violent opinions — opinions which, to say nothing more of them, would very much damage my prospects of success in life; and that I was in the habit of associating with the advocates of such opinions,— persons who, he must say, were not fit companions for a gentleman,— and of writing violent articles in low revolutionary newspapers, such as the *Wessex Freeman.* Yes, I confessed I had written. Would I give up these things? I had a great mind to say flat, No, and I believe I ought to have; but as his tone was kind I couldn't help trying to meet him. So I said I would give up writing or speaking publicly about such matters, but I couldn't pretend not to believe what I did believe. Perhaps, as my opinions had altered so much already, very likely they might again.

"He seemed to be rather amused at that, and said he sincerely hoped they might. But now came the most serious point: he had heard very bad stories of me at Oxford, but he would not press me with them. There were too few young men whose lives would bear looking into for him to insist much on such matters, and he was ready to let bygones be bygones. But I must remember that he had himself seen me in one very awkward position. I broke in, and said I had hoped that had been explained to him. I could not defend my Oxford life; I could not defend myself as to this particular case at one time; but there had been nothing in it that I was ashamed of since before the time I knew his daughter.

"On my honor had I absolutely and entirely broken off all relations with her? He had been told that I still kept up a correspondence with her.

"Yes, I still wrote to her, and saw her occasionally; but it was only to give her news of a young man from her village, who was now serving in India. He had no other way of communicating with her.

"It was a most curious arrangement; did I mean that this young man was going to be married to her?

"I hoped so.

"Why should he not write to her at once if they were engaged to be married?

"They were not exactly engaged; it was rather hard to explain. Here your uncle seemed to lose patience, for he interrupted me and said, Really, it must be clear to me, as a reasonable man, that, if this connection were not absolutely broken off, there must be an end of every thing, so far as his daughter was concerned. Would I give my word of honor to break it off at once, and completely? I tried to explain again; but he would have nothing but yes or no. Dear Katie, what could I do? I have written to Patty that, till I die, she may always reckon on me as on a brother; and I have promised Harry never to lose sight of her, and to let her know every thing that happens to him. Your uncle would not hear me; so I said, No. And he said, 'Then our interview had better end,' and rang the bell. Somebody, I'm sure, has been slandering me to him; who can it be?

"I didn't say another word, or offer to shake hands, but got up and walked out of the room, as it was no good waiting for the servant to come. When I got into the hall the front door was open, and I heard her voice. I stopped dead short. She was saying something to some people who had been riding with her. The next moment the door shut, and she tripped in in her riding-habit, and gray gloves, and hat, with the dearest little gray plume in it. She went humming along, and up six or eight steps, without seeing me. Then I moved a step, and she stopped and looked, and gave a start. I don't know whether my face was awfully miserable, but, when our eyes met, hers seemed to fill with pity and uneasiness and inquiry, and the bright look to melt away altogether; and then she blushed, and ran down-stairs again, and held out her hand, saying, 'I am so glad to see you, after all this long time.' I pressed it, but I don't think I said any thing. I forget; the butler came into the hall, and stood by the door. She paused another moment, looked confused, and then, as the library door opened, went away up-stairs, with a kind 'good-by.' She dropped a little bunch of violets, which she had worn in the breast of her habit, as she went away. I went and picked them up, although your uncle had now come out of the library, and then made the best of my way into the street.

"There, Katie, I have told you every thing, exactly as it happened. Do write to me, dear, and tell me, now, what you think. Is it all over? What can I do? Can you do any thing for me? I feel it is better in one respect. Her father can never say now that I didn't tell him all about it. But what is to happen? I am so restless. I can settle to nothing, and do nothing, but fish. I moon away all my time by the water-side, dreaming. But I don't mean to let it beat me much longer. Here's the fourth day since I saw her. I came away the next morning. I shall give myself a week; and, dear, do write me a long letter at once, and interpret it all to me. A woman knows so wonderfully what things mean. But don't make it out better than you really think. Nobody can stop my going on loving her, that's a comfort; and while I can do that, and don't know that she loves anybody else, I ought to be happier than any other man in the world. Yes, I ought to be, but I aint. I will be, though; see if I wont. Heigho! Do write directly, my dear counsellor, to your affectionate cousin,

"T. B.

"P.S.— I had almost forgotten my usual budget. I enclose my last from India. You will see by it that Harry is getting on famously. I am more glad than I can tell you that my friend East has taken him as his servant. He couldn't be under a better master. Poor Harry! I sometimes think his case is more hopeless than my own. How is it to come right? or mine?"

"*Englebourn.*

"Dear Cousin,— You will believe how I devoured your letter; though, when I had read the first few lines, and saw what was coming, it made me stop and tremble. At first I could have cried over it for vexation; but, now I have thought about it a little, I really do not see any reason to be discouraged. At any rate, Uncle Robert now knows all about it, and will get used to the idea, and Mary seems to have received you just as you ought to have wished that she should. I am thankful that you have left off pressing me to write to her about you, for I am sure that would not be honorable; and, to reward you, I enclose a letter of hers, which came yesterday. You will see that she speaks with such pleasure of having just caught a glimpse of you, that you need not regret the shortness of the interview. You could not expect her to say more, because, after all, she can only guess; and I cannot do more than answer as if I were quite innocent too. I am sure you will be very thankful to me some day for not having been your mouthpiece, as I was so very near being. You need not return the letter. I suppose I am getting more hopeful as I grow older — indeed, I am sure I am; for three or four years ago I should have been in despair about you, and now I am nearly sure that all will come right.

"But, indeed, Cousin Tom, you cannot, or ought not, to wonder at Uncle Robert's objecting to your opinions. And then I am so surprised to find you saying that you think you may very likely change them. Because, if that is the case, it would be so much better if you would not write and talk about them. Unless you are quite convinced of such things as you write in that dreadful paper, you really ought not to go on writing them so very much as if you believed them.

"And now I am speaking to you about this, which I have often had on my mind to speak to you about, I must ask you not to send me that *Wessex Freeman* any more. I am always delighted to hear what you think; and there is a great deal in the articles you mark for me which seems very fine; and I dare say you quite believe it all when you write it. Only I am quite afraid lest papa or any of the servants should open the papers, or get hold of them after I have opened them; for I am sure there are a great many wicked things in the other parts of the paper. So, please do not send it me, but write and tell me yourself any thing that you wish me to know of what you are thinking about and doing. As I did not like to burn the papers, and was afraid to keep them here, I have generally sent them on to your friend, Mr. Hardy. He does not know who sends them; and now you might send them yourself straight to him, as I do not know his address in the country. As you are going up again to keep a term, I wish you would talk them over with him, and see what he thinks about them. You will think this very odd of me, but you know you have always said how much you rely on his judgment, and that you have learned so much from him. So I am sure you would wish to consult him; and, if he thinks you ought to go on writing, it will be a great help to you to know it.

"I am so very glad to be able to tell you how well Martha is going on. I have always read to her the extracts from your letters from India which you have sent me, and she is very much obliged to you for sending them. I think there is no doubt that she is, and always has been, attached to poor Widow Winburn's son, and, now that he is behaving so well, I can see that it gives her great pleasure to hear about him. Only, I hope, he will be able to come back before very long, because she is very much admired, and is likely to have so many chances of settling in life, that it is a great chance whether her attachment to him will be strong enough to keep her single if he should be absent for many years.

"Do you know I have a sort of superstition, that your fate hangs upon theirs in some curious manner, — the two stories have been so interwoven, — and that they will both be settled happily much sooner than we dare to hope even just now?

"Don't think, my dear cousin, that this letter is cold, or that I do not take the very deepest interest in all that concerns you. You and Mary are always in my thoughts, and there is nothing in the world I would not do for you both which I thought would help you. I am sure it would do you harm to be only a go-between. Papa is much as usual. He gets out a good deal in his chair in the sun this fine weather. He desires me to say how glad he should be if you will come over soon and pay us a visit. I hope you will come *very soon.*

"Ever believe me, dear Tom,
"Your affectionate cousin,
"KATIE."

"*November.*

"DEAR TOM,—I hear that what you in England call a mail is to leave camp this evening; so, that you may have no excuse for not writing to me constantly, I am setting to spin you such a yarn as I can under the disadvantageous circumstances in which this will leave me.

"This time last year, or somewhere thereabouts, I was enjoying academic life with you at Oxford; and now here I am, encamped at some unpronounceable place beyond Umbala. You wont be much the wiser for that. What do you know about Umbala? I didn't myself know that there was such a place till a month ago, when we were ordered to march up here. But one lives and learns. Marching over India has its disagreeables, of which dysentery and dust are about the worst. A lot of our fellows are down with the former; amongst others my captain; so I'm in command of the company. If it were not for the glorious privilege of grumbling, I think we should all own that we liked the life. Moving about, though one does get frozen and broiled regularly once in the twenty-four hours, suits me; besides, they talk of matters coming to a crisis, and no end of fighting to be done directly. You'll know more about what's going on from the papers than we do, but here they say the ball may begin any day; so we are making forced marches to be up in time. I wonder how I shall like it. Perhaps, in my next, I may tell you how a bullet sounds when it comes at you. If there is any fighting, I expect our regiment will make their mark. We are in tip-top order; the colonel is a grand fellow, and the regiment feels his hand, down to the youngest drummer boy. What a deal of good I will do when I'm a colonel.

"I duly delivered the enclosure in your last to your convict, who is rapidly ascending the ladder of promotion. I am disgusted at this myself, for I have had to give him up, and there never was such a jewel of a servant; but, of course, it's a great thing for him. He is covering sergeant of my company, and the smartest coverer we have too. I have got a regular broth of a boy, an Irishman, in his place, who leads me a dog of a life. I took him chiefly because he very nearly beat me in a foot-race. Our senior major is a Pat himself, and, it seems, knew something of Larry's powers. So, one day at mess, he offered to back him against any one in the regiment for two hundred yards. My captain took him and named me, and it came off next day; and a precious narrow thing it was, but I managed to win by a neck for the honor of the old school. He is a lazy scatter-brained creature, utterly indifferent to fact, and I am obliged to keep the brandy flask under lock and key; but the humor and absolute good temper of the animal impose upon me, and I really think he is attached to me. So I keep him on, grumbling horribly at the change from that orderly, punctual, clean, accurate convict. Depend upon it, that fellow will do. He makes his way everywhere, with officers and men. He is a gentleman at heart, and, by the way, you would be surprised at the improvement in his manners and speech. There is hardly a taste of Berkshire left in his *deealect*. He has read all the books I could lend him, or borrow for him, and is fast picking up Hindustanee. So you see, after all, I am come round to your opinion that we did a good afternoon's work on that precious stormy common, when we carried off the convict from the authorities of his native land, and I was first under fire. As you are a performer in that line, couldn't you carry off his sweetheart, and send her out here? After the sea voyage there isn't much above one thousand miles to come by dauk; and tell her, with my compliments, he is well worth coming twice the distance for. Poor fellow, it is a bad look-out for him I'm afraid, as he may not get home this ten years; and, though he isn't a kind to be easily killed, there are serious odds against him, even if he keeps all right. I almost wish you had never told me his story.

"We are going into cantonments as soon as this expedition is over in a splendid pig district, and I look forward to some real sport. All the men who have had any tell me it beats the best fox-hunt all to fits for excitement. I have got my eye on a famous Arab, who is to be had cheap. The brute is in the habit of kneeling on his masters, and tearing them with his teeth when he gets them off, but nothing can touch him while you keep on his back. Howsumdever, as your countrymen say, I shall have a shy at him, if I can get him at my price. I've nothing more to say. There's nobody you know here, except the convict sergeant, and it's awfully hard to fill a letter home unless you've somebody to talk about. Yes, by the way, there is one little fellow, an ensign, just joined, who says he remembers us at school. He can't be more than eighteen or nineteen, and was an urchin in the lower school, I suppose, when we were leaving. I don't remember his face, but it's a very good one, and he is a bright, gentlemanly youngster as you would wish to see. His name is Jones. Do you remember him? He will be a godsend to me. I have him to chum with me on this march.

"Keep up your letters as you love me. You at home little know what it is to enjoy a letter. Never mind what you put in it; any thing will do from home, and I've nobody else much to write to me.

"There goes the 'assembly.' Why, I can't think, seeing we have done our day's march. However, I must turn out and see what's up.

\* \* \* \* \* \* \* \*

"*December.*

"I have just fallen on this letter, which I had quite forgotten, or, rather, had fancied I had sent off to you three weeks and more ago. My baggage has just come to hand, and the scrawl turned up in my paper case. Well, I have plenty to tell you now, at any rate, if I had time to tell it. That 'assembly' which stopped me short sounded in consequence of the arrival of one of the commander-in-chief's aides in our camp, with the news that the enemy was over the Sutlej. We were to march at once, with two six-pounders and a squadron of cavalry, on a fort occupied by an outlying lot of them, which commanded a ford, and was to be taken and destroyed, and the rascals who held it dispersed; after which we were to join the main army. Our colonel had the command; so we were on the route within an hour, leaving a company and the baggage to follow as it could; and from that time to this, forced marching and hard fighting have been the order of the day.

"We drew first blood next morning. The enemy were in some force outside the fort, and showed fight in very rough ground covered with bushes; out of which we had to drive them — which we did after a sharp struggle, and the main body drew off altogether. Then the fort had to be taken. Our two guns worked away at it till dark. In the night two of the gunners, who volunteered for the service, crept close up to the place, and reported that there was nothing to hinder our running right into it. Accordingly, the colonel resolved to rush it at daybreak, and my company was told off to lead. The captain being absent, I had to command. I was with the dear old chief the last thing at night, getting his instructions: ten minutes with him before going into action would make a hare fight.

"There was cover to within one hundred and fifty yards of the place; and there I, and poor little Jones, and the men, spent the night in a dry ditch. An hour before daybreak we were on the alert, and served out rations, and then they began playing tricks on one another as if we were out for a junketing. I sat with my watch in my hand, feeling queer, and wondering whether I was a greater coward than the rest. Then came a streak of light. I put up my watch, formed the men; up went a rocket, my signal, and out into the open we went at the double. We hadn't got over a third of the ground when bang went the fort guns, and the grape-shot were whistling about our ears; so I shouted 'Forward!' and away we went as hard as we could go. I was obliged to go ahead, you see, because every man of them knew I had beaten Larry, their best runner, when he had no gun to carry; but I didn't half like it, and should have blessed any hole or bramble which would have sent me over and given them time to catch me. But the ground was provokingly level; and so I was at the first mound and over it several lengths in front of the men, and among a lot of black fellows serving the guns. They came at me like wild-cats, and how I got off is a mystery. I parried a cut from one fellow, and dodged a second; a third rushed at my left side. I just caught the flash of his tulwar, and thought it was all up, when he jumped into the air, shot through the heart by Sergeant Winburn; and the next moment Master Larry rushed by me and plunged his bayonet into my friend in front. It turned me as sick as a dog. I can't fancy any thing more disagreeable than seeing the operation for the first time, except being stuck one's self. The supporting companies were in in another minute, with the dear old chief himself, who came up and shook hands with me, and said I had done credit to the regiment. Then I began to look about, and missed poor little Jones. We found him about twenty yards from the place, with two grape-shot through him, stone dead, and smiling like a child asleep. We buried him in the fort. I cut off some of his hair, and sent it home to his mother. Her last letter was in his breast pocket, and a lock of bright brown hair of some one's. I sent them back, too, and his sword.

"Since then we have been with the army, and had three or four general actions; about which I can tell you nothing, except that we have lost about a third of the regiment, and have always been told we have won. Steps go fast enough; my captain died of wounds and dysentery a week ago; so I have the company in earnest. How long I shall hold it is another question; for, though there's a slack, we haven't done with sharp work yet, I can see.

"How often we've talked, years ago, of what it must feel like going into battle! Well, the chief thing I felt when the grape came down pretty thick for the first time, as we were advancing, was a sort of gripes in the stomach which made me want to go forward stooping. But I didn't give in to it; the chief was riding close behind us, joking the youngsters who were ducking their heads, and so cheery and cool, that he made old soldiers of us at once. What with smoke and dust and excitement, you know scarcely any thing of what is going on. The finest sight I have seen is the artillery going into action. Nothing stops those fellows. Places you would crane at out hunting they go right over, guns, carriages, men, and all, leaving any cavalry we've got out here well behind. Do you know what a nullah is? Well, it's a great gap, like a huge dry canal, fifteen or twenty feet deep. We were halted behind one in the last great fight, waiting the order to advance, when a battery came up at full gallop. We all made sure they must be pulled up by the nullah. They never pulled bridle. 'Leading gun, right turn!' sang out the subaltern, and down they went sideways into the nullah. Then, 'Left turn;' up the other bank, one gun after another, the horses scrambling like cats up and down places that my men had to use their hands to scramble up, and away the other side to within two hundred yards of the enemy; and then, round like lightning, and look out in front.

"Altogether it's sickening work, though there's a grand sort of feeling of carrying your life in your hand. They say the Sepoy regiments have behaved shamefully. There is no sign of any thing like funk amongst our fellows that I have seen. Sergeant Winburn has distinguished himself everywhere. He is like my shadow, and I can see tries to watch over my precious carcase, and get between me and danger. He would be a deal more missed in the world than I. Except you, old friend, I don't know who would care much if I were knocked over to-morrow.

Aunts and cousins are my nearest relations. You know I never was a snuffler; but this sort of life makes one serious, if one has any reverence at all in one. You'll be glad to have this line, if you don't hear from me again. I've often thought in the last month that we shall never see one another again in this world. But, whether in this world or any other, you know I am and always shall be your affectionate friend,

"H. East."

"Camp on the Sutlej,
"January.

"Dear Master Tom,— The captain's last words was, if any thing happened I was to be sure to write and tell you. And so I take up my pen, though you will know as I am not used to writing, to tell you the misfortune as has happened to our regiment. Because, if you was to ask any man in our regiment, let it be who it would, he would say as the captain was the best officer as ever led men. Not but what there's a many of them as will go to the front as brave as lions, and don't value shot no more than if it was rotten apples; and men as is men will go after such. But 'tis the captain's manners and ways, with a kind word for any poor fellow as is hurt, or sick and tired, and making no account of hisself, and, as you may say, no bounce with him; that's what makes the difference.

"As it might be last Saturday, we came upon the enemy where he was posted very strong, with guns all along his front, and served till we got right up to them, the gunners being cut down and bayoneted when we got right up amongst them, and no quarter given; and there was great banks of earth, too, to clamber over, and more guns behind; so, with the marching up in front and losing so many officers and men, our regiment was that wild when we got amongst them 'twas awful to see, and, if there was any prisoners taken, it was more by mistake than not.

"Me and three or four more settled, when the word came to prepare for action, to keep with the captain, because 'twas known to every one as no odds would stop him, and he would never mind hisself. The dust and smoke and noise was that thick you couldn't see nor hear any thing after our regiment was in action; but, so far as I seen, when we was wheeled into line, and got the word to advance, there was as it might be as far as from our old cottage to the Hawk's Lynch to go over before we got to the guns, which was playing into us all the way. Our line went up very steady, only where men was knocked down; and, when we come to within a matter of sixty yards, the officers jumped out and waved their swords, for 'twas no use to give words, and the ranks was broken by reason of the running up to take the guns from the enemy. Me and the rest went after the captain; but he, being so light of foot, was first, by maybe ten yards or so, at the mound, and so up before we was by him. But, though they was all round him like bees when we got to him, 'twas not then as he was hit. There was more guns further on, and we and they drove on altogether; and, though they was beaten, being fine tall men and desperate, there was many of them fighting hard, and, as you might say, a man scarcely knowed how he got hit. I kept to the captain as close as ever I could, but there was times when I had to mind myself. Just as we come to the last guns, Larry, that's the captain's servant, was trying by hisself to turn one of them round, so

as to fire on the enemy as they took the river to the back
of their lines all in a huddle. So I turned to lend him a
hand; and, when I looked round next moment, there was
the captain a staggering like a drunken man, and he so
strong and lissom up to then, and never had a scratch
since the war begun, and this the last minute of it pretty
nigh, for the enemy was all cut to pieces and drowned
that day. I got to him before he fell, and we laid him
down gently, and did the best we could for him. But
he was bleeding dreadful with a great gash in his side,
and his arm broke, and two gunshot wounds. Our sur-
geon was killed, and 'twas hours before his wounds was
dressed, and 'twill be God's mercy if ever he gets round;
though they do say, if the fever and dysentery keeps off,
and he can get out of this country and home, there's no
knowing but he may get the better of it all, but not to
serve with the regiment again for years to come.

"I hope, Master Tom, as I've told you all the captain
would like as you should know; only, not being much
used to writing, I hope you will excuse mistakes. And,
if so be that it wont be too much troubling of you, and
the captain should go home, and you could write to say
how things was going on at home as before, which the
captain always gave me to read when the mail come in,
it would be a great help towards keeping up of a good
heart in a foreign land, which is hard at times to do.
There is some things which I make bold to send by a
comrade going home sick. I don't know as they will
seem much, but I hope as you will accept of the sword,
which belonged to one of their officers, and the rest to her.
Also, on account of what was in the last piece as you for-
warded, I send a letter to go along with the things, if
Miss Winter, who have been so kind, or you, would

deliver the same. To whom I make bold to send my respects as well as to yourself, and hoping this will find you well and all friends, and

"From your respectful,
"Henry Winburn,
"Color-Sergeant 101st Regiment."

"*March.*

"My dear Tom, — I begin to think I may see you again yet, but it has been a near shave. I hope Sergeant Winburn's letter, and the returns, in which I see I was put down 'dangerously wounded,' will not have frightened you very much. The war is over; and, if I live to get down to Calcutta you will see me in the summer, please God. The end was like the beginning — going right up to guns. Our regiment is frightfully cut up; there are only three hundred men left under arms — the rest dead or in hospital. I am sick at heart at it, and weak in body, and can only write a few lines at a time, but will go on with this as I can, in time for next mail.

\* \* \* \* \* \* \*

"Since beginning this letter I have had another relapse. So, in case I should never finish it, I will say at once what I most want to say. Winburn has saved my life more than once, and is besides one of the noblest and bravest fellows in the world; so I mean to provide for him in case any thing should happen to me. I have made a will, and appointed you my executor, and left him a legacy. You must buy his discharge, and get him home and married to the Englebourn beauty as soon as possible. But what I want you to understand is that, if the legacy isn't enough to do this, and make all straight with her old curmudgeon of a father, it is my first wish that whatever will do it should be made up to him. He has been in hospital with a bad flesh wound, and has let out to me the whole of his story, of which you had only given me the heads. If that young woman does not wait for him, and book him, I shall give up all faith in petticoats. Now that's done I feel more at ease.

"Let me see. I haven't written for six weeks and more, just before our last great fight. You'll know all about it from the papers long before you get this — a bloody business — I am loth to think of it. I was knocked over in the last of their entrenchments, and should then and there have bled to death had it not been for Winburn. He never left me, though the killing and plundering and roystering afterwards was going on all round, and strong temptation to a fellow when his blood is up, and he sees his comrades at it, after such work as we had had. What's more, he caught my Irish fellow and made him stay by me, too, and between them they managed to prop me up and stop the bleeding, though it was touch and go. I never thought they would manage it. You can't think what a curious feeling it is, the life going out of you. I was perfectly conscious, and knew all they were doing and saying, and thought quite clearly, though in a sort of dreamy way, about you, and a whole jumble of people and things at home. It was the most curious painless mixture of dream and life, getting more dreamy every minute. I don't suppose I could have opened my eyes or spoken; at any rate I had no wish to do so, and didn't try. Several times the thought of death came close to me; and, whether it was the odd state I was in, or what else I don't know, but the only feeling I had was one of intense curiosity. I should think I must have lain there, with Winburn supporting my head, and moistening my lips with rum and water, for four or five hours, before a doctor could be got. He had managed to drive Larry about till he had found, or borrowed, or stolen the drink, and then kept him making short cruises in search of help in the shape of hospital-stuff, ambulances, or doctors, from which Master Larry always came back without the slightest success. My belief is, he employed those precious minutes, when he was from under his sergeant's eye, in looting. At last Winburn got impatient, and I heard him telling Larry what he was to do while he was gone himself to find a doctor; and then I was moved as gently as if I had been a sick girl. I heard him go off with a limp, but did not know till long after of his wound.

"Larry had made such a wailing and to-do when they first found me, that a natural reaction now set in, and he began gently and tenderly to run over in his mind what could be made out of 'the captin,' and what would become of his things. I found out this, partly through his habit of talking to himself, and partly from the precaution which he took of ascertaining where my watch and purse were, and what else I had upon me. It tickled me immensely to hear him. Presently I found he was examining my boots, which he pronounced 'iligant entirely,' and wondered whether he could get them on. The 'serjint' would never want them. And he then proceeded to assert, while he actually began unlacing them, that the captin would never have '*bet him*' but for the boots, which 'was worth ten feet in a furlong to any man.' 'Shure 'tis too late now; but wouldn't I like to run him agin with the bare feet?' I couldn't stand that, and just opened my eyes a little, and moved my hand, and said, 'Done.' I wanted to add, 'you rascal,' but that was too much for me. Larry's face of horror, which I just caught through my half-opened eyes, would have made me roar, if I had had strength for it. I believe the resolution I made that he should never go about in my boots helped me to pull through; but, as soon as Winburn came back with the doctor, Master Larry departed, and I much doubt whether I shall ever set eyes on him again in the flesh; not if he can help it, certainly. The regiment, what's left of it, is away in the Punjaub, and he with it. Winburn, as I told you, is hard hit, but no danger. I have great hopes that he will be invalided. You may depend upon it he will escort me home, if any interest of mine can manage it; and the dear old chief is so kind to me that I think he will arrange it somehow.

"I must be wonderfully better to have spun such a yarn. Writing those first ten lines nearly finished me, a week ago, and now I am scarcely tired after all this scrawl. If that rascal, Larry, escapes hanging another year, and comes back home, I will run him yet, and thrash his head off.

"There is something marvellously life-giving in the idea of sailing for old England again; and I mean to make a strong fight for seeing you again, old boy. God bless you. Write again for the chance, directing to my agents at Calcutta, as before. Ever your half-alive, but whole-hearted and affectionate friend,

"H. EAST."

## CHAPTER XXII.

#### MASTER'S TERM.

ONE more look into the old college where we have spent so much time already, not, I hope, altogether unpleasantly. Our hero is up in the summer term, keeping his three weeks' residence, the necessary preliminary to an M.A. degree. We find him sitting in Hardy's rooms; tea is over, scouts out of college, candles lighted, and silence reigning, except when distant sounds of mirth come from some undergraduates' rooms on the opposite side of quad, through the open windows.

Hardy is deep in the budget of Indian letters, some of which we have read in the last chapter; and Tom reads them over again as his friend finishes them, and then carefully folds them up and puts them back in their places in a large pocket-case. Except an occasional explanatory remark, or exclamation of interest, no word passes until Hardy finishes the last letter. Then he breaks out into praises of the two Harrys, which gladdens Tom's heart as he fastens the case, and puts it back in his pocket, saying, "Yes, you wont find two finer fellows in a long summer's day; no, nor in twenty."

"And you expect them home, then, in a week or two?"

"Yes, I think so. Just about the time I shall be going down."

"Don't talk about going down. You haven't been here a week."

"Just a week. One out of three. Three weeks wasted in keeping one's Master's term! Why can't you give a fellow his degree quietly, without making him come and kick his heels here for three weeks?"

"You ungrateful dog! Do you mean to say you haven't enjoyed coming back, and sitting in dignity in the bachelors' seats in chapel, and at the bachelors' table in hall, and thinking how much wiser you are than the undergraduates? Besides, your old friends want to see you, and you ought to want to see them."

"Well, I'm very glad to see something of you again, old fellow. I don't find that a year's absence has made any change in you. But who else is there that I care to see? My old friends are gone, and the year has made a great gap between me and the youngsters. They look on me as a sort of don."

"Of course they do. Why, you are a sort of don. You will be an M.A. in a fortnight, and a member of Convocation."

"Very likely; but I don't appreciate the dignity; I can tell you being up here now is any thing but enjoyable. You have never broken with the place. And then, you always did your duty, and have done the college credit. You can't enter into the feelings of a fellow whose connection with Oxford has been quite broken off, and who wasted three parts of his time here, when he comes back to keep his Master's."

"Come, come, Tom. You might have read more certainly, with benefit to yourself and the college, and taken a higher degree. But, after all, didn't the place do you a great deal of good? and you didn't do it much harm. I don't like to see you in this sort of gloomy state; it isn't natural to you."

"It is becoming natural. You haven't seen much of

me during the last year, or you would have remarked it. And then, as I tell you, Oxford, when one has nothing to do in it but to moon about, thinking over one's past follies and sins, isn't cheerful. It never was a very cheerful place to me at the best of times."

"Not even at pulling times?"

"Well, the river is the part I like best to think of. But even the river makes me rather melancholy now. One feels one has done with it."

"Why, Tom, I believe your melancholy comes from their not having asked you to pull in the boat."

"Perhaps it does. Don't you call it degrading to be pulling in the torpid in one's old age?"

"Mortified vanity, man! They have a capital boat. I wonder how we should have liked to have been turned out for some bachelor just because he had pulled a good oar in his day?"

"Not at all. I don't blame the young ones, and I hope I do my duty in the torpid. By the way, they're an uncommonly nice set of youngsters. Much better behaved in every way than we were, unless it is that they put on their best manners before me."

"No, I don't think they do. The fact is, they are really fine young fellows."

"So I think. And I'll tell you what, Jack; since we are sitting and talking our minds to one another at last, like old times, somebody has made the most wonderful change in this college. I rather think it is seeing what St. Ambrose's is now, and thinking what it was in my time, and what an uncommon member of society I should have turned out if I had had the luck to have been here now instead of then, that makes me down in the mouth — more even than having to pull in the torpid instead of the racing boat."

"You do think it is improved, then?"

"Think! Why it is a different place altogether; and, as you are the only new tutor, it must have been your doing. Now, I want to know your secret."

"I've no secret, except taking a real interest in all that the men do, and living with them as much as I can. You may fancy it isn't much of a trial to me to steer the boat down, or run on the bank and coach the crew."

"Ah! I remember; you were beginning that before I left, in your first year. I knew that would answer."

"Yes. The fact is, I find that just what I like best is the very best thing for the men. With very few exceptions they are all glad to be stirred up, and meet me nearly half-way in reading, and three-quarters in every thing else. I believe they would make me captain tomorrow."

"And why don't you let them, then?"

"No; there's a time for every thing. I go in in the scratch fours for the pewters, and — more by token — my crew won them two years running. Look at my trophies," and he pointed to two pewter pots, engraved with the college arms, which stood on his sideboard.

"Well, I dare say you're right. But what does the president say?"

"Oh, he is a convert. Didn't you see him on the bank when you torpids made your bump the other night?"

"No, you don't mean it? Well, do you know, a sort of vision of black tights, and a broad-brimmed hat, crossed me, but I never gave it a second thought. And so the president comes out to see the St. Ambrose boat row?"

"Seldom misses two nights running."

"Then, carry me out, and bury me decently. Have you seen old Tom walking round Peckwater lately on his clapper, smoking a cigar with the Dean of Christchurch? Don't be afraid. I am ready for any thing you like to tell me. Draw any amount you like on my faith; I shall honor the draft after that."

"The president isn't a bad judge of an oar, when he sets his mind to it."

"Isn't he? But, I say, Jack, — no sell, — how in the world did it happen?"

"I believe it happened chiefly through his talks with me. When I was first made tutor he sent for me and told me he had heard I encouraged the young men in boating, and he must positively forbid it. I didn't much care about staying up; so I was pretty plain with him, and said if I was not allowed to take the line I thought best in such matters I must resign at the end of term. He assented, but afterwards thought better of it, and sent for me again, and we had several encounters. I took my ground very civilly but firmly, and he had to give up one objection after another. I think the turning-point was when he quoted St. Paul on me, and said I was teaching boys to worship physical strength, instead of teaching them to keep under their bodies and bring them into subjection. Of course I countered him there with tremendous effect. The old boy took it very well, only saying he feared it was no use to argue further — in this matter of boat-racing he had come to a conclusion, not without serious thought, many years before. However, he came round quietly. And so he has on other points. In fact, he is a wonderfully open-minded man for his age, if you only put things to him the right way."

"Has he come round about gentlemen-commoners? I see you've only two or three up."

"Yes. We haven't given up taking them altogether. I hope that may come soon. But I and another tutor took to plucking them ruthlessly at matriculation, unless they were quite up to the commoner standard. The consequence was, a row in common room. We stood out, and won. Luckily, as you know, it has always been given out here that all undergraduates, gentlemen-commoners, and commoners, have to pass the same college examinations, and to attend the same courses of lectures. You know also what a mere sham and pretence the rule had become. Well, we simply made a reality of it, and in answer to all objectors said, Is it our rule or not? If it is, we are bound to act on it. If you want to alter it, there are the regular ways of doing so. After a little grumbling they let us have our way, and the consequence is, that velvet is getting scarce at St. Ambrose."

"What a blessing! What other miracles have you been performing?"

"The best reform we have carried is throwing the kitchen and cellar open to the undergraduates."

"W-h-e-w! That's just the sort of reform we should have appreciated. Fancy Drysdale's lot with the key of the college cellars, at about ten o'clock on a shiny night."

"You don't quite understand the reform. You remember, when you were an undergraduate you couldn't give a dinner in college, and you had to buy your wine anywhere?"

"Yes, and awful firewater we used to get. The governor supplied me, like a wise man."

"Well, we have placed the college in the relation of benevolent father. Every undergraduate now can give two dinners a term in his own room, from the kitchen; or more, if he comes and asks, and has any reason to give.

We take care that they have a good dinner at a reasonable rate, and the men are delighted with the arrangement. I don't believe there are three men in the college now who have hotel bills. And we let them have all their wine out of the college cellars."

"That's what I call good common-sense. Of course it must answer in every way. And you find they all come to you?"

"Almost all. They can't get any thing like the wine we give them at the price, and they know it."

"Do you make them pay ready money?"

"The dinners and wine are charged in their battel bills; so they have to pay once a term, just as they do for their ordinary commons."

"It must swell their battel bills awfully."

"Yes, but battel bills always come in at the beginning of term, when they are flush of money. Besides, they all know that battel bills must be paid. In a small way it is the best thing that ever was done for St. Ambrose's. You see it cuts so many ways. Keeps men in college, knocks off the most objectionable bills at inns and pastry-cooks, keeps them from being poisoned, makes them pay their bills regularly, shows them that we like them to be able to live like gentlemen —"

"And lets you dons know what they are all about, and how much they spend in the way of entertaining."

"Yes; and a very good thing for them too. They know that we shall not interfere while they behave like gentlemen."

"Oh, I'm not objecting. And was this your doing too?"

"No; a joint business. We hatched it in the common room, and then the bursar spoke to the president, who was furious, and said we were giving the sanction of the college to disgraceful luxury and extravagance. Luckily, he had not the power of stopping us, and now is convinced."

"The goddess of common-sense seems to have alighted again in the quad of St. Ambrose. You'll never leave the place, Jack, now you're beginning to get every thing your own way."

"On the contrary, I don't mean to stop up more than another year at the outside. I have been tutor nearly three years now; that's about long enough."

"Do you think you're right? You seem to have hit on your line in life wonderfully. You like the work, and the work likes you. You are doing a heap of good up here. You'll be president in a year or two, depend on it. I should say you had better stick to Oxford."

"No. I should be of no use in a year or two. We want a constant current of fresh blood here."

"In a general way. But you don't get a man every day who can throw himself into the men's pursuits, and can get hold of them in the right way. And then, after all, when a fellow has got such work cut out for him as you have, Oxford must be an uncommonly pleasant place to live in."

"Pleasant enough in many ways. But you seem to have forgotten how you used to rail against it."

"Yes. Because I never hit off the right ways of the place. But, if I had taken a first and got a fellowship, I should like it well enough, I dare say."

"Being a fellow, on the contrary, makes it worse. While one was an undergraduate one could feel virtuous and indignant at the vices of Oxford, at least at those which one did not indulge in, particularly at the flunkeyism and money-worship which are our most prevalent and disgraceful sins. But when one is a fellow, it is quite another affair. They become a sore burden then, enough to break one's heart."

"Why, Jack, we're changing characters to-night. Fancy your coming out in the abusive line! Why, I never said harder things of Alma Mater myself. However, there's plenty of flunkeyism and money-worship everywhere else."

"Yes; but it is not so heart-breaking in other places. When one thinks what a great centre of learning and faith like Oxford ought to be — that its highest educational work should just be the deliverance of us all from flunkeyism and money-worship — and then looks at matters here without rose-colored spectacles, it gives one sometimes a sort of chilly leaden despondency, which is very hard to struggle against."

"I am sorry to hear you talk like that, Jack, for one can't help loving the place after all."

"So I do, God knows. If I didn't I shouldn't care for its shortcomings."

"Well, the flunkeyism and money-worship were bad enough, but I don't think they were the worst things — at least not in my day. Our neglects were almost worse than our worships."

"You mean the want of all reverence for parents? Well, perhaps that lies at the root of the false worships. They spring up on the vacant soil."

"And the want of reverence for women, Jack. The worst of all, to my mind!"

"Perhaps you are right. But we are not at the bottom yet."

"How do you mean?"

"I mean that we must worship God before we can reverence parents or women, or rout out flunkeyism and money-worship."

"Yes. But after all, can we fairly lay that sin on Oxford? Surely, whatever may be growing up side by side with it, there's more Christianity here than almost anywhere else."

"Plenty of common-room Christianity—belief in a dead God. There, I have never said it to any one but you, but that is the slough we have to get out of. Don't think that I despair for us. We shall do it yet; but it will be sore work, stripping off the comfortable wine-party religion in which we are wrapped up—work for our strongest and our wisest."

"And yet you think of leaving?"

"There are other reasons. I will tell you some day. But now, to turn to other matters, how have you been getting on this last year? You write so seldom that I am all behindhand."

"Oh, much the same as usual."

"Then you are still like one of those who went out to David?"

"No, I'm not in debt."

"But discontented?"

"Pretty much like you there, Jack. However, content is no virtue, that I can see, while there's any thing to mend. Who is going to be contented with game-preserving, and corn-laws, and grinding the faces of the poor? David's camp was a better place than Saul's, any day?"

Hardy got up, opened a drawer, and took out a bundle of papers, which Tom recognized as the *Wessex Freeman*. He felt rather uncomfortable, as his friend seated himself again, and began looking them over.

"You see what I have here?" he said. Tom nodded.

"Well, there are some of the articles I should like to ask you about, if you don't object."

"No; go on."

"Here is one, then, to begin with. I wont read it all. Let me see; here is what I was looking for," and he began reading: "'One would think, to hear these landlords, our rulers, talk, that the glorious green fields, the deep woods, the everlasting hills, and the rivers that run among them, were made for the sole purpose of ministering to their greedy lusts and mean ambitions; that they may roll out amongst unrealities their pitiful mock lives, from their silk and lace cradles to their spangled coffins, studded with silver knobs, and lying coats of arms, reaping where they have not sown, and gathering where they have not strewed; making the omer small and the ephah great, that they may sell the refuse of the wheat —'"

"That'll do, Jack. But what's the date of that paper?"

"July last. Is it yours, then?"

"Yes. And I allow it's too strong and one-sided. I have given up writing altogether; will that satisfy you? I don't see my own way clear enough yet, but for all that, I'm not ashamed of what I wrote in that paper."

"I have nothing more to say after that, except that I'm heartily glad you have given up writing for the present."

"But, I say, old fellow, how did you get these papers, and know about my articles?"

"They were sent me. Shall I burn them now, or would you like to have them? We needn't say any thing more about them."

"Burn them, by all means. I suppose a friend sent them to you?"

"I suppose so." Hardy went on burning the papers in silence; and, as Tom watched him, a sudden light seemed to break upon him.

"I say, Jack," he said, presently, "a little bird has been whispering something to me about that friend."

Hardy winced a little, and redoubled his diligence in burning the papers. Tom looked on smiling, and thinking how to go on now that he had so unexpectedly turned the tables on his monitor, when the clock struck twelve.

"Hullo!" he said, getting up; "time for me to knock out, or old Copas will be in bed. To go back to where we started from to-night — as soon as East and Harry Winburn get back we shall have some jolly doings at Englebourn. There'll be a wedding, I hope, and you'll come over and do parson for us, wont you?"

"You mean for Patty? Of course I will."

"The little bird whispered to me that you wouldn't dislike visiting that part of the old county. Good-night, Jack. I wish you success, old fellow, with all my heart, and I hope after all that you may leave St. Ambrose's within the year."

# CHAPTER XXIII.

#### FROM INDIA TO ENGLEBOURN.

IF a knowledge of contemporary history must be reckoned as an important element in the civilization of any people, then I am afraid that the good folk of Englebourn must have been content, in the days of our story, with a very low place on the ladder. How, indeed, was knowledge to percolate, so as to reach down to the foundations of Englebournian society — the stratum upon which all others rest — the common agricultural laborer, producer of corn, and other grain, the careful and stolid nurse and guardian of youthful oxen, sheep, and pigs, — many of them far better fed and housed than his own children? All-penetrating as she is, one cannot help wondering that she did not give up Englebourn altogether as a hopeless job.

So far as written periodical instruction is concerned (with the exception of the *Quarterly*, which Dr. Winter had taken in from its commencement, but rarely opened), the supply was limited to at most half a dozen weekly papers. A London journal, sound in church and state principles, most respectable but not otherwise than heavy, came every Saturday to the Rectory. The Conservative county paper was taken in at the Red Lion; and David the constable, and the blacksmith, clubbed together to purchase the Liberal paper, by help of which they managed to wage unequal war with the knot of village quidnuncs, who assembled almost nightly at the bar of the Tory beast above referred to, — that king of beasts, red indeed in color, but of the truest blue in political principle. Besides these, perhaps three or four more papers were taken by the farmers. But, scanty as the food was, it was quite enough for the mouths; indeed, when the papers once passed out of the parlors, they had for the most part performed their mission. Few of the farm-servants, male or female, had curiosity or scholarship enough to spell through the dreary columns.

And oral teaching was not much more plentiful, as how was it likely to be? Englebourn was situated on no trunk road, and the amount of intercourse between it and the rest of the world was of the most limited kind. The rector never left home; the curate at rare intervals. Most of the farmers went to market once a week, and dined at their ordinary, discussing county politics after their manner, but bringing home little, except as much food and drink as they could cleverly carry. The carrier went to and from Newbury once a week; but he was a silent man, chiefly bent on collecting and selling butter. The postman, who was deaf, only went as far as the next village. The wagoners drove their masters' produce to market from time to time, and boozed away an hour or two in the kitchen, or tap, or skittle-alley, of some small public-house in the nearest town, while their horses rested. With the above exceptions, probably not one of the villagers strayed ten miles from home, from year's end to year's end. As to visitors, an occasional pedler or small commercial traveller turned up about once a quarter. A few boys and girls, more enterprising than their fellows, went out altogether into the world, of their own accord, in the course of the year; and an occasional burly ploughboy, or carter's boy, was entrapped into taking the queen's shilling by some subtle recruiting sergeant. But few of these were seen again, except at long intervals. The yearly village feasts, harvest homes, or a meet of the hounds on Englebourn Common, were the most exciting events which in an ordinary way stirred the surface of Englebourn life; only faintest and most distant murmurs of the din and strife of the great outer world, of wars, and rumors of wars, the fall of governments and the throes of nations, reached that primitive, out-of-the-way little village.

A change was already showing itself since Miss Winter had been old enough to look after the schools. The waters were beginning to stir; and by this time, no doubt, the parish boasts a regular book-hawker and reading-room; but at that day Englebourn was like one of those small ponds you may find in some nook of a hill-side, the banks grown over with underwood, to which neither man nor beast, scarcely the winds of heaven, have any access. When you have found such a pond you may create a great excitement amongst the easy-going newts and frogs who inhabit it, by throwing in a pebble. The splash in itself is a small splash enough, and the waves which circle away from it are very tiny waves, but they move over the whole face of the pond, and are of more interest to the frogs than a nor-wester in the Atlantic.

So the approaching return of Harry Winburn, and the story of his doings at the wars, and of the wonderful things he had sent home, stirred Englebourn to its depths. In that small corner of the earth the sergeant was of far more importance than governor-general and commander-in-chief. In fact, it was probably the common belief that he was somehow the head of the whole business; and India, the war, and all that hung thereon, were looked at and cared for only as they had served to bring him out. So careless were the good folk about every thing in the matter except their own hero, and so wonderful were the romances which soon got abroad about him, that Miss Winter, tired of explaining again and again to the old women without the slightest effect on the parochial faith, bethought her of having a lecture on the subject of India and the war in the parish school-room.

Full of this idea, she wrote off to Tom, who was the medium of communication on Indian matters, and propounded it to him. The difficulty was, that Mr. Walker the curate, the only person competent to give it, was going away directly for a three weeks' holiday, having arranged with two neighboring curates to take his Sunday duty for him. What was to be done? Harry might be back any day, it seemed; so there was no time to be lost. Could Tom come himself, and help her?

Tom could not; but he wrote back to say that his friend Hardy was just getting away from Oxford for the long vacation, and would gladly take Mr. Walker's duty for the three weeks, if Dr. Winter approved, on his way home; by which arrangement Englebourn would not be without an efficient parson on week days, and she would have the man of all others to help her in utilizing the sergeant's history for the instruction of the bucolic mind. The arrangement, moreover, would be particularly happy, because Hardy had already promised to perform the marriage ceremony, which Tom and she had settled would take place at the earliest possible moment after the return of the Indian heroes.

Dr. Winter was very glad to accept the offer; and so, when they parted at Oxford, Hardy went to Englebourn, where we must leave him for the present. Tom went home — whence, in a few days, he had to hurry down to Southampton to meet the two Harrys. He was much shocked at first to see the state of his old schoolfellow.

East looked haggard and pale in the face, notwithstanding the sea-voyage. His clothes hung on him as if they had been made for a man of twice his size, and he walked with difficulty by the help of a large stick. But he had lost none of his indomitableness, laughed at Tom's long face, and declared that he felt himself getting better and stronger every day.

"If you had only seen me at Calcutta, you would sing a different song, eh, Winburn?"

Harry Winburn was much changed, and had acquired all the composed and self-reliant look which is so remarkable in a good non-commissioned officer. Readiness to obey and command was stamped on every line of his face; but it required all his powers of self-restraint to keep within bounds his delight at getting home again. His wound was quite healed, and his health re-established by the voyage; and, when Tom saw how wonderfully his manners and carriage were improved, and how easily his uniform sat on him, he felt quite sure that all would be soon right at Englebourn, and that Katie and he would be justified in their prophecies and preparations. The invalids had to report themselves in London, and thither the three proceeded together. When this was done, Harry Winburn was sent off at once. He resisted at first, and begged to be allowed to stay with his captain until the captain could go into Berkshire himself. But he was by this time too much accustomed to discipline not to obey a positive order, and was comforted by Tom's assurance that he would not leave East, and would do every thing for him which the sergeant had been accustomed to do.

Three days later, as East and Tom were sitting at breakfast, a short note came from Miss Winter, telling of Harry's arrival — how the bells were set ringing to welcome him; how Mr. Hardy had preached the most wonderful sermon on his story the next day; above all, how Patty had surrendered at discretion, and the banns had been called for the first time. So the sooner they would come down the better — as it was very important that no time should be lost, lest some of the old jealousies and quarrels should break out again. Upon reading and considering which letter, East resolved to start for Englebourn at once, and Tom to accompany him.

There was one person to whom Harry's return and approaching wedding was a subject of unmixed joy and triumph, and that was David the constable. He had always been a sincere friend to Harry, and had stood up for him when all the parish respectabilities had turned against him, and had prophesied that he would live to be a credit to the place. So now David felt himself an inch higher as he saw Harry walking about in his uniform with his sweetheart, the admiration of all Englebourn. But, besides all the unselfish pleasure which David enjoyed on his young friend's account, a little piece of private and personal gratification came to him on his own. Ever since Harry's courtship had begun David had felt himself in a false position towards, and had suffered under, old Simon, the rector's gardener. The necessity for keeping the old man in good humor for Harry's sake had always been present to the constable's mind; and, for the privilege of putting in a good word for his favorite every now and then, he had allowed old Simon to assume an air of superiority over him, and to trample upon him and dogmatize to him, even in the matters of flowers and bees. This had been the more galling to David on account of old Simon's intolerant Toryism, which the constable's soul rebelled against, except in the matter of church music. On this one point they agreed, but even here Simon managed to be unpleasant. He would lay the whole blame of the changes which had been effected upon David, accusing him of having given in when there was no need. As there was nothing but a wall between the Rectory garden and David's little strip of ground, in which he spent all his leisure time, until the shades of evening summoned him to the bar of the Red Lion for his daily pint and pipe, the two were constantly within hearing of one another, and Simon, in times past, had seldom neglected an opportunity of making himself disagreeable to his long-suffering neighbor.

But now David was a free man again; and he took the earliest occasion of making the change in his manner apparent to Simon, and of getting, as he called it, "upsides" with him. One would have thought, to look at him, that the old gardener was as pachydermatous as a rhinoceros; but somehow he seemed to feel that things had changed between them, and did not appreciate an interview with David now nearly so much as of old. So he found very little to do in that part of the garden which abutted on the constable's premises. When he could not help working there, he chose the times at which David was most likely to be engaged, or even took the trouble to ascertain that he was not at home.

Early on Midsummer-day, old Simon reared his ladder against the boundary wall, with the view of "doctorin'" some of the fruit trees, relying on a parish meeting, at which the constable's presence was required. But he had not more than half finished his operations before David returned from vestry, and, catching sight of the top of the ladder and Simon's head above the wall, laid aside all other business, and descended into the garden.

Simon kept on at his work, only replying by a jerk of the head and one of his grunts to his neighbor's salutation.

David took his coat off, and his pruning-knife out, and, establishing himself within easy shot of his old oppressor, opened fire at once,—

"Thou'st gi'en thy consent then?"

"'Tis no odds, consent or none—her's old enough to hev her own waay."

"But thou'st gi'en thy consent?"

"Ees, then, if thou wilt hev't," said Simon, surlily; "wut then?"

"So I heerd," said David, indulging in an audible chuckle.

"What bist a laughin' at?"

"I be laughin' to think how folks changes. Do'st mind the hard things as thou hast judged and said o' Harry? Not as ever I known thy judgment to be o' much account, 'cept about roots. But thou saidst, times and times, as a would come to the gallows."

"So a med yet—so a med yet," answered Simon. "Not but wut I wishes well to un, and bears no grudges; but others as hev got the law ov un medn't."

"'Tis he as hev got grudges to bear. He don't need none o' thy forgiveness."

"Pr'aps a medn't. But hev 'em got the law ov un, or hevn't 'em?"

"Wut do'st mean: got the law ov un?"

"Thaay warrants as wur out agen un, along wi' the rest as was transpworted auver Farmer Tester's job."

"Oh, he've got no call to be afeard o' thaay now. Thou know'st I hears how 'tis laid down at Sessions and 'Sizes, wher' I've a been this twenty year."

"Like enuff. Only, wut's to hinder thaay tryin' ov un, if thaay be minded to't? That's wut I wants to know."

"'Tis wut the counsellors calls the Statut o' Lamentations," said the constable, proudly.

"Wutever's Lamentations got to do wi't?"

"A gurt deal, I tell 'ee. What do'st thou know o' Lamentations?"

"Lamentations cums afore Ezekiel in the Bible."

"That aint no kin to the Statut o' Lamentations. But there's summut like to't in the Bible," said the constable, stopping his work to consider a moment. "Do'st mind the year when the land wur all to be guv back to they as owned it fust, and debts wur to be wiped out?"

"Ees, I minds summut o' that."

"Well, this here statut says, if so be as a man hev bin to the wars, and sarved his country like, as nothin' sha'n't be reckoned agen he, let alone murder: nothin' can't do away wi' murder."

"No, nor oughtn't. Hows'mdever, you seems clear about the law on't. There's miss a callin'."

And old Simon's head disappeared as he descended the ladder to answer the summons of his young mistress, not displeased at having his fears as to the safety of his future son-in-law set at rest by so eminent a legal authority as the constable. Fortunately for Harry, the constable's law was not destined to be tried. Young Wurley was away in London. Old Tester was bedridden with an accumulation of diseases brought on by his bad life. His illness made him more violent and tyrannical than ever; but he could do little harm out of his own room, for no one ever went to see him, and the wretched farm-servant who attended him was much too frightened to tell him any thing of what was going on in the parish. There was no one else to revive proceedings against Harry.

David pottered on at his bees and his flowers till old Simon returned, and ascended his ladder again.

"You be ther' still, be 'ee?" he said, as soon as he saw David.

"Ees. Any news?"

"Ah, news enuff. He as wur Harry's captain and young Mr. Brown be comin' down to-morrow, and hev tuk all the Red Lion to theirselves. And thaay beant content to wait for banns—not thaay—and so ther's to be a license got for Saturday. 'Tain't scarce decent, that 'tain't."

"'Tis best to get drough wi't," said the constable.

"Then nothin'll sarve 'em but the church must be hung wi' flowers, and wher' be thaay to cum from without stripping and starving ov my beds? 'Tis shameful to see how folks acts wi' flowers now-a-days, a cuttin' on 'em and puttin' on 'em about, as prodigal as though thaay growed o' theirselves."

"So 'tis, shameful," said David, whose sympathies for flowers were all with Simon. "I heers tell as young Squire Wurley hevs 'em on table at dinner-time instead o' the wittles."

"Do'ee though! I calls it reg'lar papistry, and so I tells miss; but her only laughs."

The constable shook his head solemnly as he replied, "Her've been led away wi' such doin's ever since Mr. Walker cum, and took to organ-playin' and chantin'."

"And he aint no sich gurt things in the pulpit neether, aint Mr. Walker," chimed in Simon (the two had not been so in harmony for years). "I reckon as he aint nothin' to speak ov alongside o' this here new un as hev tuk his place. He've got a deal o' move in un, he hev."

"Ah, so a hev. A wunnerful sight o' things a telled us t'other night about the Indians and the wars."

"Ah! talking cums as nat'ral to he as buttermilk to a litterin' sow."

"Thou should'st a heerd un, though, about the battles I can't mind the names on 'em — let me zee —"

"I dwun't vally the neames," interrupted Simon. "They makes a deal o' fuss ouver't aall, but I dwunt tek no account on't. 'Taint like the owld wars and fightin' o' the French, this here fightin' wi' blackamooes, let 'em talk as thaay wool."

"No more 'tain't. But 'twur a 'mazin' fine talk as he gi'n us. Hev'ee seed ought 'twixt he and young missus?"

"Nothin' out o' th' common. I got plenty to do without lookin' arter the women, and 'tain't no bisness o' mine, nor o' thine neether."

David was preparing a stout rejoinder to this rebuke of the old retainer of the Winter family on his curiosity, but was summoned by his wife to the house to attend a customer; and by the time he could get out again Simon had disappeared.

The next day East and Tom arrived, and took possession of the Red Lion; and Englebourn was soon in a ferment of preparation for the wedding. East was not the man to do things by halves; and, seconded as he was by Miss Winter and Hardy and Tom, had soon made arrangements for all sorts of merry-making. The school-children were to have a whole holiday, and, after scattering flowers at church and marching in the bridal procession, were to be entertained in a tent pitched in the home paddock of the Rectory, and to have an afternoon of games and prizes, and tea and cake. The bell-ringers, Harry's old comrades, were to have five shillings apiece, and a cricket match, and a dinner afterwards at the second public-house, to which any other of his old friends whom Harry chose to ask were to be also invited. The old men and women were to be fed in the village school-room; and East and Tom were to entertain a select party of the farmers and tradesmen at the Red Lion, the tap of which hostelry was to be thrown open to all comers at the captain's expense. It was not without considerable demur on the part of Miss Winter that some of these indiscriminate festivities were allowed to pass. But after consulting with Hardy she relented, on condition that the issue of beer at the two public-houses should be put under the control of David the constable, who, on his part, promised that law and order should be well represented and maintained on the occasion. "Arter all, miss, you sees 'tis only for once in a waay," he said, "and 'twill make 'em remember aal as hev bin said to 'em about the Indians, and the rest on't." So the captain and his abettors, having gained the constable as an ally, prevailed; and Englebourn, much wondering at itself, made ready for a general holiday.

# CHAPTER XXIV.

### THE WEDDING-DAY.

One — more — poor — man — un-done —<br>
One — more — poor — man — un-done.

THE belfry-tower rocked and reeled, as that peal rang out, now merry, now scornful, now plaintive, from those narrow belfry windows, into the bosom of the soft south-west wind, which was playing round the old gray tower of Englebourn church. And the wind caught the peal and played with it, and bore it away over Rectory and village street, and many a homestead, and gently waving field of ripening corn, and rich pasture and water-meadow, and tall whispering woods of the Grange, and rolled it against the hill-side, and up the slope past the clump of firs on the Hawk's Lynch, till it died away on the wild stretches of common beyond.

The ringers bent lustily to their work. There had been no such ringing in Englebourn since the end of the great war. Not content with the usual peal out of church, they came back again and again in the afternoon, full of the good cheer which had been provided for them; and again and again the wedding-peal rang out from the belfry in honor of their old comrade —

One — more — poor — man — un-done —<br>
One — more — poor — man — un-done.

Such was the ungallant speech which for many generations had been attributed to the Englebourn weddingbells; and when you had once caught the words — as you would be sure to do from some wide-mouthed, grinning boy, lounging over the churchyard rails to see the wedding pass — it would be impossible to persuade yourself that they did, in fact, say any thing else. Somehow, Harry Winburn bore his undoing in the most heroic manner, and did his duty throughout the trying day, as a non-commissioned officer and bridegroom should. The only part of the performance arranged by his captain which he fairly resisted, was the proposed departure of himself and Patty to the station in the solitary post-chaise of Englebourn — a real old yellow — with a pair of horses. East, after hearing the sergeant's pleading on the subject of vehicles, at last allowed them to drive off in a tax-cart, taking a small boy with them behind, to bring it back.

As for the festivities, they went off without a hitch, as such affairs will, where the leaders of the revels have their hearts in them. The children had all played, and romped, and eaten, and drunk themselves into a state of torpor by an early hour of the evening. The farmers' dinner was a decided success. East proposed the health of the bride and bridegroom, and was followed by Farmer Grove and the constable. David turned out in a new blue swallow-tailed coat, with metal buttons, of his own fabulous cut, in honor of the occasion. He and the farmer spoke like the leader of the Government and the Opposition in the House of Commons on an address to the Crown. There was not a pin to choose between their speeches, and a stranger hearing them would naturally have concluded that Harry had never been any thing but the model boy and young man of the parish. Fortunately, the oratorical powers of Englebourn ended here; and East, and the majority of his guests, adjourned to the green where the cricket was in progress. Each game lasted a very short time only, as the youth of Englebourn were not experts in the noble science, and lost their wickets one after another so fast, that Tom and Hardy had time to play out two matches with them, and then to retire on their laurels, while the afternoon was yet young.

The old folk in the village school-room enjoyed their beef and pudding, under the special superintendence of Miss Winter, and then toddled to their homes, and sat about in the warmest nooks they could find, mumbling of old times, and the doings at Dr. Winter's wedding.

David devoted himself to superintending the issue of beer, swelling with importance, but so full of the milk of human kindness from the great event of the day that nobody minded his little airs. He did his duty so satisfactorily that, with the exception of one or two regular confirmed soakers, who stuck steadily to the tap of the Red Lion, and there managed successfully to fuddle themselves, there was nothing like drunkenness. In short, it was one of those rare days when every thing goes right, and everybody seems to be inclined to give and take, and to make allowances for their neighbors. By degrees the cricket flagged, and most of the men went off to sit over their pipes, and finish the evening in their own way. The boys and girls took to playing at kissing in the ring; and the children who had not already gone home sat in groups watching them.

Miss Winter had already disappeared, and Tom, Hardy, and the captain, began to feel that they might consider their part finished. They strolled together off the green towards Hardy's lodgings, the Red Lion being still in the possession of East's guests.

"Well, how do you think it all went off?" asked he.

"Nothing could have been better," said Hardy; "and

they all seem so inclined to be reasonable that I don't think we shall even have a roaring song along the street to-night when the Red Lion shuts up."

"And are you satisfied, Tom?"

"I should think so. I have been hoping for this day any time this four years, and now it has come and gone off well, too, thanks to you, Harry."

"Thanks to me? Very good; I am open to any amount of gratitude."

"I think you have every reason to be satisfied with your second day's work at Englebourn, at any rate."

"So I am. I only hope it may turn out as well as the first."

"Oh, there's no doubt about that."

"I don't know. I rather believe in the rule of contraries."

"How do you mean?"

"Why, when you inveigled me over from Oxford, and we carried off the sergeant from the authorities, and defeated the yeomanry in that tremendous thunder-storm, I thought we were a couple of idiots, and deserved a week each in the lock-up for our pains. That business turned out well. This time we have started with flying colors, and bells ringing, and so —"

"This business will turn out better. Why not?"

"Then let us manage a third day's work in these parts as soon as possible. I should like to get to the third degree of comparison, and perhaps the superlative will turn up trumps for me somehow. Are there many more young women in the place as pretty as Mrs. Winburn? This marrying complaint is very catching, I find."

"There's my Cousin Katie," said Tom, looking stealthily at Hardy; "I wont allow that there's any face in the country-side to match hers. What do you say, Jack?"

Hardy was confused by this sudden appeal.

"I haven't been long enough here to judge," he said. "I have always thought Miss Winter very beautiful. I see it is nearly seven o'clock, and I have a call or two to make in the village. I should think you ought to get some rest after this tiring day, Captain East."

"What are you going to do, Tom?"

"Well, I was thinking of just throwing a fly over the mill tail. There's such a fine head of water on."

"Isn't it too bright?"

"Well, perhaps it is a little: marrying weather and fishing weather don't agree. Only what else is there to do? But if you are tired," he added, looking at East, "I don't care a straw about it. I shall stay with you."

"Not a bit of it. I shall hobble down with you, and lie on the bank and smoke a cheroot."

"No, you sha'n't walk, at any rate. I can borrow the constable's pony, old Nibble, the quietest beast in the world. He'll stand for a week if we like while I fish and you lie and look on. I'll be off, and bring him round in two minutes."

"Then we shall meet for a clumsy tea at nine at my lodgings," said Hardy, as he went off to his pastoral duties.

Tom and East, in due time, found themselves by the side of the stream. There was only a small piece of fishable water in Englebourn. The fine stream, which, a mile or so below, in the Grange grounds, might be called a river, came into respectable existence only about two hundred yards above Englebourn mill. Here two little chalk brooks met, and former millers had judiciously deepened the channel, and dammed the united waters back so as to get a respectable reservoir. Above the junction the little weedy, bright, creeping brooks, afforded good sport for small truants groppling about with their hands, or bobbing with lobworms under the hollow banks, but were not available for the scientific angler. The parish ended at the fence next below the mill garden, on the other side of which the land was part of the Grange estate. So there was just the piece of still water above the mill, and the one field below it, over which Tom had leave. On ordinary occasions this would have been enough, with careful fishing, to last him till dark; but his nerves were probably somewhat excited by the events of the day, and East sat near and kept talking; so he got over his water faster than usual. At any rate, he had arrived for the second time at the envious fence before the sun was down. The fish were wondrous wary in the miller's bit of water — as might be expected, for they led a dog of a life there, between the miller and his men, and their nets, and baits of all kinds always set. So Tom thought himself lucky to get a couple of decent fish, the only ones that were moving within his liberty; but he could not help looking with covetous eyes on the fine stretch of water below, all dimpling with rises.

"Why don't you get over and fish below?" said East, from his seat on the bank; "don't mind me. I can watch you from here; besides, lying on the turf on such an evening is luxury enough by itself."

"I can't go. Both sides below belong to that fellow Wurley."

"The sergeant's amiable landlord and prosecutor?"

"Yes; and the yeoman with whom you exchanged shots on the common."

"Hang it, Tom, just jump over and catch a brace of his trout. Look how they are rising."

"No. I don't know. I never was very particular

about poaching, but somehow I shouldn't like to do it on his land. I don't like him well enough."

"You're right, I believe. But, just look there. There's a whopper rising not more than ten yards below the rail. You might reach him, I think, without trespassing, from where you stand."

"Shall I have a shy at him?"

"Yes; it can't be poaching if you don't go on his ground."

Tom could not resist the temptation, and threw over the rails, which crossed the stream from hedge to hedge to mark the boundaries of the parish, until he got well over the place where the fish was rising.

"There, that was at your fly," said East, hobbling up in great excitement.

"All right, I shall have him directly. There he is. Hullo! Harry, I say! Splash with your stick. Drive the brute back. Bad luck to him. Look at that!"

The fish when hooked had come straight up-stream towards his captor, and, notwithstanding East's attempts to frighten him back, had rushed in under the before-mentioned rails, which were adorned with jagged nails, to make crossing on them unpleasant for the Englebourn boys. Against one of these Tom's line severed, and the waters closed over two beauteous flies, and some six feet of lovely taper gut.

East laughed loud and merrily; and Tom, crestfallen as he was, was delighted to hear the old ring coming back into his friend's voice.

"Harry, old fellow, you're picking up already in this glorious air."

"Of course I am. Two or three more weddings and fishings will set me up altogether. How could you be so green as to throw over those rails? It's a proper lesson to you, Tom, for poaching."

"Well, that's cool. Didn't I throw down-stream to please you?"

"You ought to have resisted temptation. But, I say, what are you at?"

"Putting on another cast, of course."

"Why, you're not going on to Wurley's land?"

"No; I suppose not. I must try the mill tail again."

"It's no good. You've tried it over twice, and I'm getting bored."

"Well, what shall we do, then?"

"I've a mind to get up to the hill there to see the sun set — what's its name? — where I waited with the cavalry that night, you know."

"Oh! the Hawk's Lynch. Come along, then; I'm your man."

So Tom put up his rod, and caught the old pony, and the two friends were soon on their way towards the common, through lanes at the back of the village.

The wind had sunk to sleep as the shadows lengthened. There was no sound abroad except that of Nibble's hoofs on the turf, — not even the hum of insects; for the few persevering gnats, who were still dancing about in the slanting glints of sunshine that struck here and there across the lanes, had left off humming. Nothing living met them, except an occasional stag-beetle, steering clumsily down the lane, and seeming, like a heavy coaster, to have as much as he could fairly manage in keeping clear of them. They walked on in silence for some time, which was broken at last by East.

"I haven't had time to tell you about my future prospects."

"How do you mean? Has any thing happened?"

"Yes. I got a letter two days ago from New Zealand, where I find I am a considerable landowner. A cousin of mine has died out there and left me his property."

"Well, you're not going to leave England, surely?"

"Yes, I am. The doctors say the voyage will do me good, and the climate is just the one to suit me. What's the good of my staying here? I sha'n't be fit for service again for years. I shall go on half-pay, and become an enterprising agriculturist at the Antipodes. I've spoken to the sergeant, and arranged that he and his wife shall go with me; so, as soon as I can get his discharge, and he has done honeymooning, we shall start. I wish you would come with us."

Tom could scarcely believe his ears; but soon found that East was in earnest, and had an answer to all his remonstrances. Indeed, he had very little to say against the plan, for it jumped with his own humor; and he could not help admitting that, under the circumstances, it was a wise one, and that, with Harry Winburn for his head man, East couldn't do better than carry it out.

"I knew you would soon come round to it," said the captain; "what could I do dawdling about at home, with just enough money to keep me and get me into mischief? There I shall have a position and an object; and one may be of some use, and make one's mark in a new country. And we'll get a snug berth ready for you by the time you're starved out of the old country. England isn't the place for poor men with any go in them."

"I believe you're right, Harry," said Tom, mournfully.

"I know I am. And in a few years, when we've made our fortunes, we'll come back and have a look at the old country, and perhaps buy up half Englebourn, and lay our bones in the old churchyard."

"And if we don't make our fortunes?"

"Then we'll stay out there."

"Well, if I were my own master I think I should make one with you. But I could never leave my father and mother, or — or —"

"Oh, I understand. Of course, if matters go all right in that quarter, I have nothing more to say. But, from what you have told me, I thought you might be glad of a regular break in your life, a new start in a new world."

"Very likely I may. I should have said so myself this morning. But somehow I feel to-night more hopeful than I have for years."

"Those wedding-chimes are running in your head."

"Yes; and they have lifted a load off my heart too. Four years ago I was very near doing the greatest wrong a man can do to that girl who was married to-day, and to that fine fellow her husband, who was the first friend I ever had. Ever since then I have been doing my best to set matters straight, and have often made them crookeder. But to-day they are all straight, thank God, and I feel as if a chain were broken from off my neck. All has come right for them, and perhaps my own turn will come before long."

"To be sure it will. I must be introduced to a certain young lady before we start. I shall tell her that I don't mean to give up hopes of seeing her on the other side of the world."

"Well, here we are on the common. What a glorious sunset! Come, stir up, Nibble. We shall be on the Lynch just in time to see him dip if we push on."

Nibble, that ancient pony, finding that there was no help for it, scrambled up the greater part of the ascent successfully. But his wheezings and roarings during the operation excited East's pity. So he dismounted when they came to the foot of the Hawk's Lynch, and, tying Nibble's bridle to a furze bush,— a most unnecessary precaution, — set to work to scale the last and steepest bit of the ascent with the help of his stick and Tom's strong arm.

They paused every ten paces or so to rest and look at the sunset. The broad vale below lay in purple shadow; the soft flocks of little clouds high up over their heads, and stretching away to the eastern horizon, floated in a sea of rosy light; and the stems of the Scotch firs stood out like columns of ruddy flame.

"Why, this beats India," said East, putting up his hand to shade his eyes, which were fairly dazzled by the blaze. "What a contrast to the last time I was up here! Do you remember that awful black-blue sky?"

"Don't I? Like a nightmare. Hullo! who's here?"

"Why, if it isn't the parson and Miss Winter!" said East, smiling.

True enough, there they were, standing together on the very verge of the mound, beyond the firs, some ten yards in front of the last comers, looking out into the sunset.

"I say, Tom, another good omen," whispered East; "hadn't we better beat a retreat?"

Before Tom could answer, or make up his mind what to do, Hardy turned his head and caught sight of them, and then Katie turned too, blushing like the little clouds overhead. It was an embarrassing moment. Tom stammered out that they had come up quite by chance, and then set to work, well seconded by East, to look desperately unconscious, and to expatiate on the beauties of the view. The light began to fade, and the little clouds to change again from soft pink to gray, and the evening star shone out clear as they turned to descend the hill, when the Englebourn clock chimed nine.

Katie attached herself to Tom, while Hardy helped the captain down the steep pitch, and on to the back of Nibble. They went a little ahead. Tom was longing to speak to his cousin, but could not tell how to begin. At last Katie broke silence, —

"I am so vexed that this should have happened!"

"Are you, dear? So am not I," he said, pressing her arm to his side.

"But I mean, it seems so forward — as if I had met Mr. Hardy here on purpose. What will your friend think of me?"

"He will think no evil."

"But indeed, Tom, do tell him, pray. It was quite an accident. You know how I and Mary used to go up the Hawk's Lynch whenever we could, on fine evenings."

"Yes, dear, I know it well."

"And I thought of you both so much to-day, that I couldn't help coming up here."

"And you found Hardy? I don't wonder. I should come up to see the sun set every night, if I lived at Englebourn."

"No. He came up some time after me. Straight up the hill. I did not see him till he was quite close. I could not run away then. Indeed, it was not five minutes before you came."

"Five minutes are as good as a year sometimes."

"And you will tell your friend, Tom, how it happened?"

"Indeed I will, Katie. May I not tell him something more?"

He looked round for an answer, and there was just light enough to read it in her eyes.

"My debt is deepening to the Hawk's Lynch," he said, as they walked on through the twilight. "Blessed five minutes! Whatever else they may take with them, they will carry my thanks forever. Look how clear and steady the light of that star is, just over the church tower. I wonder whether Mary is at a great hot dinner. Shall you write to her soon?"

"Oh, yes. To-night."

"You may tell her that there is no better Englishman walking the earth than my friend, John Hardy. Here we are at his lodgings. East and I are going to tea with him. Wish them good-night, and I will see you home."

# CHAPTER XXV.

#### A MEETING IN THE STREET.

FROM the Englebourn festivities Tom and East returned to London. The captain was bent on starting for his possessions in the South Pacific; and, as he regained strength, energized over all his preparations, and went about in cabs purchasing agricultural implements, sometimes by the light of nature, and sometimes under the guidance of Harry Winburn. He invested also in something of a library, and in large quantities of saddlery. In short, packages of all kinds began to increase and multiply upon him. Then there was the selecting a vessel, and all the negotiations with the ship's husband as to terms, and the business of getting introduced to, and conferring with, people from the colony, or who were supposed to know something about it. Altogether, East had plenty of work on his hands; and, the more he had to do, the better and more cheery he became.

Tom, on the contrary, was rather lower than usual. His half-formed hopes, that some good luck was going to happen to him after Patty's marriage, were beginning to grow faint, and the contrast of his friend's definite present purpose in life with his own uncertainty, made him more or less melancholy in spite of all his efforts. His father had offered him a tour abroad, now that he had finished with Oxford, urging that he seemed to want a change to freshen him up before buckling to a profession, and that he would never, in all likelihood, have such another chance. But he could not make up his mind to accept the offer. The attraction to London was too strong for him; and, though he saw little hope of any thing happening to improve his prospects, he could not keep away from it. He spent most of his time when not with East in haunting the neighborhood of Mr. Porter's house in Belgravia, and the places where he was likely to catch distant glimpses of Mary, avoiding all chance of actual meeting or recognition, from which he shrank in his present frame of mind.

The nearest approach to the flame which he allowed himself was a renewal of his old friendship with Grey, who was still working on in his Westminster rookery. He had become a great favorite with Mrs. Porter, who was always trying to get him to her house to feed him properly, and was much astonished, and sometimes almost provoked, at the small success of her hospitable endeavors. Grey was so taken up with his own pursuits that it did not occur to him to be surprised that he never met Tom at the house of his relations. He was innocent of all knowledge or suspicion of the real state of things, so that Tom could talk to him with perfect freedom about his uncle's household, picking up all such scraps of information as Grey possessed without compromising himself or feeling shy.

Thus the two old schoolfellows lived on together after their return from Englebourn, in a set of chambers in the Temple, which one of Tom's college friends, who had been beguiled from the perusal of Stephens' Commentaries, and aspirations after the woolsack, by the offer of a place on board a yacht and a cruise to Norway, had fortunately lent him.

We join company with our hero again on a fine July

morning. Readers will begin to think that, at any rate, he is always blessed with fine weather whatever troubles he may have to endure; but, if we are not to have fine weather in novels, when and where are we to have it? It was a fine July morning, then, and the streets were already beginning to feel sultry as he worked his way westward. Grey, who had never given up hopes of bringing Tom round to his own views, had not neglected the opportunities which this residence in town offered, and had enlisted Tom's services on more than one occasion. He had found him specially useful in instructing the big boys, whom he was trying to bring together and civilize in a "Young Men's Club," in the rudiments of cricket on Saturday evenings. But on the morning in question an altogether different work was on hand.

A lady, living some eight or nine miles to the northwest of London, who took great interest in Grey's doings, had asked him to bring the children of his night-school down to spend a day in her grounds, and this was the happy occasion. It was before the days of cheap excursions by rail, so that vans had to be found for the party; and Grey had discovered a benevolent remover of furniture in Paddington, who was ready to take them at a reasonable figure. The two vans, with awnings and curtains in the height of the fashion, and horses with tasselled ear-caps, and every thing handsome about them, were already drawn up in the midst of a group of excited children, and scarcely less excited mothers, when Tom arrived. Grey was arranging his forces, and laboring to reduce the Irish children, who formed almost half of his ragged little flock, into something like order before starting. By degrees this was managed, and Tom was placed in command of the rear van, while Grey reserved the leading one to himself. The children were divided, and warned not to lean over the sides and tumble out — a somewhat superfluous caution, as most of them, though unused to riding in any legitimate manner, were pretty well used to balancing themselves behind any vehicle which offered as much as a spike to sit on, out of sight of the driver. Then came the rush into the vans. Grey and Tom took up their places next the doors as conductors, and the procession lumbered off with great success, and much shouting from treble voices.

Tom soon found that he had plenty of work on his hands to keep the peace amongst his flock. The Irish element was in a state of wild effervescence, and he had to draft them down to his own end, leaving the foremost part of the van to the soberer English children. He was much struck by the contrast of the whole set to the Englebourn school children, whom he had lately seen under somewhat similar circumstances. The difficulty with them had been to draw them out, and put any thing like life into them; here, all he had to do was to repress the superabundant life. However, the vans held on their way, and got safely into the suburbs, and so at last to an occasional hedge, and a suspicion of trees, and green fields beyond.

It became more and more difficult now to keep the boys in; and, when they came to a hill, where the horses had to walk, he yielded to their entreaties, and, opening the door, let them out, insisting only that the girls should remain seated. They scattered over the sides of the roads, and up the banks; now chasing pigs and fowls up to the very doors of their owners; now gathering the commonest road-side weeds, and running up to show them to him, and ask their names, as if they were rare treasures. The ignorance of most of the children as to the commonest country matters astonished him. One small boy particularly came back time after time to ask him, with solemn face, "Please, sir, is this the country?" and, when, at last he allowed that it was, rejoined, "Then, please, where are the nuts?"

The clothing of most of the Irish boys began to tumble to pieces in an alarming manner. Grey had insisted on their being made tidy for the occasion, but the tidiness was of a superficial kind. The hasty stitching soon began to give way, and they were rushing about with wild locks — the strips of what once might have been nether garments hanging about their legs; their feet and heads bare, the shoes which their mothers had borrowed for the state occasion having been deposited under the seat of the van. So, when the procession arrived at the trim lodge-gates of their hostess, and his charge descended and fell in on the beautifully clipped turf at the side of the drive, Tom felt some of the sensations of Falstaff when he had to lead his ragged regiment through Coventry streets.

He was soon at his ease again, and enjoyed the day thoroughly, and the drive home; but, as they drew near town again, a sense of discomfort and shyness came over him, and he wished the journey to Westminster well over, and hoped that the carmen would have the sense to go through the quiet parts of the town.

He was much disconcerted, consequently, when the vans came to a sudden stop, opposite one of the park entrances, in the Bayswater road. "What in the world is Grey about?" he thought, as he saw him get out, and all the children after him. So he got out himself, and went forward to get an explanation.

"Oh, I have told the man that he need not drive us round to Westminster. He is close at home here; and his horses have had a hard day; so we can just get out and walk home."

"What, across the park?" asked Tom.

"Yes, it will amuse the children, you know."

"But they're tired," persisted Tom; "come now, it's all nonsense letting the fellow off; he's bound to take us back."

"I'm afraid I have promised him," said Grey; "besides, the children all think it a treat. Don't you all want to walk across the park?" he went on, turning to them, and a general affirmative chorus was the answer. So Tom had nothing for it but to shrug his shoulders, empty his own van, and follow into the park with his convoy, not in the best humor with Grey for having arranged this ending to their excursion.

They might have got over a third of the distance between the Bayswater road and the Serpentine, when he was aware of a small thin voice addressing him.

"Oh, please, wont you carry me a bit? I'm so tired," said the voice. He turned in some trepidation to look for the speaker, and found her to be a sickly undergrown little girl of ten or thereabouts, with large pleading gray eyes, very shabbily dressed, and a little lame. He had remarked her several times in the course of the day, not for any beauty or grace about her, for the poor child had none, but for her transparent confidence and trustfulness. After dinner, as they had been all sitting on the grass under the shade of a great elm to hear Grey read a story, and Tom had been sitting a little apart from the rest with his back against the trunk, she had come up and sat quietly down by him, leaning on his knee. Then he had seen her go up and take the hand of the lady who had entertained them, and walk along by her, talking without the least shyness. Soon afterwards she had squeezed into the swing by the side of the beautifully dressed little daughter of the same lady, who, after looking for a minute at her shabby little sister with large round eyes, had jumped out and run off to her mother, evidently in a state of childish bewilderment as to whether it was not wicked for a child to wear such dirty old clothes.

Tom had chuckled to himself as he saw Cinderella settling herself comfortably in the swing in the place of the ousted princess, and had taken a fancy to the child, speculating to himself as to how she could have been brought up, to be so utterly unconscious of differences of rank and dress. "She seems really to treat her fellow-creatures as if she had been studying the Sartor Resartus," he thought. "She has cut down through all clothes philosophy without knowing it. I wonder, if she had a chance, whether she would go and sit down in the queen's lap?"

He did not at the time anticipate that she would put his own clothes philosophy to so severe a test before the day was over. The child had been as merry and active as any of the rest during the earlier part of the day; but now, as he looked down, in answer to her reiterated plea, "Wont you carry me a bit? I'm so tired!" he saw that she could scarcely drag one foot after the other.

What was to be done? He was already keenly alive to the discomfort of walking across Hyde Park in a procession of ragged children, with such a figure of fun as Grey at their head, looking, in his long, rusty, straight-cut black coat, as if he had come fresh out of Noah's ark. He didn't care about it so much while they were on the turf in the out-of-the-way parts, and would meet nobody but guards, and nurse-maids, and trades-people, and mechanics out for an evening stroll. But the Drive and Rotten Row lay before them, and must be crossed. It was just the most crowded time of the day. He had almost made up his mind once or twice to stop Grey and the procession, and propose to sit down for half an hour or so, and let the children play, by which time the world would be going home to dinner. But there was no play left in the children; and he had resisted the temptation, meaning, when they came to the most crowded part, to look unconscious, as if it were by chance that he had got into such company, and had in fact nothing to do with them. But now, if he listened to the child's plea, and carried her, all hope of concealment was over. If he did not, he felt that there would be no greater flunkey in the park that evening than Thomas Brown, the enlightened radical and philosopher, amongst the young-gentlemen riders in Rotten Row, or the powdered footmen lounging behind the great blaring carriages in the Drive.

So he looked down at the child once or twice in a state of puzzle. A third time she looked up with her great eyes, and said, "Oh, please carry me a bit!" and her piteous, tired face turned the scale. "If she were Lady Mary or Lady Blanche," thought he, "I should pick her up at once, and be proud of the burden. Here goes!" And he took her up in his arms, and walked on, desperate and reckless.

Notwithstanding all his philosophy, he felt his ears tingling and his face getting red, as they approached the Drive. It was crowded. They were kept standing a minute or two at the crossing. He made a desperate effort to abstract himself wholly from the visible world, and retire into a state of serene contemplation. But it would not do; and he was painfully conscious of the stare of lack-lustre eyes of well-dressed men leaning over the rails, and the amused look of delicate ladies, lounging in open carriages, and surveying him and Grey and their ragged rout through glasses.

At last they scrambled across, and he breathed freely for a minute, as they struggled along the comparatively quiet path leading to Albert Gate, and stopped to drink at the fountain. Then came Rotten Row, and another pause amongst the loungers, and a plunge into the ride, where he was nearly run down by two men whom he had known at Oxford. They shouted to him to get out of the way; and he felt the hot, defiant blood rushing through his veins, as he strode across without heeding. They passed on, one of them having to pull his horse out of his stride to avoid him. Did they recognize him? He felt a strange mixture of utter indifference, and longing to strangle them.

The worst was now over; besides, he was getting used to the situation, and his good sense was beginning to rally. So he marched through Albert Gate, carrying his ragged little charge, who prattled away to him without a pause, and surrounded by the rest of the children, scarcely caring who might see him, and who might not. They won safely through the omnibuses and carriages on the Kensington road, and so into Belgravia. At last he was quite at his ease again, and began listening to what the child was saying to him, and was strolling carelessly along, when once more, at one of the crossings, he was startled by a shout from some riders. There was straw laid down in the street, so that he had not heard them as they cantered round the corner, hurrying home to dress for dinner; and they were all but upon him, and had to rein up their horses sharply.

The party consisted of a lady and two gentlemen,— one old, the other young; the latter dressed in the height of fashion, and with the supercilious air which Tom hated from his soul. The shout came from the young man, and drew Tom's attention to him first. All the devil rushed up as he recognized St. Cloud. The lady's horse swerved against his, and began to rear. He put his hand on its bridle, as if he had a right to protect her. Another glance told Tom that the lady was Mary, and the old gentleman, fussing up on his stout cob on the other side of her, Mr. Porter.

They all knew him in another moment. He stared from one to the other, was conscious that she turned her horse's head sharply, so as to disengage the bridle from St. Cloud's hand, and of his insolent stare, and of the embarrassment of Mr. Porter; and then, setting his face straight before him, he passed on in a bewildered dream, never looking back till they were out of sight. The dream gave way to bitter and wild thoughts, upon which it will do none of us any good to dwell. He put down the little girl outside the schools, turning abruptly from the mother, a poor widow in scant well-preserved black clothes, who was waiting for the child, and began thanking him for his care of her; refused Grey's pressing invitation to tea, and set his face eastward. Bitterer and more wild and more scornful grew his thoughts as he strode along past the abbey, and up Whitehall, and away down the Strand, holding on over the crossings without paying the slightest heed to vehicle, or horse, or man. Incensed coachmen had to pull up with a jerk to avoid running over him, and more than one sturdy walker turned round in indignation at a collision which they felt had been intended, or at least there had been no effort to avoid. As he passed under the window of the Banqueting Hall, and by the place in Charing-cross where the pillory used to stand, he growled to himself what a pity it was that the times for cutting off heads and cropping ears had gone by. The whole of the dense population from either side of the Strand seemed to have crowded out into that thoroughfare to impede his march and aggravate him. The further eastward he got the thicker got the crowd;

and the vans, the omnibuses, the cabs, seemed to multiply and get noisier. Not an altogether pleasant sight to a man in the most Christian frame of mind is the crowd that a fine summer evening fetches out into the roaring Strand, as the sun fetches out flies on the window of a village grocery. To him just then it was at once depressing and provoking, and he went shouldering his way towards Temple Bar as thoroughly out of tune as he had been for many a long day.

As he passed from the narrowest part of the Strand into the space round St. Clement Dane's church, he was startled, in a momentary lull of the uproar, by the sound of chiming bells. He slackened his pace to listen; but a huge van lumbered by, shaking the houses on both sides, and drowning all sounds but its own rattle; and then he found himself suddenly immersed in a crowd, vociferating and gesticulating round a policeman, who was conveying a woman towards the station-house. He shouldered through it, — another lull came, and with it the same slow, gentle, calm cadence of chiming bells. Again and again he caught it as he passed on to Temple Bar; whenever the roar subsided the notes of the old hymn tune came drooping down on him like balm from the air. If the ancient benefactor who caused the bells of St. Clement Dane's church to be arranged to play that chime so many times a day is allowed to hover round the steeple at such times, to watch the effect of his benefaction on posterity, he must have been well satisfied on that evening. Tom passed under the Bar, and turned into the Temple another man, softened again, and in his right mind.

"There's always a voice saying the right thing to you somewhere, if you'll only listen for it," he thought. He took a few turns in the court to clear his head, and then went up, and found Harry East reclining on a sofa, in full view of the gardens and river, solacing himself with his accustomed cheroot.

"Oh, here you are," he said, making room on the sofa; — "how did it go off?"

"Well enough. Where have you been?"

"In the city and at the docks. I've been all over our vessel. She's a real clipper."

"When do you sail?"

"Not quite certain. I should say in a fortnight, though." East puffed away for a minute, and then, as Tom said nothing, went on. "I'm not so sweet on it as the time draws near. There are more of my chums turning up every day from India at the Rag. And this is uncommonly pleasant, too, living with you here in chambers. You may think it odd, but I don't half like getting rid of you."

"Thanks: but I don't think you will get rid of me."

"How do you mean?"

"I mean that I shall go with you, if my people will let me, and you will take me."

"W-h-ew! Any thing happened?"

"Yes."

"You've seen her?"

"Yes."

"Well, go on. Don't keep a fellow in suspense. I shall be introduced, and eat one of the old boy's good dinners, after all, before I sail."

Tom looked out of window, and found some difficulty in getting out the words, "No, it's all up."

"You don't mean it?" said East, coming to a sitting position by Tom's side. "But how do you know? Are you sure? What did she say?"

"Nothing. I haven't spoken to her; but it's all up. She was riding with her father and the fellow to whom she's engaged. I have heard it a dozen times, but never would believe it."

"But, is that all? Riding with her father and another man! Why, there's nothing in that."

"Yes, but there is though. You should have seen his look. And they all knew me well enough, but not one of them nodded even."

"Well, there's not much in that after all. It may have been chance, or you may have fancied it."

"No, one isn't quite such a fool. However, I have no right to complain, and I wont. I could bear it all well enough if he were not such a cold-hearted blackguard."

"What, this fellow she was riding with?"

"Yes. He hasn't a heart the size of a pin's head. He'll break hers. He's a mean brute too. She can't know him, though he has been after her this year and more. They must have forced her into it. Ah! it's a bitter business," and he put his head between his hands, and East heard the deep catches of his laboring breath, as he sat by him, feeling deeply for him, but puzzled what to say.

"She can't be worth so much after all, Tom," he said at last, "if she would have such a fellow as that. Depend upon it, she's not what you thought her."

Tom made no answer; so the captain went on presently, thinking he had hit the right note.

"Cheer up, old boy. There's as good fish in the sea yet as ever came out of it. Don't you remember the song — whose is it? Lovelace's: —

"'If she be not fair for me,
What care I for whom she be?'"

Tom started up almost fiercely, but recovered himself in a moment, and then leant his head down again.

"Don't talk about her, Harry; you don't know her," he said.

"And don't want to know her, Tom, if she is going to throw you over. Well, I shall leave you for an hour or so. Come up to me presently at the Rag, when you feel better."

East started for his club, debating within himself what he could do for his friend — whether calling out the party mightn't do good.

Tom, left to himself, broke down at first sadly; but, as the evening wore on he began to rally, and sat down and wrote a long letter to his father, making a clean breast, and asking his permission to go with East.

# CHAPTER XXVI.

### THE END.

"My Dear Katie,—I know you will be very much pained when you read this letter. You two have been my only confidantes, and you have always kept me up, and encouraged me to hope that all would come right. And after all that happened last week, Patty's marriage, and your engagement,—the two things upon earth, with one exception, that I most wished for,—I quite felt that my own turn was coming. I can't tell why I had such a strong feeling about it, but somehow all the most important changes in my life for the last four years have been so interwoven with Patty and Harry Winburn's history that, now they were married, I was sure something would happen to me as soon as I came to London. And, indeed, it has. Dear Katie, I can hardly bring myself to write it. It is all over. I met her in the street to-day; she was riding with her father and the man I told you about. They had to pull up not to ride over me; so I had a good look at her, and there can be no mistake about it. I have often tried to reason myself into the belief that the evil day must come sooner or later, and to prepare myself for it, but I might have spared myself, for it could not have been worse than it is if I had never anticipated it. My future is all a blank now. I can't stay in England, so I have written home to ask them to let me go to New Zealand with East, and I am sure they will consent, when they know all.

"I shall wait in town till I get the answer. Perhaps I may be able to get off with East in a few weeks. The sooner the better; but, of course, I shall not go without seeing you and dear old Jack. You mustn't mind me calling him Jack. The only thing that gives me any pleasure to think about is your engagement. It is so right, and one wants to see something going right, some one getting their due, to keep alive one's belief in justice being done somehow or another in the world; and I do see it, and acknowledge it when I think over his history and mine since we first met. We have both got our due; and you have got yours, Katie, for you have got the best fellow in England.

"Ah, if I only could think that she has got hers! If I could only believe that the man she has chosen is worthy of her! I will try hard to think better of him. There must be more good in him than I have ever seen, or she would never have engaged herself to him. But I can't bear to stop here, and see it all going on. The sooner I am out of England the better. I send you a parcel with this; it contains her notes, and some old flowers, and other matters which I haven't the heart to burn. You will be the best judge what should be done with them. If you see your way to managing it, I should like her to know that I had sent them all to you, and that whatever may happen to me hereafter, my love for her has been the mainstay and the guiding-star of my life ever since that happy time when you all came to stay with us in my first long vacation. It found me eaten up with selfishness and conceit, the puppet of my own lusts and vanities, and has left me — Well, never mind what it has left me. At any rate, if I have not gone from worse to worse, it is all owing to her; and she ought to know it. It cannot be wrong to let her know what good she has scattered unknowingly about her path. May God bless and reward her for it, and you, too, dear cousin, for all your long love and kindness to one who is very unworthy of, but very thankful for, them.— Ever yours, affectionately, T. B."

The above letter, and that to his father, asking for leave to emigrate, having been written and sent off, Tom was left on the afternoon of the day following his upset, making manful, if not very successful, efforts to shake off the load of depression which weighed on him, and to turn his thoughts resolutely forward to a new life in a new country. East was away at the docks. There was no one moving in the Temple. The men who had business were all at Westminster, or out of sight and hearing in the recesses of their chambers. Those who had none were for the most part away enjoying themselves, in one way or another, amongst the mighty whirl of the mighty human sea of London. There was nothing left for him to do, he had written the only two letters he had to write, and had only to sit still and wait for the answers, killing the mean time as well as he could. Reading came hard to him, but it was the best thing to do perhaps; at any rate, he was trying it on, though his studies were constantly interrupted by long fits of absence of mind, during which, though his body remained in the Temple, he was again in the well-kept garden of Barton, or in the hazel wood under the lea of the Berkshire hills.

He was roused out of one of these reveries, and brought back to external life and Fig-tree Court, by a single knock at the outer door, and a shout of the newsman's boy for the paper. So he got up, found the paper, which he had forgotten to read, and as he went to the door cast his eye on it, and saw that a great match was going on at Lord's. This gave a new turn to his thoughts. He stood looking down-stairs after the boy, and considering whether he should not start at once for the match.

He would be sure to see a lot of acquaintance there at any rate. But the idea of seeing and having to talk to mere acquaintance was more distasteful than his present solitude. He was turning to bury himself again in his hole, when he saw a white dog walk quietly up seven or eight stairs at the bottom of the flight, and then turn round, and look for some one to follow.

"How odd!" thought Tom, as he watched him; "as like as two peas. It can't be. No. Why, yes it is." And then he whistled, and called "Jack," and the dog looked up, and wagged his tail, as much as to say, "All right, I'm coming directly; but I must wait for my master." The next moment Drysdale appeared at the bottom of the stairs, and looking up, said, —

"Oh! that's you, is it? I'm all right then. So you knew the old dog?"

"I should rather think so," said Tom. "I hope I never forget a dog or a horse I have once known."

In the short minute which Drysdale and Jack took to arrive at his landing, Tom had time for a rush of old college memories, in which grave and gay, pleasant and bitter, were strangely mingled. The night when he had been first brought to his senses about Patty came up very vividly before him, and the commemoration days, when he had last seen Drysdale. "How strange!" he thought; "is my old life coming back again just now? Here, on the very day after it is all over, comes back the man with whom I was so intimate up to the day it began, and have never seen since. What does it mean?"

There was a little touch of embarrassment in the manner of both of them as they shook hands at the top of the stairs, and turned into the chambers. Tom motioned to

Jack to take his old place at one end of the sofa, and began caressing him there, the dog showing unmistakably, by gesture and whine, that delight at renewing an old friendship, for which his race are so nobly distinguished. Drysdale threw himself down in an arm-chair, and watched them.

"So you knew the old dog, Brown?" he repeated.

"Knew him?—of course I did. Dear old Jack! How well he wears; he is scarcely altered at all."

"Very little; only steadier. More than I can say for his master. I'm very glad you knew Jack."

"Come, Drysdale, take the other end of the sofa, or it wont look like old times. There, now I can fancy myself back at St. Ambrose's."

"By Jove, Brown, you're the right sort. I always said so, even after that last letter. You pitched it rather too strong in that though. I was very near coming back from Norway to quarrel with you."

"Well, I was very angry at being left in the lurch by you and Blake."

"You got the coin all right, I suppose? You never acknowledged it."

"Didn't I? Then I ought to have. Yes, I got it all right about six months afterwards. I ought to have acknowledged it, and I thought I had. I'm sorry I didn't. Now we're all quits, and wont talk any more about that rascally bill."

"I suppose I may light up," said Drysdale, dropping into his old lounging attitude on the sofa, and pulling out his cigar-case.

"Yes, of course. Will you have any thing?"

"A cool drink wouldn't be amiss."

"They make a nice tankard with cider and a lump of ice at the Rainbow. What do you say to that?"

"It sounds touching," said Drysdale. So Tom posted off to Fleet Street to order the liquor, and came back followed by a waiter with the tankard. Drysdale took a long pull, and smacked his lips.

"That's a wrinkle," he said, handing the tankard to Tom. "I suppose the lawyers teach all the publicans about here a trick or two. Why, one can fancy one's self back in the old quad looking out on this court. If it weren't such an outlandish out-of-the-way place I think I should take some chambers here myself. How did you get here?"

"Oh, they belong to a friend of mine who is away. But how did *you* get here?"

"Why along the Strand in a Hansom."

"I mean, how did you know I was here?"

"Grey told me."

"What! Grey who was at St. Ambrose's with us?"

"Yes. You look puzzled."

"I didn't think you knew Grey."

"No more I do. But a stout old party I met last night — your godfather, I should think he is — told me where he was, and said I should get your address from him. So I looked him up this morning, in that dog-hole in Westminster where he lives. He didn't know Jack from Adam."

"But what in the world do you mean by my godfather?"

"I had better tell my story from the beginning I see. Last night I did what I don't often do, went out to a great drum. There was an awful crush of course, and you may guess what the heat was in these dog-days, with gas-lights and wax-lights going, and a jam of people in every corner. I was fool enough to get into the rooms, so that my retreat was cut off, and I had to work right through, and got at last into a back room, which was not so full. The window was in a recess, and there was a balcony outside, looking over a little bit of garden. I got into the balcony, talking with a girl who was sensible enough to like the cool. Presently I heard a voice I thought I knew inside. Then I heard St. Ambrose, and then your name. Of course I listened, I couldn't help myself. They were just inside the window, in the recess, not five feet from us, so I heard pretty nearly every word. Give us the tankard, I'm as dry as an ash-heap with talking."

Tom scarcely able to control his impatience, handed the tankard. "But who was it? — you haven't told me," he said, as Drysdale put it down at last empty.

"Why, that d———d St. Cloud. He was giving you a nice character, in a sort of sneaking deprecatory way, as if he was sorry for it. Amongst other little tales, he said you used to borrow money from Jews — he knew it for a certainty because he had been asked himself to join you and another man, meaning me, of course, in such a transaction. You remember how he wouldn't acknowledge the money I lent him at play, and the note he wrote me which upset Blake so. I had never forgotten it. I knew I should get my chance some day, and here it was. I don't know what the girl thought of me, or how she got out of the balcony, but I stepped into the recess just as he had finished his precious story, and landed between him and a comfortable old boy, who was looking shocked. He *must* be your godfather, or something of the kind. I'll bet you a pony you are down for something handsome in his will."

"What was his name? Did you find out?"

"Yes; Potter, or Porter, or something like it. I've got his card somewhere. I just stared St. Cloud in the face, and you may depend upon it he winced. Then I told the old boy that I had heard their talk; and as I was at St. Ambrose with you, I should like to have five minutes with him when St. Cloud had done. He seemed rather in a corner between us. However, I kept in sight till St. Cloud was obliged to draw off, and, to cut my story short as the tankard is empty, I think I put you pretty straight there. You said we were quits just now: after last night, perhaps we are, for I told him the truth of the Benjamin story, and I think he is squared. He seems a good sort of old boy. He's a relation of yours, eh?"

"Only a distant connection. Did any thing more happen?"

"Yes; I saw that he was flurried, and didn't know quite what to think; so I asked him to let me call, and I would bring him some one else to speak to your character. He gave me his card, and I'm going to take Blake there to-day. Then I asked him where you were, and he didn't know, but said he thought Grey could tell me."

"It is very kind of you, Drysdale, to take so much trouble."

"Trouble! I'd go from here to Jericho to be even with our fine friend. I never forget a bad turn. I met him afterwards in the cloak-room, and went out of the door close after him, to give him a chance if he wants to say any thing. I only wish he would. But why do you suppose he is lying about you?"

"I can't tell. I've never spoken to him since he left Oxford. Never saw him till yesterday, riding with Mr. Porter. I suppose that reminded them of me."

"Well, St. Cloud is bent on getting round him for some reason or another, you may take your oath of that. Now my time's up; I shall go and pick up Blake. I should think I had better not take Jack to call in Eton Square, though he'd give you a good character if he could speak; wouldn't you, Jack?"

Jack wagged his tail and descended from the sofa.

"Does Blake live up here? What is he doing?"

"Burning the candle at both ends, and in the middle, as usual. Yes, he's living near his club. He writes political articles, devilish well I hear, too, and is reading for the bar; besides which he is getting into society, and going out whenever he can, and fretting his soul out that he isn't prime minister, or something of the kind. He wont last long at the pace he's going."

"I'm very sorry to hear it. But you'll come here again, Drysdale; or let me come and see you. I shall be very anxious to hear what has happened."

"Here's my pasteboard; I shall be in town for another fortnight. Drop in when you like."

And so Drysdale and Jack went off, leaving Tom in a chaotic state of mind. All his old hopes were roused again as he thought over Drysdale's narrative. He could no longer sit still, so he rushed out, and walked up and down the river side-walk, in the Temple gardens, where a fine breeze was blowing, at a pace which astonished the gate-keepers and the nursery-maids, and children, who were taking the air in that favorite spot. Once or twice he returned to chambers, and at last found East reposing after his excursion to the docks.

East's quick eye saw at once that something had happened, and had very soon heard the whole story, upon which he deliberated for some minutes, and rejoiced Tom's heart by saying: "Ah! all up with New Zealand, I see. I shall be introduced after all, before we start. Come along, I must stand you a dinner on the strength of the good news, and we'll drink her health."

Tom called twice that evening at Drysdale's lodgings, but he was out. The next morning he called again. Drysdale had gone to Hampton Court races, and had left no message. He left a note for him, but got no answer. It was trying work. Another day passed without any word from Drysdale, who seemed never to be at home, and no answer to either of his letters. On the third morning he heard from his father. It was just the answer which he had expected, — as kind a letter as could be written. Mr. Brown had suspected how matters stood at one time, but had given up the idea in consequence of Tom's silence, which he regretted, as possibly things might have happened otherwise had he known the state of the case. It was too late now, however; and the less said the better about what might have been. As to New Zealand, he should not oppose Tom's going, if, after some time, he continued in his present mind. It was very natural for him just now to wish to go. They would talk it over as soon as Tom came home, which Mr. Brown begged him to do at once, or, at any rate, as soon as he had seen his friend off. Home was the best place for him.

Tom sighed as he folded it up; the hopes of the last three days seemed to be fading away. He spent another restless day, and by night had persuaded himself that Drysdale's mission had been a complete failure, and that he did not write out of kindness to him.

"Why, Tom, old fellow, you look as down in the mouth as ever to-night," East said, when Tom opened the door for him about midnight, on his return from his club; "cheer up, you may depend it's all to go right."

"But I haven't seen Drysdale again, and he hasn't written."

"There's nothing in that. He was glad enough to do you a good turn, I dare say, when it came in his way, but

that sort of fellow never can keep any thing up. He has
been too much used to having his own way, and following
his own fancies. Don't you lose heart because he wont
put himself out for you."

"Well, Harry, you are the best fellow in the world.
You would put backbone into any one."

"Now, we'll just have a quiet cheroot, and then turn in
and see if you don't have good news to-morrow. How
hot it is; the Strand to-night is as hot as the Punjaub, and
the reek of it — Phah! my throat is full of it still."

East took off his coat, and was just throwing it on a
chair, when he stopped, and, feeling in the pocket, said, —

"Let's see, here's a note for you. The porter gave it
me as I knocked in."

Tom took it carelessly, but the next moment was tearing it open with trembling fingers. "From my cousin,"
he said. East watched him read, and saw the blood rush
to his face, and the light come into his eyes.

"Good news, Tom, I see. Bravo, old boy. You've
had a long fight for it, and deserve to win."

Tom got up, tossed the note across the table, and began
walking up and down the room; his heart was too full for
speech.

"May I read?" said East, looking up.

Tom nodded, and he read, —

"DEAR TOM, — I am come to town to spend a week
with them in Eton Square. Call on me to-morrow at
twelve, or, if you are engaged then, from three to five.
I have no time to add more now, but long to see you.
Your loving cousin, KATIE.

"P.S. — I will give you your parcel back to-morrow,
and then you can *burn* the contents yourself, or do what

you like with them. Uncle bids me say he shall be glad if you will come and dine to-morrow, and any other day you can spare while I am here."

When he had read the note East got up and shook hands heartily with Tom, and then sat down again quietly to finish his cheroot, watching with a humorous look his friend's march.

"And you think it is really all right now?" Tom asked, in one form or another, after every few turns; and East replied in various forms of chaffing assurance that there could not be much further question on the point. At last, when he had finished his cheroot, he got up, and taking his candle said, " Good-night, Tom; when that revolution comes, which you're always predicting, remember if you're not shot or hung, you'll always find a roost for you and your wife in New Zealand."

"I don't feel so sure about the revolution now, Harry."

"Of course you don't. Mind, I bargain for the dinner in Eton Square. I always told you I should dine there before I started."

\* \* \* \* \* \*

The next day Tom found that he was not engaged at twelve o'clock, and was able to appear in Eton Square. He was shown up into the drawing-room, and found Katie alone there. The quiet and coolness of the darkened room was most grateful to him after the glare of the streets, as he sat down by her side.

"But, Katie," he said, as soon as the first salutations and congratulations had passed, "how did it all happen? I can't believe my senses yet. I am afraid I may wake up any minute."

"Well, it was chiefly owing to two lucky coincidences; though no doubt it would have all come right in time without them."

"Our meeting the other day in the street, I suppose, for one?"

"Yes. Coming across you so suddenly, carrying the little girl, reminded Mary of the day when she sprained her ankle, and you carried her through Hazel Copse. Ah, you never told me all of that adventure, either of you."

"All that was necessary, Katie."

"Oh! I have pardoned you. Uncle saw then that she was very much moved at something, and guessed well enough what it was. He is so very kind, and so fond of Mary, he would do any thing in the world that she wished. She was quite unwell that evening; so he and aunt had to go out alone, and they met that Mr. St. Cloud at a party, who was said to be engaged to her."

"It wasn't true, then?"

"No, never. He is a very designing man, though I believe he was really in love with poor Mary. At any rate, he has persecuted her for more than a year. And, it is very wicked, but I am afraid he spread all those reports himself."

"Of their engagement? Just like him!"

"Uncle is so good-natured, you know, and he took advantage of it, and was always coming here, and riding with them. And he had made uncle believe dreadful stories about you, which made him seem so unkind. He was quite afraid to have you at the house."

"Yes, I saw that last year; and the second coincidence?"

"It happened that very night. Poor uncle was very much troubled what to do; so when he met Mr. St. Cloud, as I told you, he took him aside to ask him again about you. Somehow, a gentleman who was a friend of yours at Oxford overheard what was said, and came forward and explained every thing."

"Yes, he came and told me."

"Then you know more than I about it."

"And you think Mr. Porter is convinced that I am not quite such a scamp after all?"

"Yes, indeed; and the boys are so delighted that they will see you again. They are at home for the holidays, and so grown."

"And Mary?"

"She is very well. You will see her before long, I dare say."

"Is she at home?"

"She is out riding with uncle. Now I will go up and get your parcel, which I had opened at home before I got aunt's note asking me here. No wonder we could never find her boot."

Katie disappeared, and at the same time Tom thought he heard the sound of horse's feet. Yes, and they have stopped, too; it must be Mary and her father. He could not see, because of the blinds and other devices for keeping the room cool. But the next moment there were voices in the hall below, and then a light step on the carpeted stair which no ear but his could have heard. His heart beat with heavy, painful pulsations, and his head swam as the door opened, and Mary in her riding-habit stood in the room.

# CHAPTER XXVII.

### THE POSTSCRIPT.

Our curtain must rise once again, and it shall be on a familiar spot. Once more we must place ourselves on the Hawk's Lynch, and look out over the well-known view, and the happy autumn fields, ripe with the golden harvest. Two people are approaching on horseback from the Barton side, who have been made one since we left them at the fall of the curtain in the last chapter. They ride lovingly together, close to one another, and forgetful of the whole world, as they should do, for they have scarcely come to the end of their honeymoon.

They are in country costume, she in a light plain habit, but well cut, and setting on her as well as she sits on her dainty gray; he in shooting-coat and wide-awake, with his fishing-basket slung over his shoulder. They come steadily up the hill-side, rousing a yellow hammer here and there from the furze bushes, and only draw bit when they have reached the very top of the knoll. Then they dismount, and Tom produces two halters from his fishing-basket, and, taking off the bridles, fastens the horses up in the shade of the fir-trees, and loosens their girths, while Mary, after searching in the basket, pulls out a bag, and pours out a prodigal feed of corn before each of them, on the short grass.

"What are you doing, you wasteful little woman? You should have put the bag underneath. They wont be able to pick up half the corn."

"Never mind, dear, then the birds will get it."

"And you have given them enough for three feeds."

"Why did you put so much in the bag? Besides, you know it is the last feed I shall give her. Poor dear little Gipsy," she added, patting the neck of her dapple gray; "you have found a kind mistress for her, dear, haven't you?"

"Yes; she will be lightly worked, and well cared for," he said, shortly, turning away, and busying himself with the basket again.

"But no one will ever love you, Gipsy, like your old mistress. Now give me a kiss, and you shall have your treat," and she pulled a piece of sugar out of the pocket of her riding-habit, at the sight of which the gray held out her beautiful nose to be fondled, and then lapped up the sugar with eager lips from Mary's hand, and turned to her corn.

The young wife tripped across and sat down near her husband, who was laying out their luncheon on the turf.

"It was very dear of you to think of coming here for our last ride," she said. "I remember how charmed I was with the place the first Sunday I ever spent at Englebourn, when Katie brought me up here directly after breakfast, before we went to the school. Such a time ago it seems — before I ever saw you. And I have never been here since. But I love it most for your sake, dear. Now tell me again all the times you have been here."

Tom proceeded to recount some of his visits to the Hawk's Lynch, in which we have accompanied him. And then they talked on about Katie, and East, and the Englebourn people, past and present, old Betty, and Harry and his wife in New Zealand, and David patching coats and tending bees, and executing the queen's justice to the best of his ability in the village at their feet.

"Poor David, I must get over somehow to see him before we leave home. He feels your uncle's death, and the other changes in the parish, more than any one."

"I am so sorry the living was sold," said Mary; "Katie and her husband would have made Englebourn into a little paradise."

"It could not be helped, dear. I can't say I'm sorry. There would not have been work enough for him. He is better where he is, in a great town parish."

"But Katie did love the place so, and was so used to it, she had become quite a little queen there before her marriage. See what we women have to give up for you," she said, playfully, turning to him. But a shadow passed over his face, and he looked away without answering.

"What makes you look sorrowful, dear? What are you thinking of?"

"Oh! nothing!"

"That isn't true. Now tell me what it is. You have no right, you know, to keep any thing from me."

"I can't bear to think of you having had to sell Gipsy. You have never been without a riding-horse till now. You will miss your riding dreadfully, I am sure, dear."

"I shall do very well without riding. I am so proud of learning my lesson from you. You will see what a poor man's wife I shall make. I have been getting mamma to let me do the housekeeping, and know how a joint should look, and all sorts of useful things, and I have made my own house-linen. I shall soon get to hate all luxuries as much as you do."

"Now, Mary, you mustn't run into extremes. I never

said you ought to hate all luxuries, but that almost everybody one knows is a slave to them."

"Well, and I hate any thing that wants to make a slave of me."

"You are a dear little free woman. But now we are on this subject again, Mary, I really want to speak to you about keeping a lady's maid. We can quite afford it, and you ought to have one."

"I shall do nothing of the sort."

"Not to oblige me, Mary?"

"No, not even to oblige you. There is something to be said for dear Gipsy. But, take a maid again! to do nothing but torment me and pretend to take care of my clothes, and my hair! I never knew what freedom was till I got rid of poor, foolish, grumbling Higgins."

"But you may get a nice girl who will be a comfort to you."

"No, I never will have a woman again to do nothing but look after me. It isn't fair to them. Besides, dear, you can't say that I don't look better since I have done my own hair. Did you ever see it look brighter than it does now?"

"Never, and now here is luncheon all ready." So they sat down on the verge of the slope, and eat their cold chicken and tongue with the relish imparted by youth, a long ride, and the bracing air.

Mary was merrier and brighter than ever, but it was an effort with him to respond; and soon she began to notice this, and then there was a pause, which she broke at last with something of an effort.

"What makes you look so serious, now? I must know."

"Was I looking serious? I beg your pardon, dearest, and I wont do so again any more;" and he smiled as he answered, but the smile faded away before her steady, loving gaze, and he turned slightly from her, and looked out over the vale below.

She watched him for a short time in silence, her own fair young face changing like a summer sea, as the light clouds pass over it. Presently she seemed to have come to some decision; for, taking off her riding-hat, she threw it and her whip and gauntlets on the turf beside her, and drawing nearer to his side, laid her hand on his. He looked at her fondly, and stroking her hair, said, —

"Take care of your complexion, Mary."

"Oh, it will take care of itself in this air, dear. Besides, you are between me and the sun; and now you must tell me why you look so serious. It is not the first time I have noticed that look. I am your wife, you know, and I have a right to know your thoughts, and to share all your joy, and all your sorrow. I do not mean to give up any of my rights which I got by marrying you."

"Your rights, dearest! — your poor little rights, which you have gained by changing name, and plighting troth. It is thinking of that, — thinking of what you have bought, and the price you have paid for it, which makes me sad at times; even when you are sitting by me, and laying your hand on my hand, and the sweet burden of your pure life and being on my soiled and baffled manhood."

"But it was my own bargain, you know, dear, and I am satisfied with my purchase. I paid the price with my eyes open."

"Ah, if I could only feel that!"

"But you know that it is true."

"No, dearest, that is the pinch. I do not know that it is true. I often feel that it is just not a bit true. It was a one-sided bargain, in which one of the parties had their eyes open and got all the advantage, and that party was I."

"I will not have you so conceited," she said, patting his hand once or twice, and looking more bravely than ever up into his eyes. "Why should you think you were so much the cleverer of the two, as to get all the good out of our bargain? I am not going to allow that you were so much the most quick-witted and clear-sighted. Women are said to be as quick-witted as men. Perhaps it is not I who have been outwitted after all."

"Look at the cost, Mary. Think of what you will have to give up. You cannot reckon it up yet."

"What! you are going back to the riding-horses and lady's maid again. I thought I had convinced you on those points."

"They are only a very little part of the price. You have left a home where everybody loved you. You knew it; you were sure of it. You had felt their love ever since you could remember any thing."

"Yes, dear, and I feel it still. They will be all just as fond of me at home, though I am your wife."

"At home! It is no longer your home."

"No, I have a home of my own now. A new home, with new love there to live on; and an old home, with the old love to think of."

"A new home instead of an old one; a poor home instead of a rich one — a home where the cry of the sorrow and suffering of the world will reach you, for one in which you had — "

"In which I had not you, dear. There now, that was my purchase. I set my mind on having you — buying you, as that is your word. I have paid my price, and got my bargain, and — you know, I was always an oddity, and rather wilful — am content with it."

"Yes, Mary, you have bought me, and you little know, dearest, what you have bought. I can scarcely bear my own selfishness at times when I think of what your life might have been had I left you alone, and what it must be with me."

"And what might it have been, dear?"

"Why you might have married some man with plenty of money, who could have given you every thing to which you have been used."

"I shall begin to think that you believe in luxuries, after all, if you go on making so much of them. You must not go on preaching one thing and practising another. I am a convert to your preaching, and believe in the misery of multiplying artificial wants. Your wife must have none."

"Yes, but wealth and position are not to be despised. I feel that, now that it is all done past recall, and I have to think of you. But the loss of them is a mere nothing to what you will have to go through."

"What do you mean, dear? Of course we must expect some troubles, like other people."

"Why, I mean, Mary, that you might, at least, have married a contented man; some one who found the world a very good world, and was satisfied with things as they are, and had light enough to steer himself by; and not a fellow like me, full of all manner of doubts and perplexities, who sees little but wrong in the world about him, and more in himself."

"You think I should have been more comfortable?"

"Yes, more comfortable and happier. What right had I to bring my worries on you? For I know you can't live with me, dearest, and not be bothered and annoyed when I am anxious and dissatisfied."

"But what if I did not marry you to be comfortable?"

"My darling, you never thought about it, and I was too selfish to think for you."

"There now, you see, it is just as I said."

"How do you mean?"

"I mean that you are quite wrong in thinking that I have been deceived. I did not marry you, dear, to be comfortable — and I did think it all over; ay, over and over again. So you are not to run away with the belief that you have taken me in."

"I shall be glad enough to give it up, dearest, if you can convince me."

"Then you will listen while I explain?"

"Yes, with all my ears and all my heart."

"You remember the year that we met, when we danced and went nutting together, a thoughtless boy and girl —"

"Remember it! Have I ever — "

"You are not to interrupt. Of course you remember it all, and are ready to tell me that you loved me the first moment you saw me at the window in High Street. Well, perhaps I shall not object to be told it at a proper time, but now I am making my confessions. I liked you then, because you were Katie's cousin, and almost my first partner, and were never tired of dancing, and were generally merry and pleasant, though you sometimes took to lecturing, even in those days."

"But Mary — "

"You are to be silent now, and listen. I liked you then. But you are not to look conceited and flatter yourself. It was only a girl's fancy. I couldn't have married you then — given myself up to you. No, I don't think I could, even on the night when you fished for me out of the window with the heather and heliotrope, though I kept them and have them still. And then came that scene down below, at old Simon's cottage, and I thought I should never wish to see you again. And then I came out in London, and went abroad. I scarcely heard of

you again for a year, for Katie hardly ever mentioned you
in her letters; and though I sometimes wished that she
would, and thought that I should just like to know what
you were doing, I was too proud to ask. Meantime, I
went out and enjoyed myself, and had a great many pretty
things said to me — much prettier things than you ever
said — and made the acquaintance of pleasant young
men, friends of papa and mamma; many of them with
good establishments too. But I shall not tell you any
thing more about them, or you will be going off about the
luxuries I have been used to. Then I began to hear of
you again. Katie came to stay with us, and I met some
of your Oxford friends. Poor dear Katie! she was full
of you and your wild sayings and doings, half frightened
and half pleased, but all the time the best and truest
friend you ever had. Some of the rest were not friends
at all; and I have heard many a sneer and unkind word,
and stories of your monstrous speeches and habits. Some
said you were mad; others that you liked to be eccentric;
that you couldn't bear to live with your equals; that you
sought the society of your inferiors to be flattered. I
listened, and thought it all over, and being wilful and
eccentric myself, you know, liked more and more to hear
about you, and hoped I should see you again some day.
I was curious to judge for myself, whether you were much
changed for the better or the worse. And at last came
the day when I saw you again, carrying the poor lame
child; and after that, you know what happened. So here
we are, dear, and you are my husband. And you will
please never to look serious again, from any foolish
thought that I have been taken in; that I did not know
what I was about when I took you 'for better for worse,
for richer for poorer, in sickness and in health, till death
u do part.' Now, what have you to say for yourself?"

"Nothing; but a great deal for you. I see more and more, my darling, what a brave, generous, pitying angel I have tied to myself. But seeing that makes me despise myself more."

"What! you are going to dare to disobey me already?"

"I can't help it, dearest. All you say shows me more and more that you have made all the sacrifice, and I am to get all the benefit. A man like me has no right to bring such a woman as you under his burden."

"But you couldn't help yourself. It was because you were out of sorts with the world, smarting with the wrongs you saw on every side, struggling after something better and higher, and siding and sympathizing with the poor and weak, that I loved you. We should never have been here, dear, if you had been a young gentleman satisfied with himself and the world, and likely to get on well in society."

"Ah, Mary, it is all very well for a man. It is a man's business. But why is a woman's life to be made wretched? Why should you be dragged into all my perplexities, and doubts, and dreams, and struggles?"

"And why should I not?"

"Life should be all bright and beautiful to a woman. It is every man's duty to shield her from all that can vex, or pain, or soil."

"But have women different souls from men?"

"God forbid!"

"Then are we not fit to share your highest hopes?"

"To share our highest hopes! Yes, when we have any. But the mire and clay where one sticks fast over and over again, with no high hopes or high any thing else in sight — a man must be a selfish brute to bring one he pretends to love into all that."

"Now, Tom," she said, almost solemnly, "you are not

true to yourself. Would you part with your own deepest convictions? Would you, if you could, go back to the time when you cared for and thought about none of these things?"

He thought a minute, and then, pressing her hand, said,—

"No, dearest, I would not. The consciousness of the darkness in one and around one brings the longing for light. And then the light dawns; through mist and fog, perhaps, but enough to pick one's way by." He stopped a moment, and then added, " and shines ever brighter unto the perfect day. Yes, I begin to know it."

"Then why not put me on your own level? Why not let me pick my way by your side? Cannot a woman feel the wrongs that are going on in the world? Cannot she long to see them set right, and pray that they may be set right? We are not meant to sit in fine silks, and look pretty, and spend money, any more than you are meant to make it, and cry peace where there is no peace. If a woman cannot do much herself, she can honor and love a man who can."

He turned to her, and bent over her, and kissed her forehead, and kissed her lips. She looked up with sparkling eyes, and said,—

"Am I not right, dear?"

"Yes, you are right, and I have been false to my creed. You have taken a load off my heart, dearest. Henceforth there shall be but one mind and one soul between us. You have made me feel what it is that a man wants, what is the help that is mete for him."

He looked into her eyes and kissed her again; and then rose up, for there was something within him like a moving of new life, which lifted him, and set him on his feet. And he stood with kindling brow, gazing into the autumn air, as his heart went sorrowing, but hopefully "sorrowing, back through all the faultful past." And she sat on at first, and watched his face, and neither spoke nor moved for some minutes. Then she rose, too, and stood by his side : —

> And on her lover's arm she leant,
> And round her waist she felt it fold, —
> And so across the hills they went,
> In that new world which is the old.

Yes, that new world, through the golden gates of which they had passed together, which is the old, old world after all, and nothing else. The same old and new world it was to our fathers and mothers as it is to us, and shall be to our children, — a world clear and bright, and ever becoming clearer and brighter to the humble, and true, and pure of heart, to every man and woman who will live in it as the children of the Maker and Lord of it, their Father. To them, and to them alone, is that world, old and new, given, and all that is in it, fully and freely to enjoy. All others but these are occupying where they have no title; "they are sowing much, but bringing in little; they eat, but have not enough; they drink, but are not filled with drink; they clothe themselves, but there is none warm; and he of them who earneth wages, earneth wages to put them into a bag with holes." But these have the world and all things for a rightful and rich inheritance, for they hold them as dear children of Him in whose hand it and they are lying, and no power in earth or hell shall pluck them out of their Father's hand.

www.ingramcontent.com/pod-product-compliance
Lightning Source LLC
Chambersburg PA
CBHW020536300426
44111CB00008B/690